NEW proficiency

Gold

exam maximiser

Richard Mann

with Jacky Newbrook and Judith Wilson

Longman

Contents

Introduction to the *Exam Maximiser*

What is the *Proficiency Gold Exam Maximiser*?

The *Proficiency Gold Exam Maximiser* is specially designed to maximise students' chances of success in the Cambridge Certificate of Proficiency in English examination.

The *Exam Maximiser* offers:

- *further practice* of all the important grammar and skills that you study in the *Proficiency Gold Coursebook*, plus the opportunity to revise and extend your vocabulary work.
- *the facts* about the papers and questions in the Proficiency exam. The *Exam overview* on pages 6 and 7 gives you information on each of the five papers.
- *step-by-step guidance* with the strategies and techniques you need to get a good grade in the exam. There are also *Exam Tips!* to help you to improve your performance and avoid common pitfalls.
- *exercises in exam format* so that you can practise using the strategies, and familiarise yourself with the demands of the exam task.
- *Study Tips* to guide you to more analytical and productive approaches to recording and using vocabulary.
- *practical advice* about how and when to use new language most effectively.
- *writing skills training*, including sample answers, to lead you to thoughtful planning, improving and editing of summaries and compositions.
- *a complete Practice exam* which shows you exactly what you need to do in the Proficiency exam.

Who is the *Proficiency Gold Exam Maximiser* for and in what situations can it be used?

The *Exam Maximiser* is extremely flexible and can be used by students in a variety of ways. Here are some typical situations.

1

You are doing a Proficiency course with other students, probably over an academic year. You are all planning to take the exam at the same time.

You are using the *Proficiency Gold Coursebook* in class. You may sometimes do related exercises, or even a whole unit of the *Exam Maximiser* in class. Your teacher may set exercises from it to do as homework, to revise and extend your classwork. You could use the entire *Exam Maximiser* as part of your course, or you and your teacher may use it to focus on your particular revision needs, depending on the time available.

2

You have already done a longer Proficiency course, and are now doing a short intensive course before taking the exam.

You have already worked through the *Proficiency Gold Coursebook*, or perhaps another Proficiency level coursebook, and so you will be using the *Exam Maximiser* in class. The exam-format tasks and strategies in the *Exam Maximiser* will help you to improve your performance and confidence, while the Practice exam will show you everything you need to do in the Proficiency exam.

3

You have a very short period in which to prepare for the Proficiency exam.

Your level of English is already nearing Proficiency exam standard. What you now need is an understanding of the demands of the exam and the skills and strategies necessary to pass. The *Exam Maximiser* has been designed to help you to activate what you know, and to build the exam awareness and the confidence you need in order to approach the Proficiency exam successfully.

4

> You are re-taking the Proficiency exam, as you were unfortunately not successful in your first attempt.

You may be having to retake Proficiency because you were not sufficiently familiar with the exam requirements, or the best way to approach each task. You probably have a clear idea of the areas you need to focus on. You will not need to follow a coursebook, but can use the *Exam Maximiser* to develop your exam techniques, and build up your confidence.

5

> You are preparing for the exam on your own.

- Perhaps you are in a class where the teacher is using the *Proficiency Gold Coursebook* as a general high level English course. This means there may be few or no other students in your class who feel ready to take the exam. Your teacher may already be using the *Exam Maximiser* to consolidate and extend your classwork. However, you can also use it on your own to prepare for the exam. The tips and strategies, together with the Practice exam, will guide you through all you need to know to approach the exam with confidence.
- You are not attending a Proficiency class, but wish to prepare for and take the exam independently. The *Exam Maximiser* by itself can give you the exam training and practice you need.

For the student: how to use this book

To be successful in the Proficiency exam you need to:
- revise and extend the grammar and vocabulary you already know
- organise your learning in an effective way
- understand what the exam is testing and how best to tackle each task
- practise as much as you can to get used to the exam format.

This book helps you to do all of these things through appropriate support, information and advice.

Graded support

The texts and tasks in the *Exam Maximiser* reflect the level and complexity of the exam right from the start of the book. Graded tasks in the early units focus on specific aspects of the language or skill that is being tested, so as to build your confidence.

Information and advice

- ***About the exam*** boxes give you information about the nature and timing of each paper in the Proficiency exam. Use them to make sure you are well aware of what you need to do.
- ***Exam Strategy*** boxes extend your exam skills, and are followed by tasks which practise the strategies outlined and assess their effectiveness for you. Use them to improve your approach to exam tasks.
- ***Exam checklists*** give you the opportunity to analyse any errors you make in exam tasks. Use them to gain an accurate awareness of your strengths and weaknesses.
- ***Exam Tip!*** boxes give you advice on how to handle the timing and stress of the Proficiency exam. Use them to help you be organised and effective in the exam room, so that you can avoid common pitfalls.
- ***Watch Out!*** boxes focus on the problem areas and typical student mistakes for each grammar point, while the exercises which follow them are designed to test these common pitfalls in particular. Use these boxes to test yourself and highlight where you need to revise.
- ***Study Tip*** boxes give you advice on how to organise and revise your notes. Use them to help you reproduce the vocabulary you have learnt accurately, in speaking and writing.

The revision unit

Unit 14 of the *Exam Maximiser* is a revision unit, packed with exam format tasks which revise language from the whole course. It contains Exam Strategy advice and exam checklists which you can use while revising your course, or to give yourself extra guidance at any point as you are working through the *Exam Maximiser*.

The Practice exam

The complete Practice exam gives you an opportunity to find out how it really feels to take the Proficiency exam.

The Learning Key

The *Exam Maximiser* has a Key, which provides the answers to all exercises, but also explains why many answers are right or wrong. The explanations will help you increase what you can learn from the exercises throughout the *Exam Maximiser*. There are also full tapescripts for all listening material.

Exam overview

Paper	Content	Test focus
Paper 1 Reading (1 hour 30 minutes)	Part 1: three short unthemed texts with 6 four-option multiple-choice questions on each	Vocabulary – collocations, idioms, complementation, phrasal verbs, semantic accuracy
	Part 2: four short texts with two four-option multiple-choice questions on each	Content, opinion, attitude, implications, text organisation
	Part 3: a gapped text with seven jumbled paragraphs to replace.	Cohesion, underlying ideas, text structure and overall meaning
	Part 4: a long text with seven four-option multiple-choice questions	As Part 2
Paper 2 Writing (2 hours)	Part 1: one compulsory question (article, essay, letter or proposal)	Discursive Extra information given
	Part 2: one question from a choice of four (questions 2 to 4 can be letter, report, article, review, proposal; question 5 is on the set reading text and can be letter, essay, article, review, report)	Descriptive rather than discursive No extra information given
Paper 3 English in Use (1 hour 30 minutes)	Part 1: modified open cloze text with 15 gaps	Lexical, lexico-grammatical: structure, grammatical patterns and collocations
	Part 2: one short gapped text with ten word-formation questions	Lexical
	Part 3: six sets of three discrete gapped sentences	Lexical: collocation, phrasal verbs, idioms and lexical patterns
	Part 4: eight key word transformations, discrete sentences which have to be rewritten using a given word which may not be altered	Lexical, lexico-grammatical
	Part 5: two texts with four open-ended comprehension questions and a summary writing task	Comprehension questions: identifying detail and referencing, paraphrasing, identifying rhetorical and stylistic devices Summary task: selecting and synthesising information from both texts and presenting the required information in continuous prose.

Paper	Content	Test focus
Paper 4 Listening (approx. 40 minutes)	Part 1: four short extracts with two three-option multiple-choice questions	Speaker's purpose, attitude, opinions and feelings as well as gist, main idea and detail
	Part 2: one long text with nine sentence completion questions	Abstract ideas, opinions or feelings as well as specific information
	Part 3: one long text with five four-option multiple-choice questions	Opinion, gist, detail and inference
	Part 4: one long text; candidates indicate whether six statements reflect the views of one or both speakers	Opinion
Paper 5 Speaking (19 minutes)	Part 1: conversation between the candidates and the interlocutor	Social interaction
	Part 2: two-way conversation between the candidates using visual prompts	Speculating, evaluating, comparing, expressing opinions, making decisions
	Part 3: long turn from each candidate followed by general discussion on related topics; each candidate receives a written question to talk about with prompts that may be used	Organising discourse, expressing and justifying opinions, developing topics

1 Nearest and dearest

Language Focus: Vocabulary
What's in a word?

> **Study Tip**
>
> A good knowledge of vocabulary is essential for all papers of the Proficiency exam. To understand a word fully, you need to be aware of meaning, grammar, register (level of formality), collocations and related words (derivatives like verb, noun and adjective forms). A good monolingual (English–English) dictionary will supply this information.

1 Study the following extract from the *Longman Dictionary of Contemporary English*. You will see that the words *exam*, *examination* and *examine* can be used in several different ways, and have a variety of collocations.

ex.am *n* [C] **1** a spoken or written test of knowledge, especially an important one: *How did you do in your exams?* | *an oral exam* | **pass/fail an exam** (=succeed/not succeed) *Did you pass the exam?* | **chemistry/French etc exam** (=an exam in a particular subject) | **take/sit an exam** *He failed his English exam and had to take it again* **2** *AmE* a set of medical tests: *an eye exam*. **3** *AmE* the paper on which the questions for an exam are written: *Do not open your exams until I tell you.*

ex.am.i.na.tion *n* **1** [C] *formal* a spoken or written test of knowledge: *The examination results will be announced in September.* **2** [C, U] the process of looking at something carefully in order to see what it is like: *a detailed examination of population statistics* | **be under examination** *The proposals are still under examination.* | **on closer examina.tion** *On closer examination the vases were seen to be cracked in several places.* **3** a set of medical tests **4** [C,U] the process of asking questions to get specific information, especially in a court of law – see also CROSS-EXAMINATION

ex.am.ine *v* [T] **1** to look at something carefully in order to make a decision, find something, check something etc: *After examining the evidence, I can find no truth in these claims.* | **examine sth for** *The police will have to examine the weapon for fingerprints.* **2** if a doctor examines you, they look at your body to check that you are healthy **3** *formal* to ask someone questions to test their knowledge of a subject: **examine sb on** *You will be examined on American history.* **4** *technical* to officially ask someone questions in a law court.

2

1 Use the dictionary extract to help you complete the following texts with an appropriate word or short phrase.

1 What an awful .... that was! I made so many mistakes – I bet I haven't .... it! Anyway, I suppose I can .... it again next semester. By the way, I didn't realise that we were going to be .... American history this afternoon. That'll probably be another disaster!

2 We .... the weapon .... fingerprints and found that they matched those of the suspect. After .... examination of the other evidence, we are now convinced that we have found the man responsible for the crime.

3 At present, the proposal for the new shopping centre is .... examination. The decision whether or not to proceed with the scheme will be made at a meeting later this month.

4 Mr Rawlings, would you please continue with the ....-examination of the witness?

2 Now match each text to the context in which it was said or written. Choose from the list a)–d) below. Think about how formal each text is, and look at the example sentences in the dictionary extract to help you.

a) Official notice outside the offices of a Town Hall. ....
b) Student talking to another student. ....
c) Police officer talking to reporters. ....
d) Judge talking to a barrister in court. ....

3 Are the following statements true (T) or false (F)? Use the dictionary extract and the texts in Exercise 2 to help you.

1 The word *examination* is always a countable noun.
2 The word *exam* can replace the word *examination* in any sentence.
3 The word *examination* is more formal than the word *exam*.
4 The preposition *for* is always used after the verb *examine*.
5 A successful student would say, *'I've succeeded in all my exams!'*
6 The word *examination* is used in a fixed phrase with the preposition *under*.

4   The following paragraph contains ten vocabulary errors. They are underlined to help you. Correct them in your notebook by looking up the words in a good monolingual dictionary. Check:

- spelling
- grammatical patterns
- common collocations
- dependent prepositions
- fixed phrases.

The (1) <u>big majority</u> of students who (2) <u>make well</u> in the Cambridge Proficiency Examination have learnt to use a good monolingual dictionary effectively. Such dictionaries provide (3) <u>informations</u>, not just about the (4) <u>meanings for</u> words but about their (5) <u>pronounciation</u> and grammar as well. A student who learns how to use a dictionary effectively will be able to work independently for much of the time, and will gain considerable (6) <u>insight to</u> the workings of the English language. He or she will be able to (7) <u>confirm to</u> the meanings of words in a text where contextual clues are insufficient, pronounce words accurately by studying the (8) <u>phonological transcriptions</u>, and use words accurately both when speaking and writing.

Make sure you make (9) <u>the room</u> for at least one good monolingual dictionary on your bookshelf – and then make sure you use it (10) <u>at a regular basis</u>!

5

1   Look at how a student recorded the word *information* in her notebook. Notice how her example sentences focus on grammatical patterns and errors she makes.

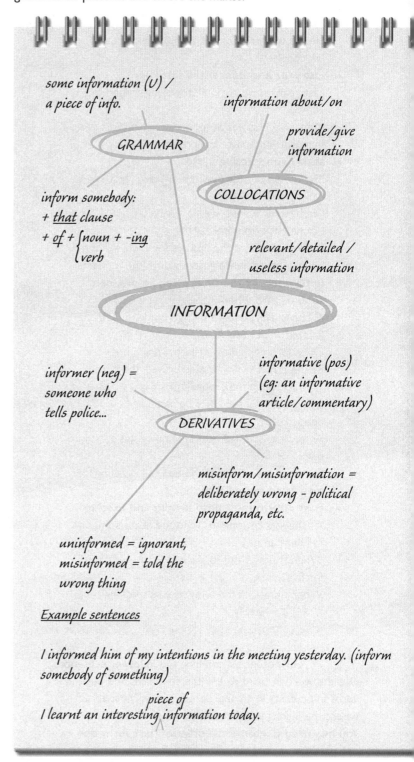

2   Now make your own vocabulary record for the word *knowledge* and its derivatives (*know, knowledgeable*, etc.). Record the information from the dictionary which you consider useful – don't simply copy the dictionary entry into your notebook!

Language Focus: Grammar
Past tenses and present perfect

Watch Out! *problem areas*

- *since*
  He has been working as a waiter since he has left college.

- *last year* and *in/over the last year*
  Last year I *spent* a month travelling around the USA. ✔
  More progress *has been made* over the last year than *was made* over the previous five years. ✔

- **stative and active verbs**
  I've known her for over a year now. I first ~~knew~~ ∧*met* her last August.
  I've been ill for two weeks. I ~~was~~ ∧*became* ill when I came back from holiday.
  I've known about the mistake for a while. I ~~knew~~ ∧*discovered* it while going through the accounts.

- *until, once, by the time, after, before, as soon as* and *when*
  My boss *didn't allow* me to go home until *I'd finished* what I was doing. ✔
  Once *I'd prepared* my speech, I *had* a break. ✔
  By the time the fire brigade *arrived*, the house ∧*had* burnt to the ground.
  Before he read the letter he ~~had taken~~ ∧*took* a deep breath.
  As soon as she ~~had~~ heard the news she burst into tears.
  Fortunately someone ~~had been~~ ∧*was* waiting for me when I arrived at the hotel.

- **past continuous, past simple and** *used to*
  As she *was crossing* the road she heard someone call her name. ✔
  When she was a child she ~~was living~~ ∧*lived* in Africa for five years.
  When he was in the army he ~~was smoking~~ ∧*used to smoke* heavily.

1 In your notebook, combine the following sentences. Use the word in **bold** to link the sentences and put the verbs in brackets in an appropriate tense. Think about where the linking word should go in your new sentence. You may need to change the order of the information, or use passives or continuous tenses for your sentence to make sense and be grammatically correct. There may be more than one correct answer.

EXAMPLE:
He (*do*) the washing-up. He (*collapse*) in a chair in front of the TV. **after**

After he had done the washing-up, he collapsed in a chair in front of the TV.

1 The mistake (*discover*) yesterday. She (*deny*) all knowledge of it. **when**
2 I finally (*win*) the lottery. I (*play*) it for thirty years. **by the time**
3 She (*overcome*) her initial reservations. She actually (*enjoy*) the concert. **once**
4 His latest novel (*publish*) last week. Tens of thousands of pounds (*spend*) on promoting it. **by the time**
5 She (*check*) all the safety catches on the windows. She (*not go*) to bed. **until**

2 There are eight mistakes with tenses in the following short text. Find and underline the mistakes, then correct them in your notebook.

When I had been a little girl, my brother and I were going every New Year to stay with grandma and grandpa in their mysterious old cottage by the sea. Like many other houses in the village it had been rumoured to be haunted.

One particular evening, a couple of days before New Year's Eve, the house was bitterly cold and rather gloomy because it was snowing heavily all day. All of us had been sitting around the fire in the living room listening to one of grandma's favourite stories, when suddenly there was a tremendous crash from upstairs. All our thoughts turned to the ghost she had been telling us about and we looked at each other in horror. When we galloped up the stairs, however, we discovered that the branch of a tree was snapped in the wind and smashed one of the bedroom windows. I will always remember the expression on grandma's face. 'I was never so scared in all my life!' was all she could whimper.

Reading

▶ Paper 1, Part 1

About the exam

In **Paper 1**, **Part 1** you have to read three gapped texts from different sources. Each text contains six gaps where a word or phrase is missing, followed by six multiple-choice questions. For each question you have to choose one option from four alternatives to fill the corresponding gap in the text. This task tests your knowledge of:

- collocations (words which are frequently found together)
- fixed phrases
- idioms
- word complementation (the grammatical patterns used with certain words)
- phrasal verbs
- semantic precision (the most appropriate word for a particular context).

Exam Strategy

Read each text carefully and try to fill the gaps **without** looking at the four options. Then look at the options and make your choice. Think carefully about both meaning and grammar.

- Look for clues before and after each of the gaps.
- Finally, read through the text again and make sure that it makes sense.
- Always guess if you're not sure. You don't lose marks for incorrect guesses.

1   Read the following three texts and dedice which answer (**A**, **B**, **C** or **D**) best fits each gap. In the Proficiency exam, the texts will be from different sources and will **not** have a common theme.

GORILLAS

Gorillas have long been the subject of (1) .... interest among zoologists for their uncanny similarity to human beings in so many aspects of their individual and social behaviour. By far the largest of the anthropoid apes, they live in the (2) .... forests of West Africa and the mountainous regions of Central Africa, in family groups (3) .... of a senior male gorilla, several females, younger males and a number of infants. Within each family group the relationships between the members are always very (4) .... defined. Almost entirely vegetarian, parties of animals roam from place to place in (5) .... of food and build their nests high up in trees for overnight use. Although gorillas are affectionate, peace-loving creatures and will even accept human beings into their midst, ruthless hunting has (6) .... to a huge decline in the numbers surviving today.

1	**A** firm	**B** utter	**C** keen	**D** sharp
2	**A** dense	**B** thick	**C** impermeable	**D** heavy
3	**A** comprising	**B** including	**C** constituting	**D** consisting
4	**A** distinctly	**B** clearly	**C** intensely	**D** heavily
5	**A** hunt	**B** search	**C** quest	**D** probe
6	**A** resulted	**B** caused	**C** attributed	**D** led

The new assistant

The first thing Inspector Highgate noticed on entering his office was the (7) .... of the cigarette. It seemed to stare menacingly at him, like the motionless red eye of a fierce animal (8) .... in the shadows in the corner of the room. He could just (9) .... the bulky contours of his new assistant's body as he leaned backwards in his chair. It was unnerving. Did he enjoy making people uneasy? 'Hello, Howard,' he said brightly, expecting no answer and (10) .... himself for the hundredth time that he would be retiring in just under a month. In that time he was expected to (11) .... this man the ropes, so that he could take over when Highgate left. He knew that Howard's appointment would be (12) .... the detriment of the department, but it had not been his decision. Someone higher up the ladder had unexpectedly taken the matter out of his hands.

7	**A** glow	**B** sparkle	**C** glimmer	**D** flicker
8	**A** creeping	**B** stalking	**C** lurking	**C** prowling
9	**A** draw out	**B** make out	**C** work out	**D** put out
10	**A** recalling	**B** remembering	**C** reminiscing	**D** reminding
11	**A** give	**B** tell	**C** show	**D** hand
12	**A** at	**B** for	**C** in	**D** to

Austen Grove, whose new novel, *A Dublin Childhood*, took the publishing world by (13) .... last week, is intensely wary of publicity. During interviews he unfailingly (and quite maddeningly) (14) .... his right to refuse to answer questions he perceives as being too personal. And that, I'm afraid, is most questions. His interview with me didn't (15) .... to be any different. 'I'm a very shy man at heart, you know,' he pointed out on first meeting me. My evident disbelief in the truth of this remark was greeted by a wry smile. 'I've always found it difficult to relate to other people. Even when I was studying in Dublin with a (16) .... to becoming an actor one day, I was regarded as being extremely antisocial and eccentric. I (17) .... up against all sorts of problems, which were the result entirely of my feeling ill at ease with other people. Fortunately for me – and for the rest of the world, I suppose – I dropped acting and became a writer of novels instead. Being in the (18) .... now doesn't come easily.'

13 **A** force   **B** tempest   **C** storm   **D** thunder
14 **A** keeps   **B** displays   **C** holds   **D** exercises
15 **A** turn out   **B** end up   **C** finish up   **D** wind up
16 **A** purpose   **B** target   **C** goal   **D** view
17 **A** came   **B** made   **C** got   **D** took
18 **A** headlight **B** limelight   **C** floodlight **D** twilight

 2 When you have checked your answers, find one example of:

- an adjective + noun collocation
- an adverb + adjective collocation
- a verb + noun collocation.

Language Focus: Vocabulary

Phrasal verbs and expressions: *keep*

1

1 Read the dictionary entry for the phrasal verb *keep on*, from the *Longman Dictionary of Contemporary English*, and then study the sentences below.

> **keep on** *phr v* **1 keep on doing sth** to continue doing something: *I've told him to stop but he keeps on scratching it!* **2** [T **keep** sb **on**] to continue to employ someone: *If you're good they might keep you on after Christmas.* **3** [I] *informal* to talk continuously in an annoying way: [+ at/about] *Do you have to keep on about your medical problems the whole time?*

1 John is getting on my nerves – he *keeps on* talking. ✓

2 I just saw Tracy crying – she says the company's in trouble, and the boss has told her that they can't *keep on* her. ✗

3 I wish you wouldn't *keep on* about the new car you've just bought. ✓

2 Is sentence 2 wrong because:

a) it has a direct object?
b) the word order is wrong?
c) an extra preposition is needed?

2 In your notebook, replace the parts of the following sentences in *italics*, using phrasal verbs with *keep*. Use a monolingual dictionary to help you.

1 If you want to do well in politics, you need to *stay friendly with* people who have power and influence.

2 *Don't get involved in* this matter, Richard. It's nothing to do with you.

3 I've had enough of working with you, because you never *obey* the rules of our agreements.

4 She *prevented them from going to sleep* by telling them one story after another.

5 When you leave school or university it is quite difficult to *continue with* friendships, even those which have been particularly intimate.

6 You haven't told me everything, have you? I'm sure there is something you are *not telling me*.

Use of English

▶ Paper 3, Part 1

> ### About the exam
>
> In **Paper 3, Part 1** you have to complete fifteen gaps in a text. You can only write one word in each gap. This task tests your knowledge of:
>
> - word combinations (collocations, fixed phrases, phrasal verbs)
> - structural items (auxiliary verbs, prepositions, pronouns, articles, etc.)
> - conjunctions and connectors (*despite*, *but*, etc.).

1   Read this extract from an article about gossip and the notes below, which a student made while doing the cloze task. He underlined the key words in the extract which helped him to find the missing words.

Gossip is enjoyable. Almost every human being in the world has <u>at some time or</u> (1)........... indulged in some form of gossip, <u>irrespective</u> (2) .... social background or education. Hard (3) .... <u>it is to believe,</u> even famous novelists and poets have been known to be notorious gossips. It (4) .... be denied, though, that gossip is something bad and possibly destructive. When friends (5) .... <u>out,</u> it is not uncommon for the cause of the argument to be gossip that has been overheard.

---

1   fixed phrase = at some time or <u>other</u>
2   'irrespective' = adjective + dependent preposition = <u>of</u>
3   clause suggesting a contrast with what follows – the meaning is 'although it is hard to believe'. Word required = <u>though/as</u>
4   modal verb is needed. It is clear from the context that gossip is bad and destructive – the connector 'though' confirms this – so appropriate modal verb = <u>cannot</u>
5   phrasal verb meaning 'argue' = <u>fall</u> out

Exam Strategy

Follow these steps whenever you do a cloze task.
*   Read the whole text first.
*   Put in words you are sure about.
*   Decide the form of other missing words (e.g. noun/verb, etc.).
*   Look for clues in the sentences **before** and after each gap.
*   Never leave any gaps.

2   Read the following text and find three things which made life pleasant for people living in the Stone Age.

3   Read the text again and fill each of the gaps with one suitable word. In this task, key words which will help you fill the gaps are underlined. There is an example at the beginning. There are also some hints to help you below

the text, although in the exam you won't be given any help. Always read through the text when you have completed the gaps, to make sure it makes sense.

Life in the Stone Age

It is a common misconception that people in the Stone Age lived (0) ...*on*..... the edge of starvation, in small groups, wandering around <u>from</u> (1) .... <u>to place.</u> <u>On the</u> (2) ...., recent studies of archaeological sites have (3) .... <u>it clear</u> that life was probably <u>a</u> (4) .... <u>deal</u> easier than it was for later farming communities. After the Ice Age, the weather was warmer than it is today and there was certainly (5) .... lack of fresh supplies of meat, fish, plants and berries.

During the Stone Age or Mesolithic Period, (6) .... it is <u>known</u> to archaeologists, men and women led an active social and spiritual life. Large encampments, where (7) .... <u>to</u> 200 people may have lived, have recently (8) .... <u>to light</u> in several parts of Europe, <u>in</u> (9) .... <u>to</u> the remains of communal tombs and temples. Making stone tools (10) .... probably <u>have been regarded</u> as a communal activity, in (11) .... even children used to participate. Nor were women <u>thought</u> (12) .... <u>as</u> inferior in these societies. <u>In</u> (13) .... <u>likelihood,</u> they <u>took</u> (14) .... actively <u>in</u> the decision-making of the tribe. Only later, with the arrival of farming, (15) .... they lose their status.

Hints

2   *This phrase introduces information which contradicts what came before.*
5   *We learn in the previous sentence that life was easier then, so this sentence has a positive meaning!*
6   *What word do you put after 'known' in the sentence 'The Stone Age is known ... the Mesolithic Period to archaeologists.'?*
7   *This is a fixed expression – in this context it means 'a maximum of 200'.*
9   *This is a connecting phrase with the meaning 'as well as'.*
10 *What kind of verb is required here?*
12 *What particle is often used after 'think'? The meaning of the phrase here is 'regarded as'.*
15 *When a sentence starts with the phrase 'Only later ...' the subject + verb word order is reversed (or inverted).*

Writing (paragraph organisation)
▶ Paper 2

1 The function of the topic sentence is to state or summarise the main idea of the paragraph. It is often, but not always, the first sentence. Read the following three paragraphs, and the three alternative topic sentences for each. Decide which alternative is:

- too general (covers areas broader than those in the paragraph)
- too specific (only refers to some of the areas covered in the paragraph)
- correct (summarises or introduces the main points appropriately).

Write the letter of the correct sentence in the space provided.

---
1 Mark had not enjoyed his childhood. .... He was only five when his parents were forced to leave the country and had to send him away to boarding school. This was difficult enough, but two years later his father went bankrupt and Mark was sent to live with his grandparents. Then, at the age of sixteen, he had a serious riding accident and had to spend six months in hospital.

---

a) It had been an unhappy time for him on the whole.
b) The routines of school life had been particularly unpleasant for him.
c) It had been spoilt by a number of unfortunate incidents.

---
2 .... For one thing, I had to work much longer hours. I often worked from six in the morning until eight at night. Another thing which was different was my social life. In England I had had a very active social life, whereas in Africa I found that there was little for me to do after work. Compared to my previous existence, I suppose my life in Africa was much healthier but it was not so much fun.

---

a) It took me a long time to get used to living abroad.

b) My job in Africa was a new experience for me.
c) Many things changed when I left England to go and live in Africa.

---
3 .... She hated the way they always found the warmest place in the house. She also disliked them because of the unnerving way they stared at you. It was almost as if they possessed an uncanny ability to penetrate the innermost secrets of your soul. Most of all, however, she hated cats because of the wailing noise they made at night. She had lost count of the number of times she had been woken up at night by the screeching of a cat in her backyard.

---

a) Dora had an almost pathological dislike of cats.
b) In Dora's view all cats were intensely selfish animals.
c) Dora was happy to live alone, without a cat.

2 Now write topic sentences for paragraphs 4 and 5. First, read the whole paragraph, and the questions which follow. These will help you focus on the most important information to include in your topic sentences.

---
4 .... At the very least it should make sure that they all receive a pension and do not have to spend the last few years of their lives in poverty. It could also give them special bus and train passes, enabling them to travel cheaply on public transport, and could offer discounts on many other things. Finally, the state could even provide housing and hospital facilities for those old people who have no relatives to look after them.

- Who or what do *it* and *they* refer to in the first sentence?
- What, in general, would the effects of the proposed changes be?

---
5 .... For example, there is a swimming pool designed for people who are confined to a wheelchair, and there is also a gym where those who are disabled in some way can work out safely and under the guidance of one of the sports centre's qualified assistants. Facilities for disabled people exist for a range of other sports and activities and everyone is given a huge amount of encouragement and help. I was extremely impressed by what I saw on my visit to the centre last week.

- Where are the pool and the gym?
- Who in particular is the paragraph concerned with?

3   It is important that all the details you include in a paragraph are **relevant** and support the main idea of the paragraph (expressed in the topic sentence). Read the following paragraph and cross out the sentences and clauses which you consider irrelevant. The topic sentence has been underlined to help you.

> When I was twelve, my sister went to university and we saw even less of her. <u>Whenever we did see her, however, we realised that she was no longer the same person</u>. Change is a part of life. Many things change in our lives, sometimes for the better but sometimes for the worse. Not only had she started to wear long, flowing dresses and lots of colourful make-up, but her hair was also quite different. Whereas previously she had always insisted on keeping it cut short, it was now startlingly long and rather unkempt. I've always longed to grow my hair myself, but my parents don't approve of long hair. Her attitude towards me had similarly undergone an enormous change. She now wanted to spend time with me, even though I was busy studying for my school exams and it was important for me to do well. She seemed to enjoy telling me all the gossip that was doing the rounds, about her life at university and her plans for the future, and she also helped me greatly with various problems I was facing at school, and there were plenty of those, I can tell you! Within a matter of weeks she had become my closest friend and confidante.

4

1   The details supporting a topic sentence should always be organised clearly. In the following box there are four common ways of organising details. Indicate which one was used in each of the five paragraphs in Exercises 1 and 2.

para. 1 ...   para. 2 ...   para. 3 ...
para. 4 ...   para. 5 ...

> ### Methods of organising paragraphs
> **A Comparison/contrast:** the writer provides details which show similarities and/or differences.
> **B Examples:** the writer uses a list of examples or an illustration in support of the main idea.
> **C Emphasis:** the writer organises the details in order of their importance, normally with the most significant detail last.
> **D Chronological order:** the writer presents details in the order in which they happened.

2   Underline any connectors or phrases in the five paragraphs which helped you decide.

5   Choose two of the topics below and write a paragraph of 120–150 words for each one.

Organise the details, linking them with appropriate connectors. For each question, a suitable method of paragraph organisation from the list **A–D** above has been suggested to help you.

1   Describe how you first met a close friend. Put the details of your paragraph in chronological order. **(D)**
2   Explain how two people you know are similar or different. Provide details which show these similarities and differences clearly. **(A)**
3   Explain what makes a good friendship. Put the details in order of emphasis. **(C)**
4   Describe how parents or teachers could reach a better understanding of young people. Provide examples or an anecdote to explain your meaning clearly or put the details in order of emphasis. **(B or C)**

> ### Study Tip
> Whenever you have to produce a piece of writing, you should plan the sequence of your paragraphs carefully, making sure one leads on naturally to the next. For each paragraph you should:
> 1 write a clear **topic sentence**, which expresses the main idea of the paragraph
> 2 support the topic sentence with **relevant details**
> 3 make sure your details are **well-organised**
> 4 use **connectors** to link the details of the paragraph.

Learning for life

Language Focus: Grammar
Conditionals and wishes

> **Watch Out!** *problem areas*
>
> - **first conditionals**
>   If you ~~will~~ go to the party tonight, you'll see Mark's new girlfriend.
>   You'll do well in the exam, as long as you ~~won't~~ *don't* do anything silly.
> - *unless*
>   *Unless is used in sentences which mean X will happen if it is not stopped by Y. It cannot be used to mean X will be the result of Y not happening.*
>   We'll go for a picnic tomorrow, unless it rains. ✓
>   I'll be quite relieved ~~unless she comes~~ ∧*if she doesn't come*.
> - **unreal present/future**
>   If you ~~would work~~ ∧*worked* harder, you would be top of the class.
> - **unreal past**
>   If she hadn't been so rude to him, he wouldn't have punished her. ✓
>   If I ~~would have~~ ∧*had* taken more interest in the course, I ~~had~~ ∧*would have* done better in the exams.
> - *wish*
>   Past: They wish they ∧*had* had the chance to go abroad last year. (= *but they didn't*)
>   Present: I wish I ~~would be~~ ∧*were* in a different class. (= *but I'm not*)
>   I wish I ~~would~~ ∧*could* speak French. (= *but I can't*)
>   Irritating habit: I wish he ~~won't~~ ∧*wouldn't* interrupt me when I'm talking to someone. (= *but he does it regularly*)
>   Future: I wish I ~~am/would be~~ ∧*was* going on holiday this year. (= *but I'm not*)
> - *wish* and *hope*
>   We use *hope* to say that we would like something to happen, although we don't know whether it will or not. When we want a situation to be different from what it already is, we use *wish*.
>   I hope he marries her. ✓
>   I hope we don't have a history test tomorrow. ✓

1 Rewrite each of the following sentences using either *if* or *wish*.

1 I couldn't write very well in the exam, because I was extremely nervous.
2 We'll have to cancel the school outing, unless the weather gets better.
3 It's a pity they are refusing to reconsider their plans.
4 Having to revise every night made me really bad tempered throughout my exams.
5 It's so annoying that my car never starts on cold mornings.
6 Thanks to all the money we received, we were able to build a new library.
7 I'll continue with my plans unless I hear from you.
8 One of the reasons that I couldn't go to the lecture was that I had too much work to do.

2 Read this example carefully before attempting the exercise below.

EXAMPLE:
I'd prefer it if you .... much noise when I'm working!

The structure *I'd prefer* and the word *noise* after the gap suggest that the general meaning is that the speaker wants you to be less noisy. The verb which collocates with *noise* is *make*. We need a past tense form because the preference is for something hypothetical, as well as a negative: *didn't make*. Before the word *much*, we also need the adverb *so*.

ANSWER:
I'd prefer it if you *didn't make so* much noise when I'm working!

3 Fill each of the gaps with a suitable word or phrase. In this exercise, you are given the number of words which are missing to help you. (Contractions like *won't* are counted here as two words.)

1 I think I would enjoy the course more if .... more feedback by the tutors.
2 It's high .... responsibility for his own problems.

3 Hadn't you .... phone?
It's already rung five or six times.

4 It looks as ....
well in his exams next summer.

5 I'd rather .... at me –
I'm not deaf, you know.

6 Gerald doesn't want you to organise the party,
because he'd .... the arrangements
himself.

7 Why are you always interfering? It's time ....
.... out of my affairs!

8 I can't understand why some of the tutors treat us
as .... still children.

Use of English
▶ **Paper 3, Part 2**

About the exam

In **Paper 3, Part 2** you have to complete ten gaps
in a text. Using the stems of the words printed in
the margin, you have to fill each gap with the form
of the word which is appropriate in the context.
This task tests your knowledge of:

• word formation (using prefixes, suffixes, etc.)
• use of parts of speech (nouns, verbs, etc.).

Exam Strategy

• Quickly read through the whole text first.
• Complete those gaps you are sure about by
forming new words from the stems.
• Decide the form of other missing words, e.g.
adjective/noun, etc. and the meaning, e.g. negative
or positive. Change the stem or add a
prefix/suffix where appropriate.
• Always check to see if the word is plural or
needs a participle ending.
• Read the text again to check that what you have
written makes sense.

1 Read the following text and find three reasons why
some young children may find it difficult to adapt to
learning in a school environment.

2 Read the text again. Use the word given in capitals
at the end of some of the lines to form a word that fits in
the space in the same line. There is an example at the
beginning (0). Read the text through again when you have
finished. (There are hints below the text to help you,
although in the exam you won't be given any help.)

Starting school

In a child's earliest years, learning takes place
within the reassuring confines of the home, where
(0) *achievements* are greeted with praise — ACHIEVE
by the parents. All this changes when the child
starts to attend school.

Two children who start school together may
have had a similar (1) .... and — BRING
be equally intelligent, but the way they
deal with the new learning environment is often
(2) .... different. One will thrive in — STRIKE
the (3) .... of the classroom, while — FORMAL
the other will struggle to keep up.

At school, the teachers are (4) .... — SIEGE
by the urgent needs of a large number of children
clamouring for their attention, and the frequent
(5) .... of classrooms means that — CROWD
the noise level is high. Despite this, a child is
expected to concentrate on what is being said,
and his (6) .... to hear or understand — ABLE
may pass unnoticed or be (7) .... — REGARD
by the teacher.

The nature of school activities will probably differ
from what the child is used to at home, and may
seem (8) .... to him. In addition, it — MEAN
is no longer possible for a child to stop what he
is doing when (9) .... sets in. Having — BORE
to sit still and concentrate is a (10) .... — REQUIRE
many children's home lives may not have prepared
them for.

Hints

1 *a noun – derived from the phrasal verb you could
also use in this context*

2 *What part of speech is required here? Do you know
the form of the adjective?*

3 *a noun – do you need to add a negative prefix or
not? Consider the meaning of the context.*

4 *a verb in the passive form, formed by adding a prefix
to the stem*

5 *an '-ing' form – is it negative or positive in
meaning? Add a prefix to the stem.*

6 *a noun – the previous sentence gives you a clue here.
What happens when noise levels are high?*

7 *a verb in the passive form, having the opposite
meaning to the stem*

8 *an adjective – is it negative or positive in meaning?
Which suffix will you add?*

9 *What part of speech is required here? How do you
form it?*

10 *The indefinite article gives you an important clue
here – what part of speech is required?*

17

Listening

▶ **Paper 4, Part 2**

 1 You will hear four extracts from a radio talk about a famous nineteenth-century scholar and explorer called Richard Burton. Each extract is similar to one of the following prompt sentences, but not the same.

1 The first time you listen, match each of the extracts to one of the following sentences. Write the letter of the extract in the space provided. Ignore the gaps in the sentences for the moment.

1 As Burton was very good at ...., his achievements were both numerous and varied. (extract ......)

2 Although the .... he made to mankind cannot be compared to those of Darwin or Einstein, he was still a very remarkable man. (extract ......)

3 Not using any 'special method', Burton could not make his foreign language learning particularly .... (extract ......)

4 In foreign language learning, Burton owed his amazing .... to the fact that he was so highly motivated. (extract ......)

 2 Now listen again to the four extracts and complete each of the sentences with a word or short phrase.

3 How are the sentences different from the extracts you heard? Which prompt sentence(s):

- rephrase(s) the extract using language of a different register (degree of formality)? Sentence(s) ......
- include(s) different forms of the same words (e.g. nouns instead of verbs)? Sentence(s) ......
- use(s) a different word order from the recording? Sentence(s) ......

 2 Now listen to the whole radio talk and complete the following sentences with a word or short phrase. Listen to the recording twice.

The speaker says that it is Burton's

[_____ 1] of sixteen volumes of the *Arabian Nights* that is most widely known.

As an explorer he searched for the

[_____ 2] and made other journeys in northern Africa and the Near East.

His most impressive achievement was that he spoke [_____ 3] as well as numerous dialects.

The speaker does not feel that his methods of studying were [_____ 4] in any way.

It seems that when Burton set out on a new learning project, he was both

[_____ 5] and persistent in his approach.

He had tremendous energy and determination, and would devote

[_____ 6] to the study of a new language.

Burton spent most of his childhood

[_____ 7]

As a child, he had to learn foreign languages in order to [_____ 8] of his own age.

On reaching [_____ 9], he had mastered impressive language skills and had a high degree of learning experience.

Use of English
▶ **Paper 3, Part 5**

About the exam

In **Paper 3**, **Part 5** you have to read two texts on a related topic, answer two comprehension questions on each text, and then write a paragraph in answer to a specific question, summarising points from **both** texts.

Exam Strategy

- Read the rubric and both texts quickly to get a general idea of the content.
- Read each text more carefully and answer the comprehension questions.
- **Go on to the summary.** Read the summary task, decide what information you need to answer it, and underline the parts of each text that contain that information.
- Make brief notes of the main points, **using your own words as far as you can**. If the same point is made in both texts, only note it once.
- Without looking back at the texts, use your notes to write a connected paragraph.
- Edit your summary, making sure that the length is correct and that you have included all the necessary information.

1 Writing a summary may be something you have never had to do before. The following exercises will help you to understand what you have to do.

1 Read the following summary task.

> In a paragraph of between 30 and 40 words, summarise what students should do to become effective learners.

2 Now read the title of the following text, to predict what it is about. Then read the text all the way through to make sure you understand it.

3 Look at the parts underlined in the text and the notes made by a student preparing to answer the summary task below it. Why has the student selected this information and omitted the rest (i.e. the parts not underlined)?

....

....

Study habits to maximise your potential

It is of the utmost importance for students to be meticulously organised in the way they occupy their time. They should avoid squandering their hours on trivia, while not devoting enough time to (*1*) tasks
5 which are of prime importance to their studies.

One aspect of time management (*2*) is the making of lists. Students should acquire the habit of making detailed lists of the things they need to do and indicating, where possible, when they need to be
10 done by. Such a list might include, for example, the written assignments which have been set for a particular week or certain books and journals which have been recommended by tutors.

While on the subject of books and journals, it is worth
15 mentioning that effective learning inevitably means (*3*) effective reading. Reading is a skill which needs to be developed. Many students are very ineffective readers and this is ultimately reflected in their poor performance in exams.

20 (*4*) Note-taking is another area where students may need help. If students are not in the habit of keeping organised notes which cover all points, most of what they read or hear in lectures will be forgotten or not clearly understood later.

25 All of which brings us to the question of exams. (*5*) Success in exams can only be achieved if preparation is approached in a systematic way. It is very important for students to start this well in advance of the exams – so many students have failed exams
30 or done badly because they have not spent enough time going over their notes beforehand.

Students should:
1 *spend their time only on important things*
2 *make lists of things they need to do by certain times*
3 *develop effective reading habits*
4 *keep organised notes which cover all points*
5 *leave enough time for studying when preparing for exams.*

2 Read the following summary, which the student wrote using his notes. Ignore the numbers and underlining for the moment. Notice he has:

- replaced the word *should* with other words and phrases to avoid monotony
- used participle clauses (*making, preparing*) and connectors (*also, finally*) to link the points.

What does the student still need to do?

....

It is (1) extremely important for students to (2) spend their time only on things which are important, making lists of (3) things they need to do by certain times. They should also develop effective reading habits and keep notes (4) which are organised and cover all points. Finally, when (5) preparing for exams, it is essential for students to leave themselves enough time for this preparation.

(62 words)

3 The first draft this student wrote is still too long. Knowing a wide range of vocabulary can give you the word-power to edit the summary further. Replace the underlined phrases with the single words in the box below, making any other necessary changes. There are two words you won't need.

revising	vital	evaluate	thorough
prioritise	deadlines	specific	

The summary should now be the correct length.

4 Now you're going to go through a similar process of reading, making notes, writing and editing a summary, based on two texts. As in the Proficiency exam, there are two comprehension questions about each text, which you should answer before you attempt the summary.

1 Read through the following two texts about the educational benefits of computer games to get a general idea of their content. Ignore the numbers and underlining for the moment.

2 Now read each text more carefully and answer the comprehension questions using a word or short phrase.

For years concern has been expressed by parents and teachers about the effect of computer games on the moral and mental make-up of the next generation. Some have warned that a relentless diet of whiz-bang 'shoot-'em-ups' fosters anti-social behaviour, even playground violence. Others believe that the age of the zombie is upon us.

But expert opinion is shifting radically. Psychologists in America and Britain now suggest that while computer games hold some dangers for children, (1) they also provide opportunities their parents never enjoyed to amplify powers of concentration and memory. Researchers have also highlighted (2) the positive response of children to the way computer games reward success, thereby spurring them on to look for greater challenges – a boon if the same attitude is applied to school work. A leading researcher at the University of Washington has even claimed that (3) children think differently when they play computer games, learning to deal with problems in parallel rather than in sequence. In effect, children are being trained to tackle problems in a fashion which is not only more rapid but also more effective. It is this apparent facility to deal with certain kinds of problems and unfamiliar situations that is so intriguing and could be of particular benefit to children in the long term.

1 Which phrase in the first paragraph implies that children spend a lot of time playing computer games?
2 What is the particular feature of computer games that could be exploited by schools to encourage children to look for greater challenges?

Perched on a tower of cushions in front of his father's desktop computer, five-year-old Elliott Smith flicks his fingers nimbly over the keyboard. As the screen lights up, so does his face. The gun-toting electronic heroine of the game he is playing greets him once again and off they go together into the realms of cyberspace.

Teacher Mark Collar, head of English at Caister High School in Great Yarmouth, is less concerned by the bloodthirsty images of such games than by the long periods spent by players alone with their screens. 'In my view these games can discourage the development of verbal and literacy skills, and have a stifling effect on the imagination,' he said.

Educational expert Julie Wright does not agree. 'We know that (*) <u>games can improve children's concentration and we know that children think quickly when using them.</u> They shouldn't be discouraged.'

Her views are shared by teachers at Lanterns, a private nursery school in east London, where computer games make up a part of the syllabus.

'Every day the pre-school pupils attend a special class, such as dance or drama,' said Janet Viola, the director. 'On Tuesdays (4) <u>they have a computer workshop where they spend an hour playing games which are designed to encourage reading and writing skills.</u> So far the results have been extremely encouraging – learning to read and write need no longer be the chore it sometimes is for many young children. All the children love it. There is not one technophobe among them.' ■

3   In the first paragraph, what does the writer imply about Elliott Smith's ability to play computer games?

4   What use of computer games does the writer mention which suggests that the views of Mark Collar may not be correct?

5   Read the summary question and underline the words in the question that tell you what information you need to include in your answer.

> In a paragraph of between 50 and 70 words, summarise in your own words as far as possible, the educational benefits of computer games mentioned in the texts.

6   Look back at the underlined sections of the two texts. Each underlined section refers to a point you need to mention in your summary. Why is one underlined section in the second text marked with an asterisk (*), not with a number?

7   Using the underlined sections 1–4, complete the notes below.

1   *increase children's powers of* ....
2   *potentially have a positive effect on children's* .... *by encouraging* .... *look for greater challenges when they complete tasks*
3   *game players think* .... *and learn to deal with problems more* ....
4   *can help* .... *to learn* ....

8   Using the notes from Exercise 7, write the first draft of your summary in your notebook. Since you are writing about people's opinions, you will probably need to use modal verbs (e.g. *may*) and expressions such as *it is believed that* or *games are thought to.*

9   Check and edit your summary. Have you included all the information you need? Is it the right length or do you need to shorten it? Use this checklist to help you.

> ### Methods of editing summaries
> * Make sure each sentence makes a new point.
> * Remove examples which support your points.
> * Remove adjectives and adverbs.
> * Look for repetition and remove it.
> * Replace particular phrases with single words.
> * Replace full clauses with participle clauses.

10   Read through the second draft of your summary. Look back at the original task, and make sure that all your points are relevant to it, then check for spelling, punctuation or grammatical mistakes.

Writing

▶ Paper 2, Part 1 (essay)

1 Read the following writing task.

> **TASK**
>
> You have read the following extract from a letter to a newspaper, in which the writer expresses his feelings about the value of educating children at home. It has prompted you to write an essay for your tutor discussing the points raised and expressing your own views.
>
> (300–350 words)

I'm convinced that parents should be allowed to educate their children at home if they so desire. Some experts suggest that children need the company of their peers if they are to develop properly. I'm not so sure about that. Anyway, such considerations pale into insignificance when compared with the benefits of such an education: the personal attention and support that such children would undoubtedly receive can only be positive. In fact, I have supervised private tutoring on a number of occasions and have always been deeply impressed by what I have seen.

1 Underline the main points to be covered in the essay.

2 Now read the following outline, which was written in answer to the task. There is one detail, or set of details, in each paragraph of the outline, which is irrelevant or repetitive. Find these details and cross them out.

Introduction
Opening comments: situation nowadays
1 low standards which may prevail in state schools
2 family relationships/effect of TV responsible for low standards
3 parents send children to private schools
4 education at home is another option

First supporting paragraph
Main idea (+): emotional support children would receive at home
1 children supported by parents/tutors at home
2 many schoolchildren not encouraged by teachers
3 many schoolchildren cannot adapt to impersonal environment/bullied
4 school buildings often in bad condition

Second supporting paragraph
Main idea (+): personal attention children would receive at home
1 education tailored to needs/abilities of children
2 parents teach themselves or employ tutors
3 important for tutors to be reliable/trustworthy
4 abilities/skills of children spotted and developed

Third supporting paragraph
Main idea (–): effect of home education on personal/ social development
1 personal and social development of children could suffer
2 need to be given time to relax from studies
3 need to move away from parents to gain self-confidence – learn to 'stand on their own two feet'
4 need to form relationships with others – could feel lonely/different

Closing paragraph
1 many benefits of home education – should be allowed
2 however – must make sure that children are not isolated – have opportunities to meet other children
3 the education laws should be changed in many countries

2   Read the following essay, which was written using the outline in Exercise 1. Ignore the underlined words and phrases for the moment. Check that your ideas about which information was irrelevant were correct.

Many parents these days are concerned about the low standards that seem to prevail in state schools. As a result, <u>many more</u> parents are sending their children to private schools. Perhaps another option, however, should be for parents to be able to educate their children at home if they wish to do so.

Educating children at home would be beneficial for two main reasons. The first, and probably more important, of these reasons is the emotional support that they would receive at home from their parents and tutors. It is well known that <u>many</u> children at school do not receive the support or the encouragement they need if they are to succeed. What is more, <u>it is well known that</u> many children do badly at school because they cannot adapt to the impersonal environment or because they are bullied by other children.

Educating children at home could also be beneficial because they would receive an education which was tailored to their particular needs and abilities. Parents could teach their children themselves, if they were qualified to do so, or employ tutors. In this way, the children's interests and talents would be spotted quickly and could be developed to a high degree.

However, <u>we must say that</u> children might suffer in their personal and social development if they were educated only at home. Children need to move away from the influence of their parents in order to gain self-confidence and learn to 'stand on their own two feet'. They also need to form relationships with other children. It is possible that a young boy or girl who was being educated at home could feel extremely lonely and different from other children of the same age.

In conclusion, <u>we can say that</u> educating children at home does have important benefits, and parents should be allowed to educate their children in this way if they wish to do so. Nevertheless, it would be necessary to make sure that such children do not become isolated and are given opportunities to meet other children.

(340 words)

3   Some of the words and phrases used in the essay are repetitive (e.g. *many*) or inappropriate in terms of style and register. Improve the essay by replacing each of the underlined words or phrases with one of the following phrases. Use each phrase once only.

1   large numbers of
2   it would seem that
3   it is a sad fact that
4   an increasing number of
5   it is important to point out that

4   In your notebook, answer these questions about the essay.

1   Did the student who wrote this essay cover all the points raised in the letter to the newspaper? Look back at the task in Exercise 1 to check.
2   Was the essay a 'balanced essay' or not?
3   What method was used to organise the details within each paragraph? (Refer to the list in Unit 1, page 15, for guidance.)
    Underline the statement of topic in the introduction, the topic sentences in the middle paragraphs, and the summing up phrase in the closing paragraph.

5   Now plan and write an essay in answer to the question below. Follow the procedure in the *Exam Strategy* box on page 22.

TASK

You have read the following extract from a magazine article in which the writer expresses her feelings about school and college examinations. It has prompted you to write an essay for your tutor discussing the points raised and expressing your own views.

(300–350 words)

There is little doubt that school and college examinations prove nothing more than that certain students have good memories. Admittedly, they are a convenient way of assessing students, and it may be possible to find other points in their favour. It does seem wrong, however, that every year thousands of young people suffer such enormous stress and spend so much time preparing for and taking examinations in our educational institutions. They should be abolished once and for all.

6   Exchange your essay with another student if you can. Evaluate each other's work and suggest improvements.

3 The moving image

Language Focus: Grammar
Inversion

> **Watch Out!** *problem areas* ←
>
> • **hardly/no sooner**
>   Hardly had he arrived at the office *when* his boss summoned him to a meeting. ✔
>   No sooner had we sat down to watch TV *than* the doorbell rang. (sooner *is a comparative, so we use* than *after it*) ✔
>
> • **word order**
>   Not ~~did~~ for one moment ∧*did* Sarah believe that the news she had heard was true.
>   Not until ~~has your report been checked you will~~
>   ∧*your report has been checked will you* be allowed to publicise your views.
>
> • **auxiliary verbs**
>   Rarely did he ∧*do* his homework on time.
>   Hardly ever did she ~~talked~~ ∧*talk* to anyone she didn't know.
>   Because these inversions are emphatic, it's **impossible to use contractions** in the inverted verb.
>   ~~Hadn't Peter~~ ∧*Had Peter not* helped us, we wouldn't have been able to cope.
>
> • **little and few**
>   *Little* and *few* usually have a negative meaning, and are often used to start inverted sentences. *A little* and *a few* have a positive meaning, and are never used to start these types of inversion.
>   Little did she realise (= *she little realised*) what the results of her action would be. ✔
>   In few cases do new actors find work easily. ✔
>   In a few cases, new actors may find they have more work than they can cope with. (= *this occasionally happens*) ✔
>
> • **agreeing**
>   When agreeing with a statement which is negative (or negative in meaning) we can use *neither/nor* + inversion, while for a positive statement we can use *so* + inversion.
>   'I can't sing at all.' – 'Nor can I.' ✔
>   'I'm not interested in this film.' – 'Neither am I.' ✔
>   'I left the theatre early.' – 'So did I.' ✔

1 Rewrite each of the following sentences, beginning with the words given and using an inversion. The part of each sentence which needs to be rewritten has been underlined to help you.

EXAMPLE:
You will *only* be allowed to leave *when* you have finished the job.

Not until *you have finished the job will you be allowed to leave.*

1 It *never* seemed likely that the disagreement would be settled.
   At no ....

2 We were *not* allowed into the country *until* our visas had been double-checked.
   Only ....

3 You are *not* to visit the old part of town on your own, *whatever happens*.
   Under no ....

4 *This is the first time that* television has played such an important role in our lives.
   Never ....

5 You do *not often* come across someone as well-informed as Charles Osborne.
   Seldom ....

6 He would not have learned the news *if he hadn't been* listening to the radio.
   Had ....

7 We had *just* sat down to eat *when* the telephone rang.
   No sooner ....

8 I *refuse* to work for that company again.
   Never ....

9 She did*n't really* realise what was about to happen.
   Little ....

10 He *acts so well* that the audience hang on his every word.
   So ....

11 *It was to be another* six months *before* Sally met him again.
   Not ....

12 He *doesn't normally* do his fair share of the work.
   Rarely ....

2 Fill each of the gaps in the following sentences with a suitable word or phrase. In some, but **not all**, of the gaps you need to use an inversion.

1 The first night of the play was a disaster. Hardly .... a good word to say about it afterwards.

2 I thought my father would be pleased, but not once .... me on my exam results.

3 On no .... you to mention what happened to your colleagues.

4 Not .... the book, it is difficult for me to say what I think of the writer's views.

5 So .... with his performance, they offered to give him a permanent job.

6 Other students had poorer exam results – he is by no means .... in the class.

7 We looked everywhere for him but nowhere .... found.

8 Every week we go to the cinema! Not once since we arrived here .... to the theatre!

9 So .... came to the meeting that we had to put it off till next week.

10 Not .... without saying goodbye, but he slammed the door behind him as well.

Language Focus: Vocabulary
Dependent prepositions and prepositional phrases

Rewrite each of the sentences below, using a prepositional phrase containing the word in brackets. **Do not change the given word in any way**. If you are unsure what the prepositional phrase is, try looking up the key word you are given in a dictionary. The phrase you need to replace is in italics to help you.

EXAMPLE:
He can tell how much a picture is worth *immediately he sees it*. (glance)
He can tell at a glance how much a picture is worth.

1 She didn't want to leave the room *because she was afraid of* missing the beginning of the film. (fear)
....

2 *I don't want you to tell anyone else* what I am telling you now. (confidence)
....

3 *Whatever happens* we must avoid a scandal. (costs)
....

4 *As far as I know*, she is still working for the same company. (knowledge)
....

5 I wanted to find a new job because I felt *bored with my life*. (rut)
....

6 They *don't get on well* with their neighbours. (terms)
....

7 I *was thinking of* something particular. (mind)
....

8 We *couldn't possibly* sell this painting. (question)
....

9 Mr Smith said a few words at the board meeting *as the representative of* the older employees. (behalf)
....

10 The book you want is *no longer available from a publisher*, so it may be difficult to find. (print)
....

> **Study Tip**
>
> For all the papers of the Proficiency exam it is important to have a good knowledge of dependent prepositions (e.g. *insist on*, *interested in*, etc.) and prepositional phrases (e.g. *at a glance*, *in time*, etc.). Make sure you keep a record of such prepositions as you come across them on a separate page of your notebook.

Reading

▶ **Paper 1, Part 4**

1 Read the following text
quickly. What type of novel could it
be from? (More than one is
possible.)

a) gothic horror
b) science fiction
c) historical
d) romantic
e) detective

26

Mandy Price, aged nineteen years two months, and the
acknowledged star of Mrs Creasley's Nonesuch Secretarial
Agency, set out on the morning of Tuesday, 14th September
for her interview at the Peverell Press with no more apprehension than
she usually felt at the start of a new job, an apprehension which was
never acute and was rooted less in an anxiety as to whether she would
satisfy the expectations of the prospective employer than in whether
the employer would satisfy hers. She had learned of the job the
previous Friday when she called in at the agency at six o'clock to
collect her pay after a boring two-week stint with a director who
regarded a secretary as a status symbol but had no idea how to use
her skills, and she was ready for something new and preferably
exciting although perhaps not as exciting as it was subsequently to
prove.

Mrs Creasley, for whom Mandy had worked for the past three
years, conducted her agency from a couple of rooms above a
newsagent and tobacconist's shop off the Whitechapel Road, a
situation which, she was fond of pointing out to her girls and clients,
was convenient both for the City and for the towering offices of
Docklands. Neither had so far produced much in the way of business,
but while other agencies foundered in the waves of recession, Mrs
Creasley's small and underprovisioned ship was still, if precariously,
afloat. Except for the help of one of her girls when no outside work
was available, she ran the agency single-handed. The outer room was
her office in which she propitiated clients, interviewed new girls and
assigned the new week's work. The inner was her personal sanctum,
furnished with a divan bed on which she occasionally spent the night
in defiance of the terms of the lease, a drinks cabinet and a
refrigerator, a cupboard which opened to reveal a minute kitchen, a
large television set and two easy chairs in front of the gas fire in which
a lurid red light rotated behind artificial logs. She referred to her room
as the 'cosy', and Mandy was one of the few girls who was admitted
to its privacies.

It was probably the cosy which kept Mandy faithful to the agency,
although she would never have openly admitted to a need which
would have seemed to her both childish and embarrassing. Her
mother had left home when she was six and she herself had been
hardly able to wait for her sixteenth birthday when she could get
away from a father whose idea of parenthood had gone little further
than the provision of two meals a day which she was expected to
cook, and her clothes. For the last year she had rented one room in a
terraced house in Stratford East where she lived in acrimonious
camaraderie with three young friends, the main cause of dispute being
Mandy's insistence that her Yamaha motorbike should be parked in
the narrow hall. But it was the cosy in Whitechapel Road, the mingled
smells of wine and take-away Chinese food, the hiss of the gas fire,
the two deep and battered armchairs in which she could curl up and
sleep which represented all Mandy had ever known of the comfort
and security of home.

Mrs Creasley, sherry bottle in one hand and a scrap of jotting paper
in the other, munched at her cigarette holder until she had
manoeuvred it to a corner of her mouth where, as usual, it hung in
defiance of gravity, and squinted at her almost indecipherable
handwriting through immense horn-rimmed spectacles.

'It's a new client, Mandy, the Peverell Press. I've looked them up in
the publisher's directory. They're one of the oldest – perhaps the
oldest – publishing firm in the country, founded in 1792.'

2 Find and underline the answers to these questions in the text.

1 Why was Mandy Price usually slightly apprehensive when going to a new job?

2 What was the main reason the director had hired Mandy?

3 Why did Mrs Creasley consider the agency's position in relation to the City and Docklands to be advantageous?

4 In what way could Mrs Creasley be considered a more successful businesswoman than others?

5 Why did Mandy continue to work for Mrs Creasley?

6 What kind of relationship did Mandy have with the other girls in the house in Stratford East?

7 What impression does the author give us of Mandy's values and personality?

3 The multiple-choice options for the questions in Exercise 2 are given below. In each case, tick the option (**A**, **B**, **C** or **D**) which is closest to the answer you found in the text.

1 **A** She was worried her new employer would not be pleased with her.
 B She was afraid of being disappointed by her new employer.
 C She felt uncomfortable with people she didn't know well.
 D She had high expectations of herself and her performance.

2 **A** He wanted an attractive secretary so that others would envy him.
 B He didn't have the skills she had.
 C He had a lot of work he needed her to do.
 D He felt that a man in his position ought to have a secretary.

3 **A** She expected business from the Docklands area.
 B A lot of business came from these two areas.
 C It was near potential employers.
 D It was easy to go shopping in the City.

4 **A** She had invested successfully in shipping.
 B Business at her agency was thriving.
 C She had remained in business while other agencies had closed.
 D She ran the business virtually single handed.

5 **A** Very few of the girls were allowed in the cosy.
 B She liked the other girls who worked at the agency.
 C She looked upon her as a mother figure.
 D The cosy provided the kind of home she craved.

6 **A** She always got on well with them.
 B She often quarreled with them.
 C She found their company boring.
 D She disliked them.

7 **A** She had a much stronger attachment to places than people.
 B Her independence was more important to her than anything else.
 C She was more sentimental than she wanted to be.
 D She didn't like to admit to things she had done.

4 For each question in a multiple-choice exercise there are four options: one option is the correct answer and the other three are 'distractors' or incorrect answers. Distractors can be:
- **wrong in relation to the text** (what they say is not exactly what the text says), or
- **wrong in relation to the stem or question** (they contain information which is in the text, but do not give a good and complete answer for the question stem).

Some distractors **both** fail to answer the question fully, **and** contain information not in the text.

For questions 1–7 above, option **A** in each case is one of the distractors. Look at the statements below, and match an option **A** distractor to each.

a) A word in the text has been repeated in the distractor, but here it is used differently, and has a different meaning. ....

b) The statement in the distractor is definitely not what the text tells us – it may even be the opposite. ....

c) The distractor gives us true information from the text, but only partly answers the question. ....

d) The distractor may well contain information which is true, but the text doesn't actually tell us this – we are inferring it, and it is our opinion, rather than the truth. ....

Language Focus: Grammar

Participle clauses

Watch Out! *problem areas*

- **the subject of the participle clause**
  The subject of the participle clause is usually the same as that of the main clause, and a subject, noun or pronoun, must appear in the main clause.
  Reading through the script, ~~there were~~ *I noticed* lots of mistakes.
  ~~Not~~ *Nobody* having any more questions to ask, the meeting came to a close.
  Not knowing what to say, *he* fumbled with his papers and sat down.
  In some common expressions, however, the participle clause can be given its own subject.
  Generally speaking, women perform this task better than men. ✔

- **present, past and perfect participles**
  Present (*wanting to ...*), past (*wanted by ...*) and perfect participles (*having wanted to ...*) can all be used to make participle clauses.
  ~~Irritating~~ *Irritated* by her remark, he glowered at her and started to shout.
  ~~Having wanted~~ *Wanting* to catch his attention, she whistled shrilly.

- **double negatives**
  Not having read the book, ~~was he able~~ *he was not able* to answer any of their questions.

1 Match each sentence 1–10, with one of the functions of participle clauses a)–e).

1 Sitting on his balcony, he watched the people below going about their business.
2 Putting down the telephone, he went into the lounge and made himself a drink.
3 Having already seen the play, he decided not to go with his friends to the theatre.
4 Wanting to forget the events of the evening, he turned on the television and watched a film.
5 Although thrilled by the good news, I decided not to celebrate until it had been confirmed.
6 Having been searched by the police, he was taken to a room for questioning.
7 He left the room, humming to himself as he went.
8 Not being a cinema buff, I am not able to comment on the quality of the film.
9 Allowed to leave the country, he would disappear without a trace.
10 Working as hard as he does, it's not surprising he's had a nervous breakdown.

The participle clause is used to describe:
  a) events happening one after the other
  b) events happening at the same time
  c) a reason
  d) a concession
  e) a condition

2

1 Read the following extract, featuring the spy, Tom Sloane.

(1) .... Tom Sloane kept his eye on the exceptionally fat man who was moving ponderously towards him. Something about the fat man was not quite right. Maybe it was the slightly insane grin which made Sloane feel uneasy. (2) .... He naturally felt vulnerable. He wondered what he should do. (3) .... He stood up and strolled towards the man. (4) ....
(5) .... He understood that a moment's carelessness could cost him his life. Sloane was ready for anything. (6) .... Especially a fat man wearing a black bowler hat – the steel hat! Why hadn't he noticed it before? (7) .... Sloane dived for cover. Zzzzzz! The steel hat just missed him. (8) .... The fat man continued to grin at Sloane. (9) .... 'Good afternoon, Mr Sloane. How nice to see you,' he muttered. (10) ....

2 The information from sentences 1–10 below fits in the gaps in the story. Rewrite the story, using participle clauses and **changing the order of the details** where you think appropriate.

EXAMPLE:

Sitting under a palm tree, sipping his cocktail, Tom Sloane kept his eye on the exceptionally fat man ...

1 Sloane was sitting under a palm tree and sipping his cocktail at the time.
2 He had not brought his gun with him to the beach.
3 He put his glass down.
4 He whistled nonchalantly as he went.
5 He understood this even though he was exhausted from his previous mission.
6 He had been attacked by a knife-wielding nun the previous week.
7 He had just seen the man reach for the weapon on his head.
8 It buried itself in the sand beside him.
9 He was unperturbed.
10 He was clenching his teeth as he said it.

Listening

▶ Paper 4, Part 1

About the exam

In **Paper 4, Part 1** you have to listen to four short extracts (from talks, interviews, conversations, etc.) and answer two **three-option** multiple-choice questions about each extract. These eight questions test your understanding of factual details as well as the speakers' feelings, attitudes and opinions. You will hear each extract twice.

Exam Strategy

- Before you listen to each extract, look at the questions carefully so that you know what you are listening out for.
- When you listen, choose the answer (A, B or C) which fits each of the questions best. The first time you hear the extract, eliminate those answers you are sure are wrong.

 1 You will hear six short extracts taken from different contexts. Listen carefully and match each extract to one of the contexts (a–f) below. What features helped you to decide?

Extract 1 .... Extract 2 .... Extract 3 ....
Extract 4 .... Extract 5 .... Extract 6 ....

a) a radio talk
b) a business presentation
c) a college or university lecture
d) a radio interview
e) a conversation between friends
f) live radio coverage of a public event

 2 You will now hear four extracts from various contexts. Before listening, read the context or situation for each extract, so that you know how many people you will hear and the way they will probably be speaking. Then read the questions carefully.
Now listen and for each question choose the answer (**A**, **B** or **C**) which fits best according to what you hear. Listen to each extract twice.

Extract One

You hear two friends talking about how they learn about current events.

1 What do the two speakers disagree about?
   A the accuracy of television news coverage
   B the value of TV commercials
   C the way television reporting has changed
2 How did the man feel when using the Internet?
   A confident
   B excited
   C intimidated

Extract Two

You hear a lecturer talking about the early history of the cinema.

3 Which method of adding sound to film was usually used in the 1920s?
   A accompaniment by a pianist
   B accompaniment by an orchestra
   C accompaniment by actors and musicians from behind the screen
4 What does the lecturer find amazing?
   A Scientists were able to add sound to film in the 1900s.
   B Film studios were so reluctant to adopt innovations.
   C Photography was so developed in the early twentieth century.

Extract Three

You hear a psychologist talking about the television series *Star Trek*.

5 Why does Dr Wolfson mention the woman he interviewed?
   A She is an example of someone who needed help.
   B She is typical of many fans who record every episode.
   C She illustrates his point about withdrawal symptoms.
6 According to Dr Wolfson, what is a positive aspect of *Star Trek*?
   A It can be inspiring.
   B It is informative.
   C It develops the imagination.

Extract Four

You hear a reporter providing live TV coverage of a film awards ceremony.

7 Who does the reporter think will win the Best Actress of the Year Award?
   A Vanessa O'Connor
   B Jenny Jarvis
   C He cannot be sure.
8 How does the reporter describe the film *Beyond the Horizon*?
   A It was not as successful as it should have been.
   B It was unexpectedly successful.
   C It was a box office hit because it was controversial.

Writing

▶ Paper 2, Part 1 (article)

About the exam

In **Paper 2, Part 1** you may have to write an **article** of 300–350 words for a newspaper, magazine or newsletter. You will be given information on which to base your writing, including a description of your target audience. In your article you may have to describe an event or situation, as well as present a reasoned discussion of the issues which are involved. There will usually be at least three clear points for discussion.

Exam Strategy

- Make sure you are clear about what kind of article you have to write. Newspaper articles are usually slightly different from magazine articles in the way they present information.
- Why are you writing the article? Who will read it? Think about the tone you should adopt – what degree of formality or informality is appropriate?
- Read the information and the instructions you are given carefully. Underline any points you are asked to cover in your article.
- Spend time writing a clear, organised outline of your article. Think about what information you will include in each of the paragraphs **at the planning stage**. Make sure you include:
  a) an introduction which makes an impact on the reader. What has happened or what will happen in the near future?
  b) the views of someone involved in the event(s) or situation you describe. In a newspaper article, direct speech is usually used for this purpose.
  c) a closing paragraph which reflects on the issue or issues described in the article and leads back to your opening comments.
- Write your article, following your outline closely.
- When you finish, check your work for grammar, punctuation and spelling mistakes.

1 Read the following writing task. Write **in your own words** the main reasons for the closure of the cinema in London Road.

TASK

You have read the following announcement about the closure of a local cinema. You have spoken to the manager of the cinema on several occasions, and decide to write a short article for a local newspaper describing the closure, discussing the reasons for it, and expressing your own views about the changing forms of entertainment.

(300–350 words)

> It is with regret that I have to announce the closure on Friday 24 April of the Royal Cinema, 35 London Road. Rising prices, together with improved television and video technology, mean that it is no longer feasible for the cinema to continue to operate. This will come as no surprise to some, perhaps, who have been aware of the steady fall off in audience attendance in recent years and the constant battle I have had with planners who want to turn the building into luxury flats. The planners, I am sorry to say, have won. After more than thirty years it is now time to close.
>
> Mr Frank Smythe, Manager

2 Now read the following detailed outline which was written in answer to the task. Underline the information (in three places) which you think should be expressed using direct speech.

Paragraph 1
(the news event)
This Friday cinema will close - projectors dismantled - Mr Smythe will leave/builders will arrive. Their job? →luxury flats.

Paragraph 2
Reactions/feelings of manager to closure

Paragraph 3
(discussion of reasons for closure)
Dwindling audiences in recent years - TV/videos - people stay at home
Developments in technology: TV screens bigger/better sound + pictures/specialist TV channels

Paragraph 4
(times change)
Views of manager about technological changes TV/Video obviously not the same as cinema - unique experience - but has become expensive Manager powerless to bring down prices - why?

Paragraph 5
(concluding remarks)
End of an era - many people sad - part of

3 Read the finished newspaper article and see whether you were correct. Ignore the underlined words for the moment. What effect do the parts in direct speech have on the reader?

This Friday evening at 7 o'clock the Royal Cinema in London Road will open its doors for the last time to members of the public. On Saturday morning the projectors will be dismantled, and the manager of the cinema, Mr Frank Smythe, will leave the premises quietly, before the builders move in. Their job? To transform the building into luxury flats over the next six months.

'It really is awful to think that this is all coming to an end,' Mr Smythe <u>says</u>. 'And to think that I've been here for over thirty years. I can't take it in.'

The problem, of course, is that in recent years cinema audiences have been dwindling. People prefer to stay in and watch television or a video. No longer are they forced to go out in the cold and wet to see the latest blockbuster – they can simply order it from the nearest video store and enjoy it in the warmth and comfort of their home. Developments in technology mean that television screens are bigger than ever, and sound and picture quality have improved tremendously over the past ten years. Furthermore, specialist television channels are now widely available, making even videos obsolete.

How does Mr Smythe view the new technologies? 'It's progress of a sort, I suppose,' he <u>says</u>, 'but I still don't believe it has the same magic as going to the cinema.' That is quite true, of course. Watching TV or a video is not the same as going to the cinema. Despite improvements in technology, nothing can replace the experience of watching a film on the 'big screen'. Unfortunately, however, this is now an expensive option. 'People say I should cut prices,' Mr Smythe <u>says</u>, 'but I wouldn't survive for a week if I did that! I'm utterly powerless to do anything.'

On Friday evening an era comes to an end. Like Frank Smythe, many people here will feel sad about the closure of the Royal Cinema in London Road. For large numbers of locals, an important part of their lives will disappear forever.

(350 words)

4 The student who wrote the article uses *says* to indicate direct speech. The verb *say* is used by journalists in this way, of course, but other verbs are also used in order to make their writing clearer and more interesting.

Look at the three parts of the article where direct speech is used, and replace *says* with one of the verbs in the box below. There are three verbs you do not need to use.

urges   smiles   concedes   confesses
sighs   enthuses

5 Now plan and write an article in answer to the following task.

> ### TASK
>
> You received the following invitation to a demonstration of TV and video equipment at a local store. You went along to see the demonstration and spoke to the manager. Write an article for a local newspaper about the event, discussing the advantages or disadvantages of the new equipment now available and expressing your own views.
>
> (300–350 words)

Public Demonstration

On Saturday 25th March we will be giving a public demonstration of our new range of wide-screen televisions and video equipment. Technology REALLY IS revolutionising the way we live! At last …

- the kind of prices you can afford
- an enormous number of TV channels at your fingertips
- new, improved sound (wow!) and picture quality
- the cinema experience in the comfort of your home.

Don't miss out! Come to 'Just TV and Video' on Saturday morning and talk to the manager, Mr John Taylor, about what is now available.

6 Exchange your article with another student if you can. Evaluate each other's work and suggest improvements.

The hard sell

Language Focus: Grammar
Determiners and substitution

> **Watch Out!** *problem areas*

- **the**

  The war is a terrible thing. It brings ~~the~~ terrible hardship to the people involved. ~The Second World War is a prime example of this.

  ~The computer has offered ~the young all sorts of opportunities not available to their parents.

- **it and this**

  The photocopier has broken down again.

  It needs to be replaced. (= *the photocopier*) ✔

  This is bound to cause a lot of problems.

  (= *the breakdown*) ✔

  When referring to a previous sentence, *it* usually refers to the *subject* of that sentence.

  This usually refers to something *later* in the sentence.

  We can also use *this* to refer to an idea or to a *number* of things previously mentioned.

  There have been so many problems today. People shouting at each other, work piling up and customers complaining. All ~~these have~~ ~*this has* been caused by the breakdown of the photocopier.

- **one(s)**

  Have you seen any good films recently? I saw ~~one really good film~~ ~*a really good one* yesterday.

  Old people spend less money on clothes than young ~~ones~~ ~*people*. (*or* the young)

  I couldn't find the new chair I wanted, so I bought several second-hand *ones* from the market. ✔

- **that and those**

  The one and *the ones* are often replaced by *that* and *those*.

  The book I'm reading now is far better than *the one/that* which I struggled to finish last month. ✔

  The books I bought in Germany are more useful than *the ones/those* I found in France. ✔

Fill each of the gaps in the following text with **one** suitable word. Most, but not all, of the words you need are **articles**, **determiners** or **reference words**. There is an example at the beginning (0).

The value of marketing

When someone sees (0) .....*a*...... new food product for sale in the supermarket, (1) .... decision whether or not to buy (2) .... depends on various factors. Among the most important of (3) ...., of course, are price and packaging. It is obvious that (4) .... highly-priced product will not sell well. If a consumer is faced with two different brands of baked beans, one of which is twice as expensive as the other, he will probably choose (5) .... which is cheaper. Nowadays, economic recession has made people even more reluctant to buy what (6) .... be thought of as luxury items. Interestingly, however, (7) .... is strong evidence to suggest that if the price of (8) .... product is too low, the effect on sales will be the same. (9) .... simply makes no difference whether the product is top quality or not. The public will not buy something it considers to be too cheap. Inevitably, (10) .... comes as a surprise to most people, but market research has shown (11) .... to be true. (12) .... goes without saying that the colour and the quality of the packaging also (13) .... a vital role in the success or failure of a new product. For example, people tend to opt for brands of frozen vegetables in green or blue packets rather than (14) .... packaged in red or yellow. The implications of all (15) .... are obvious: it is essential that manufacturers and advertisers research the market carefully before they launch a new product.

Use of English
▶ **Paper 3, Part 4**

About the exam

In **Paper 3, Part 4** you have to rewrite eight sentences using a given word, **which you must not change in any way,** to produce sentences similar in meaning to the originals. You are given the beginning and the ending of the sentences you have to write and you must only use **three to eight words** (including the key word) in each case. This task tests your knowledge of grammatical patterns associated with certain words, together with phrases and expressions.

Exam Strategy

- Read the sentence carefully for meaning.
- Look at the key word you are given. Do you recognise it as part of a grammatical pattern, phrase or idiom?
- Very often you will need to change the form of a word, e.g. adjective to noun. In many cases, this change means you will also need to add a new dependent preposition, or use a different one from that in the prompt sentence. It may also mean that you need to use the -ing form of a verb, rather than the infinitive. **Don't change the word you are given**.
- Pay particular attention to verb forms. For example, if the continuous form of a verb is used in the prompt sentence, you are likely to need a continuous form in the sentence you write.
- Complete the second sentence, using no more than three to eight words. Don't leave out or change any important information.

---

1 Read the following examples carefully. They give you an idea of what you need to consider when doing this type of task.

EXAMPLES:

1 They were well known for their fondness for practical jokes.
   love
   Their *love of practical jokes was* well known.

   The possessive adjective *their* tells us that *love* here is a noun, not a verb. It is followed by the dependent preposition *of*. Other changes: *were* changes to *was*.

2 This cleaning fluid is highly inflammable.
   catches
   This *cleaning fluid catches fire very* easily.

   Knowing what the word *inflammable* means, it is obvious that the expression we need to use is *catches fire*. Other changes: *highly* changes to *very*.

2 For each of the sentences in the following exercises, complete the second sentence with three to eight words so that it has a similar meaning to the first sentence, using the word given. **Do not change the word given**.

1 In this exercise, which tests your knowledge of various **grammatical patterns**, you have been given the number of missing words and the position of the key word to help you.

1 Petrol is very expensive these days.   **cost**
   The *cost* .... these days.

2 Over the past year the number of house buyers has risen considerably.   **increase**
   Over the past year there .... *increase* .... the number of house buyers.

3 When the theft was discovered, Mike was immediately dismissed.   **led**
   The discovery of the theft *led* .... dismissal.

4 We only realised what had happened after the accident.   **unaware**
   We .... *unaware* .... after the accident.

5 They think that Alex caused the problem.   **suspected**
   Alex .... *suspected* .... the problem.

2 In this exercise, you have been given the number of missing words. The sentences test your knowledge of **phrasal verbs** and **dependent prepositions**.

1 I don't think you should get involved in this argument.   **keep**
   I think you .... this argument.

2 Would my bringing a friend with me to dinner inconvenience you?   **put**
   Would it .... a friend with me to dinner?

3 I can't understand why he is unwilling to tell us the truth. **baffled**

I .... to tell us the truth.

4 She is a very valuable helper at the shop. **relied**

She .... at the shop.

5 One of the reasons the enterprise failed was that the manager was so inefficient. **contributed**

The manager's .... of the enterprise.

3 In this exercise you are not given any help. The sentences test your knowledge of **idioms** and **expressions**.

1 Mark's brother suddenly decided to go home by bus. **spur**

Mark's brother decided ....

.... the bus home.

2 I won't settle for anything less than an exotic foreign holiday. **set**

I ....

.... an exotic foreign holiday.

3 Sandra didn't get any sleep at all last night. **wink**

Sandra ....

.... last night.

4 The mistake was not discovered until we counted the money. **light**

The mistake only ....

.... counted the money.

5 I don't mind lending you money, but I refuse to pay for a new car. **draw**

I don't mind lending you money but I ....

.... a new car.

4 As in the exam, the sentences in this exercise test your knowledge of a range of different language features.

1 I spend much less money on groceries than she does. **nearly**

I don't ....

.... she does.

2 These two brands of ketchup are almost the same. **hardly**

There ....

.... these two brands of ketchup.

3 I really can't understand why she so desperately needs to be popular. **craving**

Her ....

.... I really can't understand.

4 Ten years ago, this shop's turnover was half of what it is today. **doubled**

Over the past ten years this ....

.... turnover.

5 A fight broke out almost immediately at the start of the match. **than**

No ....

.... a fight broke out.

6 She asked you to leave only because she wanted you to be safe. **heart**

She only had your ....

.... she asked you to leave.

7 It was only with great difficulty that he could understand what they were saying. **virtually**

It was ....

.... what they were saying.

8 When we returned to the shop the manager was nowhere to be seen. **sign**

When we returned to the shop ....

.... manager.

9 It was only at the age of eighteen that Heather started to do ballroom dancing. **take**

Heather didn't ....

.... she was eighteen.

10 George lost his job six months ago. **out**

George has ....

.... six months.

11 Provided our fuel supply continues, we'll be fine. **run**

Unless we ....

.... we'll be fine.

12 Watch my children for me while I'm away, won't you? **eye**

Can you ....

.... I'm away?

✓ **3** When you have checked your answers to Exercise 2, analyse any errors you made. Did you miss:

- a change of tense?
- a necessary dependent preposition?
- where an opposite or negative was necessary?
- a change of the form of a word, e.g. noun to adjective?
- a phrasal verb or fixed expression?

Listening

▶ Paper 4, Part 2

About the exam

The gapped sentences in sentence completion exercises focus on the main ideas in the text. These sentences always follow the order of information in the recording. As with all of the Listening tasks, you will hear the recording twice.

1 Before you listen to the recording, think of some ways in which shops (e.g. clothes shops, supermarkets, etc.) encourage customers to spend money. Make a list in your notebook.

2 Now listen and see if you agree with Sandra Adams. You will hear her talking in a radio report about the ways some big fashion stores encourage customers to spend money on clothes. Before listening, read the sentences and try to predict the type of information missing. Then listen and complete the sentences with a word or short phrase. Listen to the recording twice.

Sandra Adams reports that the customer first notices how [____1____] the air is in the shop.

An impression of [____2____] is created by the amount of open space just inside the shop entrance.

To the immediate right of the entrance, the most [____3____] are displayed.

Items of clothing are [____4____] arranged on the tables to encourage customers to pick them up.

Sandra compares the path customers take through the shop to a [____5____]

Some customers may be lucky enough to find clothes with a [____6____] in the bargain baskets.

Sandra believes that many women have grown to dread using the [____7____] of a shop.

It is the job of 'style consultants' to [____8____] the customers of the shop.

Sandra was amazed to hear that [____9____] are sometimes used to make customers feel more alert.

Exam Tip!

The first time you listen to the recording, fill in those gaps you are sure of. When you hear the recording the second time, check what you have written and fill in the remaining gaps.

Language Focus: Grammar

Structures with *it*

> **Watch Out!** *problem areas*
>
> - ***it* + adjective**
>   It must be difficult *to know* what brand of detergent to buy. ✔
>   It's amazing *that* she left the shop without paying. ✔
> - ***should***
>   *Should* can be used when referring to things which are important or must be done.
>   It is essential *that you (should)* do exactly what I say. ✔
>   It is also used to describe personal reactions.
>   It is amazing *that he should* speak to you like that. ✔
> - **sentence transformations**
>   She'll probably be late. = It's probable *that* she'll be late. (= *more formal*)
>   He's unlikely *to* arrive on time. = It's unlikely *that* he'll arrive on time.
>   We had difficulty *paying* the rent last week.
>   = We found it difficult *to pay* the rent last week.
>   There's no point (in) *asking* her for help. = It's no use *asking* her for help.

Rewrite each of the following sentences beginning and ending with the words given.

1 Nobody is expected to work during the lunch break.
   It .... lunch break.
2 Her reluctance to take part in the event seemed rather strange to me.
   I found it .... event.
3 The burglar appeared to have broken in through a window.
   It looked .... window.
4 Your success or failure is of no interest to me.
   It doesn't .... fail.
5 What time you decide to come to work is up to you.
   I'll leave it .... work.
6 I'm surprised by the number of people who still believe whatever advertisements say.
   It's .... say.
7 It seems futile for you to continue writing to him every week.
   There .... to him every week.
8 Didn't you realise that he might be lying?
   Didn't it .... the truth?

9 It is my intention not to comment on the recent decision.
   I have .... on the recent decision.
10 It can easily be shown that the claims of the advertisement are false.
   The claims .... true.

Language Focus: Vocabulary

Phrasal verbs and expressions: *set*

1 Complete the sentences below with the correct form of *set up* or *set off*. Use a dictionary to help you if necessary.

1 It was six o'clock in the morning when we .... for the monastery in the mountains.
2 One of the most memorable things which happened was when someone .... a fire alarm by mistake and everyone rushed out of the hotel screaming.
3 The police have .... road blocks everywhere in an attempt to catch the thieves.
4 She wore a black evening dress that .... her pale complexion beautifully.
5 Could you come and help me .... the video – I can't make head or tail of these instructions.
6 My wife and I are thinking of .... a small business together.
7 The police were asking me lots of questions about something I knew nothing about. I think I've been ....
8 The officer in charge of the operation said that even someone slamming a door could .... the bomb.

> ### Study Tip
>
> Some phrasal verbs have many meanings. Sometimes meanings change when the grammar is different (e.g. compare *set something up*, with *set somebody up*). Check typical contexts, grammar and usage in a good dictionary, and record example sentences like those in Exercise 1 in your notebook

2 Rewrite each of the following sentences using an expression with *set* and the word in brackets. Check these words in a dictionary if necessary. The sentences have been started for you.

1 I've never seen him before.
   I've .... (*eyes*)

2   'I'll never enter this house again!' she
    screamed.
    'Never ....
    (*foot*)

3   She desperately wants to win the competition.
    She's ....
    (*heart*)

4   His ideas and habits are too fixed for him to
    cope with the changes.
    He's too ....
    (*ways*)

5   When I go to a restaurant I see the
    attentiveness of the waiters as being of prime
    importance.
    When I go to a restaurant I ....
    (*store*)

Connectors and adverbial phrases

1   In each of the following sentences, one or
more of the words or phrases in italics is wrong.
Decide which are **correct** and underline them.

1   *While/Despite/Even though* most people know
    that they have certain rights as consumers,
    very few people understand what these rights
    actually are.

2   Children are not usually taught about banking
    and insurance when they are at school. They
    are *thus/consequently/correspondingly* ill-
    equipped to deal with their money wisely
    when they grow up.

3   Passing lorries cause a lot of damage to roads
    in cities. *Also/Besides/Furthermore*, they shake
    and slowly destroy the foundations of old
    buildings.

4   *Since/Due to/Owing to* the lack of effective
    legislation controlling advertising, many
    companies still get away with misleading
    consumers about the qualities of their products.

5   People were not unwilling to support the new
    measures. *At least/As a matter of fact/Actually*,
    most people were extremely enthusiastic about
    them.

6   John told me that he was going to resign.
    Or rather/At least/Besides, that's what I thought
    he said – I might have been mistaken.

2   Fill each of the gaps in the following text with
one suitable word. Most, but not all, of the words you
need are **connectors** or part of **adverbial phrases**.
There is an example at the beginning (0).

Nowadays, it goes without (0) *..saying..* that the success
or failure of a new product depends, to a large
(1) ...., on the ingenuity of the advertising
campaign. In other (2) .... money spent on
advertising is preferable to money spent on efforts to
improve the quality of the product. What exactly is it,
(3) ...., that makes an advertisement 'ingenious'?

What (4) .... innovations in packaging and product
design, advertising as a 'science' has developed in leaps and
(5) .... over the past fifty years.

People have become a lot more aware of advertising
techniques and tricks. No (6) .... is it enough to
show men and women in white coats poring over
microscopes or appearing in front of washing machines.
Nor is it enough to show photographs of Mrs X 'before and
after'. (7) .... the same token, advertisements which
simply repeat the name of a product over and over again, or
which play on people's feelings of guilt, are regarded as
being rather old-fashioned these days. What is
(8) ...., certain types of advertisement are just not
acceptable these days. Those which are thought to
encourage anti-social behaviour or racist behaviour, for
(9) ...., have been banned in many countries.

One of the problems advertisers have (10) .... up
against in recent years is that consumers are more
sophisticated and more demanding than they were in the
past. They face the challenge of (11) .... to promote
products which are probably identical to an enormous
number of other products on the market. As a
(12) ...., advertising agencies have been forced to
find ways to make the particular item they are promoting
unique in (13) .... way or other, or to create a
particular image or association for that item. In the world
of modern advertising, it is essential to create an
'atmosphere' around a product which will appeal to the
consumer. (14) .... is amazing, perhaps, is that
(15) .... the competition they face, advertisers can
still find ways of making particular brand names seem more
attractive than others.

Exam Tip!

Use connectors and adverbial phrases in **Paper 2** and
Paper 3 (summary) to link together ideas and points in
your writing.

Writing

▶ **Paper 2, Part 2 (formal letter)**

1 The following sentences come from a formal letter. Read them quickly to establish the situation: the writer of the letter, who the letter is written to, and the reason for writing. Make a note of these details in your notebook.

1 Had I known that the food and service in your restaurant would be so unsatisfactory, I would never have considered taking my wife there.
2 From the outset we were treated with indifference by the waiters who 'served' us.
3 I am writing to complain about the quality of service at your restaurant in Oxford Street.
4 Unless I receive an apology and some form of compensation, you will be hearing from the Association of Restaurants in due course.
5 To add insult to injury, the waiter insisted that the misunderstanding had been our fault.
6 Disgusted by the standard of the service, and not expecting the quality of the food to improve, I decided it was time for us to leave.
7 Surely the wine waiter should be able to open a bottle of wine correctly?

2 The list a)–g) below contains the functions you might need to use to write a successful letter of complaint. Match each function to one of the sentences 1–7 from Exercise 1 and write the number of the sentence in the space provided. One has been done for you as an example.

a) stating your reason for writing ......
b) mentioning the first in a list of complaints ......
c) asking a rhetorical question ...7..
d) mentioning something which was 'the last straw' ......
e) describing your response to the situation ......
f) expressing 'hindsight' (the wisdom of experience) ......
g) making a threat/demanding action ......

3 The following sentences are from a different letter of complaint. Rewrite each of them in such a way that the new sentence is as similar as possible in meaning to the original. In this exercise, you have been given both the beginning and the ending of the new sentence, and your changes should make the register **more formal**.

1 I visited your shop because I wanted to return a faulty mini CD player.
   My purpose .... a faulty mini CD player.
2 I was offended more by the attitude of the young man than by what was said.
   It was not so .... of the young man.
3 I would have asked from the start to see the manager, if I had known I would be treated like this.
   Had .... to see the manager.
4 I'm writing to complain about the way the staff behaved in your shop.
   I am writing .... of the staff in your shop.
5 She seemed to find the whole situation amusing, and it was also obvious she didn't intend to do anything about it.
   Not .... intention of doing anything about it.
6 As far as these two members of staff are concerned, I want you to tell me what action you will take.
   I would like you to inform .... regard to these two members of staff.
7 I asked whether they could give me a cash refund.
   I asked .... be possible.
8 If inadequate action is taken, I shall be forced to publish this letter.
   Unless .... option but to publish this letter.

4

1   The sentences in Exercise 3 come from a letter written in answer to the following task.

> **TASK**
>
> You were badly treated by the staff of a shop recently when you tried to return an item you had bought in a sale there. Write to the manager of the shop to complain, explaining what happened and what you would like her to do about it.
>
> (300–350 words)

2   Read the letter below. Identify the sentences from Exercise 3 and check if your rewritten versions are correct. Ignore the gaps for the moment.

Dear Madam

   I am writing to complain about the behaviour of the staff at your shop last Thursday morning, 12th July.

   My purpose in visiting the shop was to return a faulty mini CD player which I had bought the previous week in the sale.

   (1) .... the rather surly tone of voice of the young man who served me, I explained why I was returning the mini CD player and asked whether a cash refund would be possible. You can imagine my anger and amazement when he snatched the mini CD player out of my hands and walked away without saying a word. (2) ...., he told me in no uncertain terms that a cash refund was out of the question. He then walked away again, leaving the mini CD player on the counter.

   Had I known that I would be treated like this, I would have asked from the start to see the manager. It was not so much what was said that offended me, as the attitude of the young man. (3) ...., I was treated with the same indifference by another member of staff. When I asked this assistant for the name of the first young man, she simply laughed. Not only did she seem to find the whole situation amusing, but it was obvious that she had no intention of doing anything about it. (4) ...., I decided to leave the shop immediately.

   I feel that I must protest about such appallingly rude behaviour towards a regular customer of yours. Would a letter of apology be too much to expect? (5) ...., I would like you to inform me of the action you will take with regard to these two members of staff, and what you propose to do about the faulty mini CD player. Unless adequate action is taken, I shall have no other option but to publish this letter in the local newspaper.

   I look forward to hearing from you.

   Yours faithfully

   Ronald Scott

5   Look at the numbered gaps in the letter. Choose the best word or phrase (**A**, **B** or **C**) to fill each gap.

1   **A** Ignoring
     B Having ignored
     C On ignoring

2   **A** Returning
     B On returning
     C Returned

3   **A** To make matters worse
     B To mention another matter
     C As a matter of fact

4   **A** Quite unexpectedly
     B Somewhat reluctantly
     C Not surprisingly

5   **A** Last but not least
     B To say the least
     C At the very least

6   Read the following writing task and write a letter of complaint, including as many as possible of the elements from Exercise 2 and language from Exercises 3–5, where appropriate.

> **TASK**
>
> A holiday you had arranged to go on was cancelled at the last moment. When you went to the travel agency to ask for your deposit back, the person you spoke to was rude and unhelpful. Write to the manager of the travel agency to complain about the behaviour of this employee, explaining the situation and what you expect the travel agency to do.
>
> (300–350 words)

7   Exchange your letter with another student if you can. Evaluate each other's work and suggest improvements.

5 A life of crime

Language Focus: Grammar
Modal verbs

> **Watch Out!** *problem areas*
>
> - **must (have) and can't (have)**
>   You ~~mustn't~~ *can't* have seen Anne yesterday –
>   she's in America at the moment.
>   You ~~can~~ *could/may/might* have seen her sister –
>   she looks quite similar to Anne.
> - **can and don't have to/don't need to/needn't**
>   *Can* expresses freedom to do things we might
>   choose to do, while *don't have to/needn't*
>   expresses freedom from restrictions.
>   In some open prisons, inmates *can* wear what
>   they want. ✔
>   They *don't have to/needn't* stay inside their cells all
>   day if they don't want to. ✔
> - **could(n't) (have) and might (not) (have)**
>   The positive forms of *could* and *might* have very
>   similar meanings.
>   He *might* be guilty. = He *could* be guilty.
>   But the negative forms have very different
>   meanings.
>   He *might not have* committed the crime.
>   (= *I'm not sure if he did it or not*) ✔
>   He *couldn't have* committed the crime.
>   (= *I'm sure he didn't do it*) ✔
> - **supposed to**
>   I should do it. = *I'm supposed to* do it. ✔
>   I shouldn't. = I ~~don't~~ *'m not* supposed to.
> - **could and was able to**
>   We use *could* when talking about general ability
>   in the past and *was able to* for specific success on
>   one occasion.
>   The robber *could* run like the wind (= *general
>   ability*), and so he *was able to* escape (= *specific
>   success on one occasion*) the policeman chasing
>   him. ✔
>   However, we use *couldn't* to express both general
>   ability and specific failure on one occasion.
>   The kidnapper *couldn't* read or write, so he
>   *couldn't* make the ransom note himself, and had to
>   get an accomplice to help. (= *general ability and
>   specific failure*) ✔

1 Fill each of the gaps in the following sentences with a suitable word or phrase.

1 How on earth .... told all those lies to the police?
2 You .... sense than to buy that gold watch from him. It's probably stolen.
3 The witness is almost blind, so he .... seen what happened.
4 The judge was satisfied with my written statement, so I .... give evidence in person.
5 You .... trusted him if you gave him your cheque book!
6 I wouldn't walk on those floorboards if I were you – .... be safe.

2 For each question below, complete the second sentence with three to eight words so that it has a similar meaning to the first sentence, using the word given. Do not change the word given.

1 He was supposed to telephone yesterday but he didn't have time. **should**
  Although he ....
  .... round to it.
2 All those who stay longer than six months have to register with the police. **obligatory**
  Registration ....
  .... who stays longer than six months.
3 It was in your power to have him arrested for behaving so badly. **could**
  You ....
  .... bad behaviour.
4 It was remiss of you not to tell me to cancel the meeting. **might**
  You ....
  .... off the meeting.
5 Given the staff's lack of interest, her attempts to solve the problem were pointless. **bothered**
  Given the staff's lack of interest, she ....
  .... a solution to the problem.
6 The cashier did what he was told, so it was unnecessary for the robber to use force. **need**
  The robber ....
  .... the cashier did what he was told.

Reading

▶ Paper 1, Part 2

About the exam

In **Paper 1**, **Part 2** you have to read four short texts with a common theme and answer two multiple-choice questions on each text. The texts will be extracts from newspaper and magazine articles, novels, essays, advertisements, etc. and will therefore be different in style and register. The questions require you to think about:

- the main idea of the text and supporting details
- the purpose of the text or parts of the text
- the writer's message and attitude
- the writer's implication in certain parts of the text
- text organisation features, e.g. comparisons, examples, reference.

Exam Strategy

- Look at the instructions, the titles and opening sentences of each text to get an idea of the main theme and the types of text.
- Read through the first text to get a general idea of what it is about.
- Look at the two questions or unfinished stems and try to find the answer without looking at the four options. Then look at the options and choose the one which most closely resembles your own answer.
- If you are unsure of the answer, have a guess and move on to the other texts.

1   In both Part 2 and Part 4 of Paper 1, there will be words and expressions you do not know. It may be necessary for you to understand these words in order to answer particular questions. This is often possible by using clues from the context.

When working out the meaning of an unknown word, look for:

- a definition or explanation
- an example that makes the meaning clear
- repeated use of the word in other parts of the text
- words in the text that have a similar or opposite meaning.

Read the text below and try to work out the meaning of the following words and phrases, all of which occur in the text. Use the words and phrases printed in bold and the hints to help you.

My first time in prison

My first experience of prison was when I was just eighteen. I will never forget my first days of **incarceration**, of being surrounded on all sides by grim walls topped with barbed wire, of knowing that this awful place was to be my home for the next six months. A terrible feeling of **desolation** had settled upon me. I was completely alone, abandoned by everyone I had ever loved or cared for. Try as I might, I found it impossible to **stem the flow** of negative thoughts and emotions. I just gave in completely to the despair which seemed to wash over me in wave after merciless wave. What on earth had I done which deserved such terrible punishment?

Rather than **take stock of** my new situation, I steadfastly avoided any attempt at calm, logical thought, and, in doing so, offered myself up wholly to the demons that lurked within me. My life would never be the same again. It seemed to me to be inevitable that I was destined for a life of crime. How could it be avoided? With such a black mark against my name, how could anybody ever trust me again? Why would anybody in their right mind give me even the smallest bit of responsibility? From now on, I was to be an outcast; a **pariah** to society.

1 incarceration: ....
   (**HINT**: *Look at the next part of the sentence, which gives a definition of the word.*)
2 desolation: ....
   (**HINT**: *The next sentence gives a definition.*)
3 stem the flow: ....
   (**HINT**: *You will find a phrasal verb in the next sentence which conveys the opposite meaning.*)
4 take stock of: ....
   (**HINT**: *Look at the next part of the sentence, which is opposite in meaning.*)
5 pariah: ....
   (**HINT**: *Look at what comes immediately before this word.*)

── Exam Tip! ◀

Try to deduce the meaning of difficult words **only** if you need them to help you to answer a question.
When you need to work out the meaning of a word to complete the task, use the whole paragraph to help you, not just the one sentence containing the word.

2 You are going to read four texts which are all connected with crime or the punishment of crime. When you have read each text, answer the two questions which are printed beneath it. To do this, you may need to know the meaning of the words and phrases which have been underlined. Where possible, try to work out the meaning of these words and phrases from the context.

Life in a new part of town

When I had moved to my new house in a rather run-down part of town, I had done so with my eyes wide open. I was more than aware of the level of crime there. Being forewarned, however, does not prepare you for the overwhelming sense of <u>outrage</u> you experience 'when it happens to you'; when you are confronted by a gang of youths demanding your purse, quite brazenly and in broad daylight. This happened to me last week, and the feeling of helplessness I experienced was compounded by the fact that people <u>turned a blind eye</u> to what was going on. Nobody wanted to get involved.

When I duly reported the incident to the police, they were sympathetic but <u>non-committal</u> about the chances of bringing the boys to justice. Such things were commonplace in that part of town and rarely resulted in a conviction, let alone someone being sent to prison. The police, it seemed, were at the <u>end of their tether</u>, struggling to stem the tide of even more violent forms of crime.

After half an hour or so, I left the police station feeling that I had been patronised and wondering why on earth I had gone there in the first place.

1 What does the writer say about her feelings on being mugged in the street?
   A She was not particularly surprised when it happened.
   B She was deeply shaken by her experience.
   C She felt that it was a warning to her to leave the area.
   D She was angry that people seemed to support her attackers.

2 What was the attitude of the police to the crime the writer reported?
   A They were not willing to look for the culprits.
   B They were resigned to the prevailing lawlessness.
   C They considered the incident to be of no importance.
   D They felt that the writer was wasting their time.

The purpose of punishment in British society

What is the purpose of the punishment meted out to a convicted criminal? If it is purely retributive, one can argue that conditions of imprisonment should be as punitive and restrictive as possible. But most commentators these days wish to add an element of reform or <u>rehabilitation</u> to the concept of punishment. One of its consequences, they argue, should be that the person who is subjected to the punishment will be less likely to commit further offences or crimes in the future and will be helped to lead a useful life in society. The change in behaviour will come about either because of the deterrent effect of the punishment or because it has led the person being punished to a greater awareness of the need to live differently in the future. The judge, like the parent of the wayward child, punishes an offender for his or her 'own good', in order to help the offender to become a better person.

The difficulty with this worthy ambition is that the British criminal justice system finds it very difficult to cope with such complex objectives. The offender who goes to prison regards imprisonment primarily as retributive and is not convinced by arguments about their potential for rehabilitation. The victim of the original offence is likely to be confused by a series of mixed messages about how he or she is meant to benefit from the outcome of court proceedings. The public is at best <u>ambivalent</u> – unsure, that is, whether the process of justice is working or not.

3 Nowadays, it is widely believed that the purpose of prison is
   A to be as punitive and as restrictive as possible.
   B to reform and rehabilitate prisoners.
   C to act as a deterrent against offending again.
   D to punish criminals and make them useful, honest citizens.

4 The writer thinks that the use of imprisonment in Britain
   A is an effective means of punishment.
   B encourages criminals to re-offend when released.
   C leaves everyone involved feeling dissatisfied.
   D has no place in a modern society.

Hi-tech helps fight crime

In many parts of the world, modern technology has come to the aid of homeowners in the fight against crime, as ever more sophisticated burglar alarms are peddled to the security conscious. But do these <u>devices</u> make much difference? Or is installing them little more than a <u>self-deceptive gesture</u> towards peace of mind?

The police in most countries are strong advocates of alarms to protect against crime, and are usually willing to give impartial advice. They are the best placed, of course, to be able to assess how effective an alarm would be for a particular flat or house. One thing to keep in mind is that one of the biggest problems for the homeowner and the police is the 'false alarm' syndrome. In Barcelona recently, a crackdown by the police was launched to combat this now endemic problem, which is the bane of many a street. Alarms now have to meet local environmental regulations on noise, and automatically switch off after 20 minutes. The key to avoiding false alarms lies in the installation, and the police have taken measures to ensure that registered companies follow certain procedures. Needless to say, 'do-it-yourself' kits are <u>frowned upon</u>. Not that this dissuades people in Barcelona, or anywhere else for that matter, from installing them. After all, upsetting the neighbours is the last thing on most people's minds when it comes to protecting their property.

Brilliant art forger convicted

It was hard to say what was wrong – the way the paint had been applied or maybe the colours the artist had used. The paintings up for auction certainly looked the part, but – well – Leslie Waddington had not been an art dealer for as long as he had without learning a thing or two.

Within days Mr Waddington had phoned the police to express his concerns. His call added another piece to the jigsaw of evidence being gathered to <u>crack</u> one of the most ingenious art frauds of all time. Shortly afterwards, the police arrested John Drewe, a brilliant but flawed criminal who 'took an intellectual delight in fooling people'.

Drewe's scheme relied on creating histories or provenances for fake works of art he procured, and over the months he set about altering and supplementing official art archives to include details of his non-existent 'works'. He also faked catalogues from exhibitions which had never taken place. The scam took in galleries and even the families of the artists he imitated, and he was described as being '<u>devious</u> to the point of genius'. When one dealer complained that the painting he had bought was a fake, Drewe promptly gave him four sketches by the famous painter Sutherland as compensation. These also turned out to be fakes.

5 What does the writer imply about the effectiveness of most burglar alarms?
  A They may give property owners little protection.
  B They are more effective than is commonly supposed.
  C They are only effective if installed by a registered company.
  D Their effectiveness is exaggerated by the companies who sell them.

6 Why does the writer mention 'do-it-yourself' burglar alarm kits?
  A They have been banned by the police.
  B They have been responsible for most 'false alarms'.
  C Their installation cannot be regulated by the police.
  D They are the most popular type of burglar alarm.

7 What led to John Drewe's downfall?
  A the carelessness of the artist who painted the pictures
  B Drewe's overconfidence and arrogance
  C Mr Waddington's certainty that the paintings were fakes
  D the accumulated suspicions of police and art experts

8 The writer mentions the case of the dealer who complained as an example of
  A Drewe's desire to demonstrate his superior intellect.
  B Drewe's extraordinary talent for deceiving people.
  C behaviour you would expect from an art forger.
  D the technical excellence of the fake paintings.

Use of English

▶ **Paper 3, Part 3**

1

1 Read the following example carefully. It shows the sort of thing you need to consider when doing this type of task.

EXAMPLE:

The whole of the region has been affected by .... flooding and is now under several feet of water.
The punishment meted out to the accomplice in the crime seemed unnecessarily ...., given the fact that he was so young and gullible.
As soon as I noticed the .... expression on the face of the judge, I realised that I was going to be sent to prison.

Here the missing word is an adjective. In the first sentence, several words are possible – *severe*, *disastrous*, *recent* and *sudden*. The word in the second sentence has a negative meaning, so *severe*, *heavy* or *harsh* would fit. We realise by now that the word is probably *severe* – this is confirmed by the last

sentence, in which *severe* is one of several words which would collocate with *expression*.

2 Now find the missing word for these three sentences, using the hint below to help you.

The chemist's in the centre of town can .... your holiday snaps perfectly well.
There is a pressing need to .... new drugs and treatments in the fight against cancer.
I know your apple trees are rather small at the moment, but if you give them lots of fertiliser they'll soon .... and become strong and healthy.
(**HINT:** *The missing word is a verb. It collocates with 'snaps' (= 'photographs') in the first sentence, and 'new drugs/treatments' in the second. It is used in the third sentence as an intransitive verb to mean 'something grows or changes from being weak/small to being strong and healthy'.*)

2 For the following six sets of sentences, think of **one** word only which can be used appropriately in all three sentences.

1 Living in a city was difficult at first, as we had grown up in a small village, surrounded by the beauties of ....
Since she has a very easygoing ...., she probably won't object to the changes.
The support which the families of the victims are receiving is primarily of a practical ....

2 From what your colleagues tell me, I .... you've been having one or two problems at work recently.
It is expected that a huge crowd will .... outside the embassy later today.
Not being an expert herself, she is trying to .... some ideas from the police for her forthcoming article on juvenile delinquency.

3 Supporters of the defendant came from all parts of the country to .... outside the courtroom during the trial.
The findings of the survey clearly .... the relationship between poverty and crime.
The new manager is unlikely to .... much generosity towards those who work for the company.

4 In order to enter the building, we had to force our way through a .... crowd.
Aircraft are unable to take off at the moment owing to the .... fog which has settled over the runway.
I find his writing so .... that it is difficult to take in all the ideas he puts forward in his books.

5   Screaming with disgust, she .... on the beetle as it crawled across the kitchen floor.
His years as an army officer have .... him with an air of authority and importance.
The official took my passport and .... the date of my arrival in the country on one of its pages.

6   One .... on the agenda that we really need to discuss at today's meeting is what pay rise we should ask for this year.
At a particular .... in his talk, the lecturer put down his notes and walked out into the audience.
Since we cannot decide what to do, there seems to be no .... in our continuing this discussion, does there?

Use of English

▶ **Paper 3, Part 2**

Exam Strategy

If the word you need to fill a particular gap is negative in meaning, think very carefully about the prefix or suffix you have to add. In English, there are many prefixes and several suffixes which make words negative, and it is often possible to add two or more of these to a particular stem to make words which have very different meanings.

1   Fill in the gaps in the following sentences with the correct negative form of the word in capitals.

1   I found it hard to believe that anyone could be as .... as Alex. AGREE
2   The .... of the same thing happening twice will be of little comfort to most people. PROBABLE
3   Her lawyers were .... with the verdict of the trial and decided to lodge an appeal. SATISFY
4   The effects of the poison are ...., I'm afraid. REVERSE
5   Room 12 is .... at the moment, so we could go there to talk. USE
6   The .... of the remark he made just takes my breath away. THINK
7   Her .... to the company will end in her being dismissed. LOYAL
8   The doctor told us that the disease was unfortunately .... CURE

2   Read the following text quickly to get a general idea of what it is about. Then use the word given in capitals at the end of some of the lines to form a word that fits in the space in the same line. In this exercise, one of the words you have to form has a negative meaning.

Europe's debt to Rome

It is often said that Roman law has been of (0) *immeasurable* importance in the development of European civilisation. The Romans knew that only just laws could (1) .... sound government, commercial confidence and an orderly society. The idea of the law as being something 'which binds' still (2) .... all legal contracts drawn up by lawyers today. Once agreed by two parties, the contract cannot be broken.

MEASURE

SURE

LIE

The legal traditions of Rome, however, were not bequeathed to modern Europe by any direct line of (3) .... Most of the Roman Empire's law codes fell into (4) .... with the disintegration of the Empire, and had to be rediscovered in the Middle Ages. Their (5) .... was longest in Byzantium, but they did not strongly influence modern law-making by that route.

INHERIT

USE

SURVIVE

The revival of Roman traditions had to compete with other non-Roman, and often (6) ...., legal practices. Even so, the Roman (7) .... of codified principles suited the purposes of Europe's growing states better, and civil law in most countries (8) .... came to be based on the Roman model. In this regard, the most (9) .... institution was the French Code Napoleon, which was written in 1804.

CONTRADICT
CONCEIVE

INCREASE

INFLUENCE

Nowadays, whatever their connection, all educated European lawyers readily (10) .... their debt to Rome.

KNOW

Writing

▶ Paper 2, Part 1 (proposal)

About the exam

In **Paper 2, Part 1** you may have to write a **proposal** of 300–350 words, based on information which you are given. Most of this proposal will be devoted to making **recommendations or suggestions** for a **future project or course of action**.

The layout and organisation of a proposal is very important, as is the register of the language used. The points and ideas you mention should be organised into sections with **headings**, and the tone you adopt should be formal and impersonal.

It is vital that you plan carefully before you write your proposal.

Exam Strategy

- Read the information and the instructions you are given carefully. Make sure you understand what points you are being asked to cover in your proposal.
- Write a detailed plan of what each section of the proposal should contain, and its heading. You should include:
  a) an introduction or brief summary of the present situation.
  b) an outline of the proposals you are making, together with other relevant details, e.g. the benefits they will bring.
  c) a conclusion, perhaps in which you state clearly why you think it is important for your proposals to be adopted.
- Check again that you have covered the relevant points, then write your proposal.

1 Read the following writing task. Underline the main points which need to be covered in the proposal.

TASK

You have read the following advertisement in a national newspaper, offering funding for any project considered likely to be successful in preventing young offenders from re-offending. As the leader of a team of social workers, you decide to send in your proposal to the organisation, outlining your suggestions about how these people should be dealt with.

(300–350 words)

social workers

We are a government organisation which has been set up to fund projects designed to deter young people from embarking upon a life of crime. At present, young offenders receive only a police caution and little guidance as to how to avoid breaking the law again. They never fully understand the consequences of their actions, or appreciate how hard a prison sentence can be.

If you are a social worker, we want to hear what you have to propose. Tell us your ideas, mentioning how the young people concerned would benefit from what you suggest, and how they would be monitored. Successful proposals of schemes will be awarded government funding.

2 Read the proposal which was written in answer to the task, ignoring the gaps and underlining for the moment. Has it covered all the points fully? Which points have been forgotten or not dealt with in enough detail?

Introduction
Juvenile crime is on the increase. At present very little is done to prevent young offenders from re-offending and eventually being sent to prison. The proposals outlined below would go some way to improving this situation.

Recommendations
We feel that <u>a good</u> way of dealing with young offenders is to show them the consequences of their crimes and the way in which they will be punished if they continue to break the law.

We suggest that teenagers guilty of crimes of violence should <u>see</u> the consequences of their actions by visiting those they have hurt and the families of their victims. (1) . . . .

(2) . . . . We feel that it would be particularly beneficial to arrange for prison officers to tell young offenders about the <u>awful</u> conditions which prevail inside prisons. The prison officers' talk could be accompanied by a video, and it might even be a good idea for these young people to meet <u>people who have been in prison</u>, whose lives have been ruined by their time in prison. (3) . . . .

Finally, the progress of each young
offender would be <u>checked</u> by a social worker.
(4) ....

Conclusion

Juvenile crime needs to be dealt with quickly
and effectively. The measures suggested here
would achieve this by helping young offenders
to understand the destructiveness of crime,
and by showing them the future which awaits
them if they continue to break the law. Police
warnings are not enough; unless young offenders
are given guidance, crime levels will continue
to rise.

3 Use the phrases in the box below to rewrite the parts of the proposal which have been underlined so that they are more appropriate and effective. There are two phrases you do not need to use.

> former inmates   humiliating and often violent
> monitored closely   ex-cons   the most effective
> be made fully aware of   terrible

4 The proposal fails to mention satisfactorily how the measures suggested would be of benefit to the young offenders; nor does it say much about how they would be monitored. Match one of the sentences or set of sentences from the following list (a–f) to each of the gaps in the proposal. There are two letters you don't need to use.

a) This experience would certainly make them think twice before they broke the law again.

b) This would have to be done under the supervision of a social worker, of course, but it would be a valuable experience for them to listen to the details of the harm and suffering they have caused.

c) This would allow them to withstand more effectively the influence of their peers in the future.

d) Understanding exactly what having to serve a prison sentence involves would also act as a powerful deterrent to potential re-offenders.

e) He or she would meet the teenager and their family on a regular basis to talk about their progress and any problems which might have arisen. It would be made clear that should a crime be committed again in the future, the case would have to go to court.

f) It is important for young people to feel confident in their ability to earn a living. Those who took part in the session would feel able to look for honest work and would not find it necessary to break the law.

5 Now write a proposal for the following writing task.

TASK

You have read the extract below as part of a letter to a major national newspaper. As a member of the public, you agree with the sentiments expressed in the letter and decide to write a proposal to the appropriate government authorities making suggestions about how petty offenders should be punished.

(300–350 words)

> I'm amazed that for so many petty crimes nowadays, imprisonment seems to be the only form of punishment available. This is expensive and also means that our prisons are full of people who are not particularly dangerous to society. Why can't we find other ways of punishing them? Why not get them doing some kind of community service, or find ways to make them repay those they have robbed or cheated? That would seem to benefit everyone concerned. And for situations where the police needed to know the whereabouts of offenders, they could implant harmless electronic chips somewhere in their bodies. After all, we already do that for animals, don't we?

If appropriate, use words and phrases from the box below to help you make suggestions in your writing.

Useful ways of making suggestions

I feel that ... should ...

I (would) suggest that ... (should) ...

I propose that ... (should) ...

I would like to put forward the idea of ...

I feel that it would be particularly
   beneficial/effective ...

One solution (to this problem) might
   be to ...

Another possible way of dealing with the
problem would be for ...

6 Exchange your proposal with another student if you can. Evaluate each other's work and suggest improvements.

Bright lights, big city

Language Focus: Grammar
The passive

> **Watch Out!** *problem areas*
>
> - **avoiding continuous passive tenses**
>   Continuous passive tenses are not incorrect, but sound 'clumsy', and so are often avoided.
>   We will be ~~being~~ met in five minutes.
>   ~~It will have been being done by Robert.~~ *Robert will have been doing it.*
>   The town has ∧*been* ~~being attacked~~ ∧*under attack* for three days now.
> - *make* and *let*
>   They made me do it. = I was made ∧*to* do it.
>   They let me see her. = I was allowed to see her. ✔
> - **sentence transformations**
>   They heard him complain about the service at the restaurant. = He was heard ∧*to* complain about the service at the restaurant.
>   Information about the hotel is available at the reception desk. = Information about the hotel ~~is found~~ ∧*can be found* at the reception desk.
>   New anti-pollution measures will be introduced next month. = Next month will ~~be~~ ∧*see* the introduction of new anti-pollution measures.
>   If we want to do something about the traffic problem, we should act now. = If the traffic problem is ∧*to be* resolved, we should act now.

1 For questions 1–8 below, complete the second sentence with three to eight words so that it has a similar meaning to the first sentence, using the word given. Do not change the word given.

1 The mayor will give a prize to the best architect.

                                            presented

    The best architect ....
.... the mayor.

2 This year the police have arrested more drivers than usual for speeding.   **number**
    This year an ....
.... for speeding.

3 The sea is gradually eroding the cliff face in this area.   **worn**
    The cliff face in this area ....
.... the sea.

4 Smoking is to be totally banned from next month.   **takes**
    A ....
.... from next month.

5 Refusal to obey the local laws about noise could lead to your arrest.   **for**
    You ....
.... local laws about noise.

6 They insisted that my brother should complete all the application forms again.   **made**
    My brother ....
.... in all the application forms again.

7 The completion of the project should have taken place last month.   **completed**
    The project was ....
.... last month.

8 A quick solution to the housing problem is an urgent priority.   **needs**
    The housing problem ....
.... as possible.

2 Fill each of the gaps in the sentences below with a suitable word or phrase.

1 The disused chimney .... up by demolition experts last week.
2 The decision whether or not to proceed with the plan .... by the end of today.
3 It was suggested that an attempt .... to save the old Town Hall building.
4 'Where's your daughter?' – 'She .... after at the day care centre today.'
5 Since we last met, another sentence .... to the contract, to avoid any possible misunderstanding.
6 Six months' free insurance .... in the purchase price.

> ── *Exam Tip!* ◄
>
> Use passive forms in **Paper 2** in your discursive and formal writing in order to convey an impersonal tone.

Listening

▶ Paper 4, Part 4

About the exam

In **Paper 4, Part 4** you have to listen to a
conversation or discussion between two speakers.
You have to say whether each statement, from a list
of six you are given, reflects the opinions of one or
other of the speakers, or of both of them. You will
hear the recording twice.

Exam Strategy

- Listen carefully to the stated facts, the attitudes
  and opinions of the speakers.
- Try to determine which points are mentioned by
  only one of the speakers, and which points they
  agree or disagree on. Pay attention to the **way**
  the speakers talk, as this is very often an
  indication as to whether or not they agree.
- Sometimes the speakers may express their views
  using colloquial language. If you don't understand
  particular words or expressions, try to work out
  the meaning from the context or from the tone
  of voice of the speaker.

1 You will hear four short extracts from a
conversation between two friends. They are talking about
a town they have both visited on holiday.

1 Listen to the recording. For each extract, try to decide
whether they **agree or disagree** about the four issues
below.

1 The town council should begin to restore the
town's historic buildings.
Agree ☐ **Disagree** ☐

2 The sculpture in front of the National Museum has
no artistic merit whatsoever.
Agree ☐ **Disagree** ☐

3 A new road system within the town has its
advantages and disadvantages.
Agree ☐ **Disagree** ☐

4 The Green Dragon Hotel is to be particularly
recommended.
Agree ☐ **Disagree** ☐

2 Listen to the recording again, and for each extract note
down the **words or method** used by the second speaker
to signal his/her agreement or disagreement.

2 You will now hear a conversation between two
friends, Alan and Sally, about a council proposal to
pedestrianise the centre of the town where they live.
As you listen, decide whether the opinions below are
expressed by only one of the speakers, or whether the
speakers agree. Listen to the recording twice.

Write   **A**   for Alan,
        S   for Sally,
or   **B**   for Both, where they agree.

1 The traffic congestion in town has been caused
by people's unwillingness to use buses. ☐

2 Pedestrianising the town centre will make the
construction of a bypass essential. ☐

3 There are very few trees in the town centre at
present. ☐

4 The council's intention to renovate certain old
buildings in the town is praiseworthy. ☐

5 Pedestrianising the centre will mean that many
small retailers have to close down. ☐

6 The council's plans will involve considerable
disruption. ☐

Exam Tip!

It is very important in **Paper 4, Part 4** to be able
to understand when speakers agree or disagree
about a particular matter. They may use a variety of
colloquial expressions (e.g. *I'd go along with that ...*)
or adopt a certain tone of voice. It is also very
common for people to signal agreement by
**finishing a sentence which the other speaker
has started.**

Use of English
▶ **Paper 3, Part 5**

1

1 Think about a big city in your country. Are parts of the centre of this city run-down or not safe? What could be done to 'regenerate' these areas? Write down some ideas in your notebook.

2 Now read through the following two texts about what should be done to reverse the decline of many inner-city neighbourhoods. Do this quickly to get an idea of the content. Are the points mentioned by the writers similar to yours?

2 Read each text carefully and answer the comprehension questions using a word or short phrase. You don't need to write complete sentences. In this exercise there are hints to help you, although in the exam you will get no extra help.

Cities are places of extremes. The very wealthy and the very poor often live as near neighbours, with walls, visible or invisible, in between. The gradual recovery of many city centres around the world has pushed up property prices far beyond expectations, making them unaffordable to all but a lucky few. Their density, night life, busy streets and original spaces make them highly attractive to some, but unsuitable or unattainable to others. [5]

City centres often sit cheek by jowl with some of the poorest and increasingly abandoned inner-city neighbourhoods. People who cannot afford, or do not want, luxury city centre apartments, warehouses or canalside flats often reject the inner neighbourhoods that ring city centres and prefer to leapfrog to the quieter, safer, greener suburbs. [10] [15]

But as land becomes scarcer and smaller households multiply, the poorer inner areas of successful cities are becoming increasingly attractive. These large, run-down areas hold the key to affordable housing. 'Urban pioneers' need to be encouraged to take advantage of this situation, thereby helping to reclaim and restore these neighbourhoods to their former vibrancy. After all, they are often only minutes on foot from successful and flourishing centres. [20] [25]

To overcome the long legacy of social exclusion, cities must also hold on to rich and poor residents alike. The two groups need each other. They both want good homes in a pleasant, safe environment; they both want good schools for their children. The rich pay in, and gain, alongside the poor – and both benefit. [30]

50

1 Using your own words, say what point mentioned in paragraph 1 is echoed by the phrase 'cheek by jowl' (line 10).
(**HINT:** *Don't worry if you don't know this idiomatic expression – think about what it means in this sentence. Think also about what characterises 'city centres' and 'inner-city neighbourhoods'. Now look back at paragraph 1 and see if you can find the answer.*)

2 Explain why the writer has chosen to use the expression 'urban pioneers' in line 20.
(**HINT:** *What is a pioneer? What qualities do they possess? The writer uses this expression as a metaphor in this part of the text for people who go to live in inner city areas.*)

3 Explain in your own words what was primarily responsible for the lack of success of the 'ghetto housing estates' described in paragraph 1.
(**HINT:** *Note that the question asks you to say 'what' and not 'who' was responsible. It refers here to the attitude or behaviour of a certain group of people.*)

4 What exactly does the phrase 'pull it off' (line 23) refer to?
(**HINT:** *This question does not ask you to explain anything; it asks you simply to say what is being referred to. Look back at the previous few sentences.*)

3

1 Read the following summary task.

In a paragraph of between **50 and 70** words, summarise, **in your own words as far as possible**, what needs to be done, according to the texts, to regenerate run-down inner cities.

2 Look back at the two texts. Underline the parts of these texts which you feel are relevant, and write a list of the points you need for this summary. Make sure each point is really relevant to the question and that you don't mention the same point twice.

3 Now write the first draft of your summary. Remember to use connectors and try not to use the same grammatical structures in each sentence. For further advice on answering the summary question, see page 19.

I've often thought that city planners are very bad at listening to the voices of ordinary citizens. When I was young, people got out of the filthy, impoverished neighbourhoods of the big cities if
5 they could, and most never returned. Then the planners moved in. Without community consent, they tore apart existing urban patterns and created the ghetto housing estates that nobody wanted to live in. People are now beginning to come back to
10 the cities. I hope that the planners take notice of people's views this time. If they are to regenerate these inner-city areas successfully, they must take careful note of what the residents really want and need. What kind of services and amenities do they
15 require? What kind of job and leisure opportunities might be created in the area?

People come to live in compact cities because they like their energy, opportunity, diversity and excitement. But attractive, integrated urban
20 environments don't just happen, of course. They come about as a result of good design and sound organisation. It is obvious that no one individual or group can pull it off on its own. Cities require collective action. Vision and leadership are necessary,
25 of course, but so are architecture, engineering, social and communication skills.

We are living at a time when people want to rediscover social contact and interchange. What would have been unthinkable ten or twenty years
30 ago is now happening around us – people are beginning to see the older, poorer inner-city neighbourhoods as actually desirable. This is something we should all welcome and encourage. The alternative is that these run-down areas in our
35 inner cities will eventually become barren wastelands of crime, poverty and disease.

4   Read the following first draft and compare the points you made in your summary in Exercise 3 with the points made in this student's summary. Ignore the sentence numbers for the moment. Have you included the same information?

> (1) According to the writers of the texts, it is extremely important to encourage people to take advantage of the affordable housing in the poor and run-down neighbourhoods which surround many city centres. (2) Rich people as well as poor people should be strongly encouraged to live in the inner city. (3) Planners should take into account the desires and needs of the people who live there. (4) Finally, it needs to be realised that nothing which is worthwhile will be achieved unless individuals and groups agree to work together and are willing to learn to cooperate.

(93 words)

5

1   The summary above is too long. Read the following instructions, which refer to the sentence numbers in Exercise 4, to edit the summary to an appropriate length.

- **Sentence 1** Remove the introductory phrase, which is obvious and therefore a waste of words, as well as the unnecessary adverb. The phrase *affordable housing* was used by the writer, so replace it with a phrase of your own. Replace the relative clause at the end of the sentence with a participle clause.
- **Sentences 2 and 3** Shorten the phrase which begins Sentence 2 by using the connector *both* and omitting the word *people*; remove the unnecessary adverb. Combine Sentence 2 with Sentence 3, and replace the phrase *people who live there* with one word.
- **Sentence 4** Replace the whole of the first part of this sentence with *It is essential for ...* . Remove the phrase which repeats information already used and is therefore unnecessary.

2   Look again at Unit 2, page 21, for guidance on further things you can do to edit a summary.

Look again at Unit 2, page 21, for guidance on further things you can do to edit a summary.

─ **Exam Tip!** ◄

The summary is worth a lot of marks. For this reason you should not get stuck on the comprehension questions. Always leave yourself about **25 minutes** to write the summary. You can go back to those questions you were unsure about (or other parts of Paper 3) when you have completed the second draft of your summary.

Language Focus: Vocabulary

Phrasal verbs and expressions: *make*

1   Rewrite each of the following sentences using a phrasal verb with *make*, making any necessary changes. Use a dictionary to help you if necessary.

1   Perhaps he invented that story in order to gain our sympathy.
   He might .... we would sympathise with him.
2   'Atoms consist of even smaller particles,' the lecturer told us.
   The lecturer told us that atoms .... even smaller particles.
3   Pushing me to the ground, the man grabbed my wallet and ran away.
   The man pushed me to the ground and .... my wallet.
4   They tried to get us to believe that they were collecting the money for charity.
   They .... collected for charity.
5   What impression do you have of the new mayor?
   What .... the new mayor?
6   It was so foggy that I couldn't see any of the signposts.
   Due .... any of the signposts.

2   Rewrite each of the following sentences using an expression with *make*. You have been given key parts of each expression in brackets.

1   What can I do to show you I am sorry for forgetting your birthday?
   How can I .... your birthday? (*amends*)
2   You are making this exercise more difficult and complicated than it actually is.
   You are .... this exercise. (*weather*)
3   I can't understand these instructions at all.
   I can't .... instructions. (*sense*)
4   I really can't decide where to go on holiday!
   I .... where to go on holiday! (*mind*)

52

Language Focus: Grammar
Relative clauses

Watch Out! *problem areas*

- **pronouns**

  Prague, ∧*which* it is the capital of the Czech Republic, is world-famous for its baroque architecture.

  Rawlings, ∧*whose* his knowledge of medieval architecture is well known, was given the job of restoring the church.

  Climb up to the top of the hill, where ∧*there* is a castle.

  Who is the man (who) you were talking ∧*to*?
  (= *informal/spoken*)

  Who is the man to who ∧*whom* you were talking?
  (= *formal*)

- **prepositional phrases and quantifiers**

  The use of prepositional phrases and quantifiers in relative clauses is rather formal.

  In 1978 the factory closed, as a result of them ∧*which* many people lost their jobs.

  There were a number of workmen in the street, none of them ∧*whom* seemed to be doing very much.

1 Fill each gap in the following text with one suitable word. Some, but not all, of the missing words are parts of **relative clauses**. There is an example at the beginning (0).

2 **Where possible**, shorten the following sentences, using participle clauses instead of relative clauses, or by omitting relative pronouns.

1 People who work in large cities often long to escape from 'the rat race'.
2 Most houses which were built more than a hundred years ago have problems with damp.
3 The tram starts from the castle, which is the oldest surviving building in the town.
4 The house which I lived in as a child has just been knocked down.
5 The City Council, which is well known for its radical ideas, recently developed this dock area.
6 Visitors who are caught taking photographs inside the church are usually asked to leave.
7 The mosaic was discovered by workmen who were digging in the street.
8 The square is surrounded by old buildings, which are now on the verge of collapse.
9 The river which flows through the town centre is liable to flood in winter.
10 The man who I have been talking to used to live in this neighbourhood.

Exam Tip!

Use relative clauses in **Paper 2** to create more complex sentences and in **Paper 3**, **Part 5** summaries to link sentences concisely.

In many countries of Europe (0) *there* has been a steady drift of people away from villages to large cities. These people, many of (1) .... have grown up in great poverty and deprivation, hope to improve their standard of (2) ...., and see the metropolis as the (3) .... to all their problems. In many ways, they find what they are looking for. Large cities do offer a huge number of facilities, (4) .... which better education, better health care and improved housing are perhaps the most important. Large companies and factories, the vast (5) .... of which pride (6) .... on looking after the interests of their employees, also open up any (7) .... of career opportunities for those willing to work hard. Inevitably, however, there comes a time when people begin to long for the simplicity of the village or small town.

Traffic problems and pollution, (8) .... of which affect most large cities today, cause the most unhappiness. For people (9) .... whom fresh air, unpolluted water and beautiful countryside are distant – (10) .... nonetheless painfully clear – memories of a previous, peaceful life in a village, the situation must at (11) .... be unbearable. The pressure of overpopulation has meant that, in the last thirty or forty years, thousands (12) .... thousands of new flats have been built, often with (13) .... regard to architectural beauty, and the surrounding countryside has all (14) .... disappeared in many cases. It is no (15) .... such an easy matter to escape the noise and turmoil of the streets and find a field or a forest where the children can play in safety.

Writing

▶ Paper 2, Part 1 (formal letter)

About the exam

In **Paper 2, Part 1** you may be asked to write a **formal letter**. You will be given some information, such as an extract or extracts from an article in a newspaper, and asked to respond appropriately to the points which are raised. You can agree or disagree with these points, but you will be expected to present, support and develop your arguments both clearly and logically.

Exam Strategy

- Look at the information and the instructions carefully. What points do you need to respond to?
- Make a **detailed outline** of your letter, including structures and vocabulary you intend to use. Check your **outline** against the task before you start to write.
- Check your letter for **register** and **style**. Is the language you have used **appropriate** for the people who will read your letter? Check your grammar, punctuation and spelling.

1 Letters written to a newspaper or magazine in response to a recently published article usually contain a number of references to what was mentioned in that article. Match each of the following phrases (1–10) with its function (a–c) below.

1 it is/was claimed/suggested that ...
2 this is blatantly/obviously untrue ...
3 contrary to what the article/writer suggests ...
4 it is suggested that '*short quote from the article*' is/are ...
5 certain points, admittedly, cannot be argued with ...
6 you mention the fact that ...
7 (not) everyone is able to ..., as the article recommends ...
8 the writer of the article is quite correct here ...
9 what you do not mention/fail to mention is ...
10 I fail to see how this ...

a) reporting an opinion mentioned in the article
b) agreeing with an opinion
c) disagreeing with an opinion

2 The following sentences could be written in an informal letter. Rewrite each of them more formally, using the word given in brackets. Remember to change both the vocabulary and the structures. The beginning of the new sentence is given to help you.

1 I'll be generous and call his behaviour unhelpful. (*described*)
   His behaviour can at ....
2 I want to say that I don't agree with your views on that bank. (*express*)
   I would ....
3 We should be trying really hard to prevent such situations from developing. (*effort*)
   We should be making ....
4 That restaurant is a place where local business people really like to go. (*destination*)
   That restaurant is a ....
5 I really don't think their proposal is such a good thing as they pretend. (*beneficial*)
   I strongly ....
6 Unfortunately, I can't see my lawyer next week. (*unable*)
   I regret that ....

3

1 Read the following writing task.

TASK

You have read the extract below as part of a newspaper article on the benefits of hypermarkets. Readers were asked to send in their opinions. You decide to write a letter responding to the points raised and expressing your own views.

(300–350 words)

> People who have yet to discover those enormous supermarkets, known in the States as hypermarkets, really are missing out. Nothing can beat them for prices and quality of service. And for those of us who are mothers, baby-sitting facilities are usually available. No longer need shopping be the nightmare experience it so often is! Most hypermarkets are situated just outside town, so you need to jump in your car and drive a short distance to get there. Hardly a problem these days! What's more, we needn't feel an ounce of guilt about using them — research in America has convincingly shown that hypermarkets do not affect the character of a town, as is commonly supposed.

2 Now read the following letter, which was written by a student in answer to the task. The letter as a whole is well written, but it would be even more effective if the underlined parts were rewritten in a more formal way. Rewrite the underlined parts using more formal expressions, and making any other necessary changes.

Dear Sir

I am writing with reference to the article, published recently in your newspaper, on the effect of hypermarkets on our way of life. I (1) <u>want to say that I don't agree</u> with many of the views put forward in that article.

Firstly, it was claimed that hypermarkets do not affect the character of a town. This, of course, is blatantly untrue. Small local shops (2) <u>just can't</u> compete with such enterprises and, as a result, are frequently forced to close down. Local people then have to travel several kilometres to do their shopping, in an environment which (3) <u>I'll call impersonal (and that's being generous)</u>. The friendly, helpful service many of these people are used to has gone forever. Furthermore, not everyone is able to 'jump in their car' and head for the nearest hypermarket, as the article recommends. What about those who do not possess a car or other means of transport?

You mention the fact that hypermarkets are usually located on the outskirts of towns and villages. What you do not mention, however, is that they are often built in areas of natural beauty. In the town where I live a hypermarket recently sprang up in an area which is famed for its abundant wildlife and is (4) <u>a place where local people really like to go at weekends</u>. Surely we should be (5) <u>trying really hard</u> to protect the countryside around out towns rather than destroying it?

Admittedly, there are certain points made by the writer of the article which cannot be argued with. Yes, prices in hypermarkets are usually lower than elsewhere. Yes, they often do have baby-sitting facilities for mothers. What should be pointed out, however, is that many people are beginning to oppose the consumerism which hypermarkets encourage. They realise that the majority of people spend far more money in such places than they ever did in small local shops.

To sum up, it has to be said that, contrary to what your article suggests, hypermarkets are not (6) <u>such a good thing</u> as they are often made out to be. Instead, they are an unwelcome product of our modern materialistic way of life.

Yours faithfully,

(350 words)

4 Now write a letter in response to the following writing task.

TASK

You have read the extract below as part of a newspaper article calling for more modern architecture in towns. You decide to write a letter responding to the points raised and expressing your own views.

(300–350 words)

There are too many old and dilapidated buildings in our cities. We should knock them all down and have done with it. Local people don't want them and most tourists don't care much about them either. There are those who go on about how important it is for us to renovate such buildings, wanting to persuade us that they have some historical importance. I simply cannot see what they mean. Why waste money on doing up old, obsolete buildings, when we should be looking to the future and designing blocks of offices and flats which meet the needs of a modern society?

5 Exchange your letter with another student if you can. Evaluate each other's work and suggest improvements.

The living planet

Language Focus: Grammar
Mixed and open conditions

> **Watch Out!** *problem areas*
>
> - **unreal past**
>   It was only when I spoke to her that I realised we were very similar. ✔ → If I hadn't spoken to her, I *wouldn't/might not/would never* have realised that we ~~had been~~ *were* so similar.
>
> - **mixed conditionals**
>   If he hadn't been *so* careless during the experiment, he might not ~~have been~~ *be* in hospital now.
>   If he ~~hadn't been~~ *wasn't/weren't* such a good reporter, he wouldn't have been promoted last week.
>   If you hadn't listened to me, you wouldn't be doing *so* well now. ✔
>
> - **inversions**
>   These structures are rather formal.
>   Should you see Alice, give her my regards. ✔
>   If he doesn't let me go, I don't know what I'll do. ✔ = ~~Shouldn't I~~ *Should I not* be allowed to go, I don't know what I'll do. ✔
>   Were you to go on the expedition, you wouldn't be able to complete your research. ✔
>   If I could help you, I would do so. ✔ = Were I able to help you, I would do so. ✔
>
> - ***but for***
>   ~~Hadn't you~~ *Had you not* helped me, I wouldn't have known what to do. = But for your help, I wouldn't have known what to do. ✔
>
> - **open conditions**
>   The tenses used in open conditions are no different from the tenses which would be used if the clauses were separate.
>   Have you finished your work? + you can go = If you have finished your work, you can go. ✔
>   In the past hunters didn't catch anything + they went hungry = In the past, if hunters didn't catch anything, they went hungry. ✔

1 Combine the information in the following pairs of sentences to make sentences with conditional forms. Put the verb(s) in brackets in the correct form, and make any other necessary changes. You have been given the beginning of each sentence to help you.

1 You didn't go on the expedition. You are still alive. (*might/kill*)
   If ....

2 The government took little action. The disaster occurred. (*could/avoid*)
   The disaster ....

3 Few people listened to the warnings of the ecologists. Some species of animals have disappeared. (*could/save*)
   Had ....

4 I may not be allowed to enter the USA. I'll have to reconsider my options. (*prevent*)
   Should ....

5 They may make me take the exams again. I'll probably stop doing the course. (*make*)
   Were I ....

6 The Minister of Agriculture listened to the advice of so-called 'experts'. Large tracts of farmland are no longer productive. (*ignore*)
   Had ....

2 Fill each of the gaps in the following sentences with a suitable word or phrase.

1 You will be permitted to fish in the river .... as you obey the regulations.

2 Nobody needs to leave their houses .... river seems likely to flood.

3 If we are to save the whale from extinction, we .... action now.

4 If you really have seen the film, why .... me what happens in the end?

5 If you don't have a jeep, don't even .... crossing the Sahara.

6 If .... a way of saving the giant panda, we need to start looking now.

Reading

▶ Paper 1, Part 3

Exam Strategy

- Read through the gapped text quickly to get a general idea of what it is about.
- Underline any words or phrases which obviously refer to something which has been mentioned in the previous paragraph. Look specifically for pronouns such as *he, it, they, them,* etc. as well as words such as *this, that* and *these.* Also look for words or phrases which make no sense unless something mentioned earlier is taken into account: *another, still, also, such,* etc., as well as nouns and gerunds appearing for the first time.
- Now look at the jumbled paragraphs. Again, underline any words or phrases which make no sense on their own.
- Some paragraphs will be easy to place, others will require more thought. Remember that the final words of one paragraph often lead on to the main idea of the next paragraph. If the text is part of a story, think about the sequence of events and look for any time references.
- When you have finished, it is very important to read through the whole text again to make sure that it makes sense.

1 To help you think about the way paragraphs are connected, look at the following text about the Monkey Sanctuary in Cornwall, England. The first and last paragraphs have been provided, but the six middle paragraphs are in the wrong order. Paying particular attention to the underlined parts of each paragraph and the words in bold, put the paragraphs in the correct order.

Paragraph 2 ....   Paragraph 3 ....
Paragraph 4 ....   Paragraph 5 ....
Paragraph 6 ....   Paragraph 7 ....

Jordi Casamitjana, the 33-year-old research co-ordinator at the Monkey Sanctuary in Cornwall, needs no encouragement to talk. It doesn't really matter what the subject is – he will speak rapidly, enthusiastically and, if you don't interrupt, at length on almost anything. And if you ask this irrepressible ethnologist about the social life of the Spanish wasp (something of a speciality) or woolly monkeys (something of an obsession) there is no stopping him.

A
This pioneering conservation centre was set up in 1964 by Len Williams (father of John Williams, the classical guitarist) and soon after produced the first woolly monkeys bred successfully in captivity – its first world record. Now it is a leading force in developing practical methods to **rehabilitate** captive monkeys which were once kept as pets or caged zoological exhibits.

B
Rather than introduce them into the wild, where they might perish because of habitat destruction (woolly monkeys live in the tree tops of primary forest) or endanger indigenous monkeys by carrying human diseases into their midst, they will be living in an environment which is large enough for them never to realise any geographical limits but which is nevertheless **protected** and allows for the monkeys to be monitored and observed.

C
This is just as well, as this summer he intends to raise much-needed funds by attempting to set the world record for the longest uninterrupted science lecture – at least 12 hours.

D
Over the next two to three years, the centre aims to **relocate** all the Cornish monkeys **back** to Brazil. The plan is to house them on some of the 3,600 forested **islands** which pepper Lake Balbina, about 180 kilometres north of the city of Manaus.

E
Casamitjana and about 15 other conservationists live and work with 23 Amazonian grey woolly monkeys at the Monkey Sanctuary, near Looe in Cornwall. The listed Victorian mansion has been cleverly joined to several large monkey enclosures and houses both sets of primates in idyllic surroundings.

F
The project will also help the Brazilian authorities in their campaign against the large illegal pet trade. Seizing illegally captured monkeys, known as **orphans**, creates a problem as there is no obvious place to put them.

They have some experience of the forest but, since capture, no social experience. On the other hand, the Cornish monkeys have developed the social skills but in enclosures. The idea is that they should be able to teach each other – a hypothesis that received strong verification when two socialised Cornish monkeys 'adopted' several **orphans** and were then able to 'learn' (through mimicry) how to negotiate the forest environment.

2 Ignoring the seven missing paragraphs for the moment, read the following extract from a magazine article to find out:

- **who** the group of people mentioned are and **where** they live
- **what** the main problem facing them is
- **how** the problem might be solved.

Just what is Ramiro thinking about, I wonder, as we crash clumsily along the rainforest path behind him. For us, our walk reveals a thousand new sensations – giant tree trunks, insects camouflaged as leaves, the sounds of birds and bugs and crickets, splashes of colour among endless shades of green, scarlet flowers, strange yellow fruit, white fungus on rotting logs, electric-blue butterflies.

1 ....

It is more than likely that he has the oil company Occidental on his mind. Apparently, they are determined to build an oil-well where we now stand. Ramiro says he will die fighting rather than let the oil workers move in. Ramiro, a stocky, muscular 28-year-old dressed in T-shirt and football shorts, is a Siecoya Indian. This beautiful stretch of primary rainforest along the Aguarico river in the Oriente, Ecuador's part of the Amazon, is Siecoya land.

2 ....

Ramiro still hunts and fishes, but nowadays he is also a tourist guide. He has little choice since the oil companies, loggers and settlers have seized huge tracts of forest. The hunting is poorer and the Siecoya's freedom to move through the forest is gone. Increasingly, they have to find alternatives. Most, such as working for the oil companies or logging, involve destroying the forest. Only tourism seems to offer a sustainable future.

3 ....

It is not so much these details as the overall feeling that is different. The feeling of being, not in a wilderness, but guests in someone's home, with children and pets running around your feet, women cooking, neighbours visiting.

4 ....

But this is no fantasy trip to a make-believe paradise, a place where people live in some kind of blissful harmony with nature and their fellow men. We also learn about the problems the Indians face. We learn about the politics of the forest and the pressures on the Siecoya to abandon their traditional way of life.

5 ....

Occidental recently persuaded the Siecoya president to sign a contract to build their oil-well, with a road connecting it to the town of Coca, in return for five outboard motors and a well. Luckily, he was able to retract his signature in front of lawyers, but nobody thinks that Occidental will give up. Yet Ecuador's oil reserves will barely be enough for the next twenty or thirty years.

6 ....

Despite their problems, I left with a sense of hope. The Siecoya had taught me to see the Amazon in a new way – neither as uninhabited nor as a wilderness. People have lived here for millennia (evidence of settlement goes back to 5000 BC) and humans are as much a part of the rainforest as the birds and insects. The forest has its dangers, of course, but the savage jungle of Western imagination is more a reflection of our own mistrust of nature – an attitude that has led to environmental crisis.

7 ....

Tourism plays a major role in the Oriente's economy and for the small Indian communities even a few tourists make a big difference. But most tour operators make vague claims about using native guides. So it is important for tourists to look for the involvement of communities' representative organisations and to find out what the project is putting back. Siecoya Trek, for instance, provides money for school materials and training, for an outboard motor, and to send people to hospital in Quito. They also pay everyone who works with tourists roughly double what most agencies pay their native guides.

3 Read the extract again and look at the following jumbled paragraphs **A–H**. Underline words and phrases which refer to something already mentioned, then choose the paragraph which best fits each gap. There is one extra paragraph which you do not need to use.

There are some hints below to help you, though in the exam you will be given no help.

A Although Ecuador has many jungle tours, few involve or benefit the indigenous Indians. It is our loss – for the Indians have much to teach us. But this trip is different. Although the itinerary is much the same as for other jungle tours, it is run by the Siecoya themselves. We see monkeys, travel in dugout canoes, fish for piranha; we learn about the different ecosystems in the forest.

B We learn about how the Siecoya use the forest. For instance, they exploit a range of plants for medicinal or other purposes, and even make use of a type of ant to stitch wounds. Holding it so that it pinches the wound shut, they break off the body of the ant, leaving the head and pinchers in place.

C But Ramiro has walked this way a thousand times before. After all, this is where he grew up. So maybe he is thinking about his wife and three young children. Or of rebuilding his house, which burnt down last week while he was out hunting.

D Seeing the forest as the Siecoya do, as a home, a provider of food, shelter, materials and medicines, reminds us that there is another way. Man can live harmoniously with nature, without having to destroy it. And that, ultimately, is worth more than photos or exotic souvenirs or trips by canoe.

E It was time for us to go. Ramiro and his wife, Betty, waved to us from the little beach in front of their home. As we set off in the motorised canoe, they were soon swallowed up by the wall of green forest, mirrored in the brown waters of the Aguarico.

F The Siecoya have fished, hunted and farmed here for centuries. Today, like the neighbouring Cofan and Siona, the once-feared Hiapramo and the Achua, they number less than a thousand. Two other groups, the Shuar and the Quichua, are slightly bigger.

G The ultimate aim of these tours is to help them maintain that way of life and remain in the forest. By generating income, of course, and by encouraging the children to value their culture. It is not just the Siecoya's future that is at stake, but the future of the forest as well. The Indians' presence is a major factor keeping the oil-men out of Ecuador's remaining forest. But the situation is precarious.

H He may be thinking that it is better to stay in his village rather than go to work there. After all, he will probably make less money working for the settlers than he will as a tourist guide.

Hints
- Some paragraphs end with words which suggest the main idea of the next paragraph. 'This beautiful stretch ... is Siecoya land.' (just before gap 2) and 'Only tourism seems to offer a sustainable future.' (just before gap 3) are good examples of this.
- The sentence 'But the situation is precarious ...' (at the end of paragraph G) will probably be followed by an example of this precariousness.
- One paragraph begins 'Although Ecuador has many jungle tours ...' (paragraph A) another begins 'The ultimate aim of these tours is ...' (paragraph G). Which paragraph is more likely to come first?
- The paragraph which begins with the phrase 'It is not so much these details ...' (just after gap 3) is obviously going to be preceded by a paragraph supplying a number of details.
- The paragraph which begins with the phrase 'But this is no fantasy trip to a make-believe paradise ...' (just after gap 4) is likely to be preceded by some information about the incredible ways the Indians exploit the forest.
- Paragraph D begins with the words 'Seeing the forest as the Siecoya do ...' This seems to suggest that the previous paragraph is about the way the Siecoya view the forest.

4 Make sure you read through the completed text a final time to check that the order of the paragraphs makes sense.

Language Focus: Vocabulary

Dependent prepositions and prepositional phrases

Fill each of the gaps in the following text with the correct preposition.

Global warming in Arctic regions

According to the World Wide Fund, the polar bear could be faced (1) .... extinction and a large number of other animals reduced (2) .... very small remnant populations by global warming in Arctic regions.

Warmer winters are responsible (3) .... the thinning or disappearance of ice sheets in many parts of the Arctic, resulting (4) .... a situation where polar bears are (5) .... risk of starvation because they cannot travel to their normal breeding and hunting grounds.

Even in places where there is still much ice around, polar bears are (6) .... threat because they rely (7) .... snow caves to rear their young. Due to the warmer weather, these caves are prone (8) .... sudden collapse, burying the youngsters (9) ....

Other effects of the changes (10) .... climate are also being noticed. Animals such as reindeer (also known (11) .... 'caribou' in North America) have adapted (12) .... the extreme cold and are able to cope (13) .... the Arctic climate. For millions of years they have been migrating to places where they can breed and find food. These migrations coincide (14) .... the growing season for the plants they feed (15) .... Ecologists have found, however, that they are now arriving (16) .... their spring feeding grounds too late. The plants they eat have grown and gone to seed. This is having a serious impact (17) .... the herds of caribou. A substantial number of calves are being lost and there is already a substantial reduction (18) .... herds. Scientists are concerned, but powerless to do anything (19) .... response to the situation – everything they have tried has been (20) .... vain. It is simply one of the unforeseen consequences of global warming.

Phrasal verbs and expressions: *run*

1 Rewrite each of the following sentences using a phrasal verb with *run*, making any necessary changes.
Use a dictionary to help you if necessary.

1 By chance I met someone I hadn't seen for years.
I .... for years.
2 'Soon we'll have no more fuel,' she said.
She said we .... fuel.
3 He spent much more money than he could afford while he was at college.
While .... debt.
4 There was a lot of unexpected opposition to the government's proposal.
The government's .... unexpected opposition.
5 A car hit and seriously injured an old woman today.
An .... today.
6 I disapprove of the way my colleagues say unpleasant things about me.
I object .... by my colleagues.
7 Try to control your imagination.
Don't .... with you.
8 Could I explain again quickly what you have to do?
Would you mind .... again?

2 Rewrite each of the following sentences using an expression with *run*. You have been given key parts of each expression in brackets.

1 Don't eat those mushrooms because I think they may be poisonous.
If you .... poisoned. (*risk*)
2 There will be enough supplies if we are careful.
As long .... of supplies. (*short*)
3 The woman's scream really frightened me.
My .... the woman's scream. (*blood*)
4 The problems we've been having are very ordinary, and we'll have no difficulty solving them.
These problems are very ...., and we can solve them easily. (*mill*)

Listening

▶ Paper 4, Part 3

About the exam

In **Paper 4**, **Part 3** you have to listen to a conversation or interview and answer five **four-option** multiple-choice questions. These questions follow the order of the information in the recording and test your understanding of factual details, abstract ideas and the opinions and attitudes of the speakers. You will hear the recording twice.

Exam Strategy

- Read the questions and multiple-choice options before listening. Sometimes, a number of options seem to mean similar things. It is vital to notice the differences between them before you listen.
- The first time you listen, you may find it helpful to eliminate those answers you are sure are wrong.

1

1   You will hear a short extract from an interview in which a scientist talks about how stars in space may have been responsible for a number of environmental catastrophes on Earth. Look at the question below and the multiple-choice options which follow it. Listen carefully and decide which option is correct.

What do many scientists believe caused the dinosaurs to disappear?
A Large amounts of iridium in the Earth's crust.
B A meteorite crashing into the Earth.
C An asteroid which passed very close to the Earth.
D Changes in the Earth's climate.

2   When you have checked the answer, identify the option which:

1   contains information **not mentioned at all** in the extract

2   contains **a word used** in the extract but in a statement which is false

3   contains correct information but which **does not answer the question**.

2   Now listen to the complete interview and for questions 1–5, choose the answer (**A**, **B**, **C** or **D**) which fits best according to what you hear.
Read the five questions first and notice any differences between the options. Underline any key differences to make sure you don't forget them.

1   What convinced Arnon Dar that collapsing neutron stars have been the cause of the mass extinction of life on Earth?
   A Nothing else would be powerful enough.
   B There is no evidence for volcanic activity.
   C Supernova explosions are far too rare.
   D The two events happen with the same frequency.

2   According to Dar, muon particles cause
   A much heavier rain than normal.
   B cosmic rays to be created.
   C the death of animals and plants.
   D showers of high energy particles.

3   Why does Dar consider the evidence about marine life to be significant?
   A It shows how rich marine life was at that time.
   B It suggests his theory is correct.
   C It produced a valuable fossil record for scientists.
   D Scientists have always ignored it.

4   How does Dar explain the survival of many insects?
   A Radiation does not affect insects.
   B They can survive any environmental disaster.
   C The environment was ideal for insects 251 million years ago.
   D They are more resistant to radiation than large animals.

5   When Dar talks about the possibility of another large mass extinction happening, his attitude is
   A optimistic.
   B sarcastic.
   C indifferent.
   D slightly concerned.

── Exam Tip! ◄

Watch out for multiple-choice options with the same wording as that used by the speaker in the recording.
The meaning could be very different.

Writing

▶ **Paper 2, Part 2 (report)**

About the exam

In **Paper 2, Part 2** you may have to write a **report**. A report is **an account of something (e.g. a meeting) which has recently happened**, and is normally written for a specific purpose and audience. It tends to summarise and explain facts often for the purpose of making suggestions or recommendations. The layout and organisation of a report is very important, as is the style and register of the language used. Reports should have information organised into **headings**, and a formal, impersonal tone. Clear and thorough planning is essential to writing a successful report.

1 Read the following writing task and decide what points you will cover in your answer. Make a list in your notebook of at least four.

TASK

As the local councillor in charge of energy policy, you recently attended a meeting about the proposed building of a nuclear power station near your city. At this meeting, the reasons for switching to nuclear energy were discussed, as well as the potential effect this might have on the environment and the local community. Write a report on the plan for your fellow councillors, giving your opinion of the proposal and making any recommendations you think appropriate.

(300–350 words)

2 Now read the following report, which was written in answer to the task. Ignore the gaps for the moment. Are the ideas included similar to your own?

1 ....
I attended a meeting on 12th July to discuss the proposed building of a nuclear power station near the city. A spokeswoman for the Nuclear Energy Advisory Group summarised the reasons for opting for nuclear energy, the benefits it would bring, and then went on to talk about matters of safety.

2 ....
Atmospheric pollution of the area around the city is at present very high. There is also the problem of acid rain, which is responsible for widespread damage to nearby forests and lakes, as well as to the city's historic buildings. It was pointed out that nuclear energy does not add to the greenhouse effect or produce acid rain, so using nuclear energy would result in a much cleaner environment.

3 ....
The spokeswoman for the Nuclear Energy Advisory Group was eager to point out that fears of possible dangers to health or to the environment were unfounded. She assured us that very strict safety measures would be taken and there would be no question of nuclear waste being dumped near the city or in the surrounding area. The NEAG ruled out the possibility of an accident ever occurring.

4 ....
It was mentioned that were we to use nuclear energy as an energy source the cost of electricity would decrease significantly. Apparently, once the power station was in operation, we could expect reductions in the cost of electricity of up to 30%. Another benefit to the community would be the creation of several hundred jobs.

5 ....
The plan to switch to nuclear energy has much to recommend it. I did feel, however, that matters of safety were glossed over somewhat. Most people are worried about potential accidents, and these fears are not altogether unfounded – there have been several such accidents in the last twenty years. I feel that we should not reject the proposals outright, but would recommend that the question of safety be considered more carefully. At the very least, the advice of nuclear scientists not connected with the NEAG should be sought and efforts made to consult environmentalists from countries where there are already nuclear power stations in operation.

(349 words)

3 Give each paragraph of the report an appropriate heading. One of the paragraphs is not in the most logical place. Which one? (para. ....)

4

1   Read the following extract from a different report, ignoring the numbers and underlining for the moment. What is the main purpose of this extract?

> (1) The plan to build a car factory in the suburb of Westham <u>sounds really good</u>. (2) <u>It would provide unemployed people with jobs</u> and <u>make the whole area wealthier</u>, because it would offer over 2,000 jobs. (3) <u>Another thing is that</u> it would not only provide opportunities for work, but it would also offer lots of other services, <u>which would include</u> baby-sitting facilities, a free health-care scheme and a company pension. (4) <u>The biggest problem, though</u>, seems to be that the factory is <u>going to be</u> 30 miles from the town centre. (5) This would <u>without a doubt</u> be a problem for <u>the people who don't have their own car</u>, as bus and train services <u>don't run very often</u>. (6) If the factory management <u>didn't want</u> to provide company transport, the town council would have to <u>think about</u> improving the services which already exist.

2   This extract would not be successful in the exam because the register is too informal and the tone too personal. Rewrite the extract in your notebook using the following suggestions.

1   The underlined phrase in the first sentence is too informal and personal in tone. Replace it with an expression containing the words *much* and *recommend*.

2   Rewrite the whole of this sentence. Start with the present participle *Offering* ... and then rewrite the underlined phrases, using the words *solve*, *unemployment* and *increase*.

3   The connecting phrase is inappropriate, so replace it with a more formal expression, and rewrite the clauses which follow using an inversion. Replace *which would include* with a present participle.

4   The first part of this sentence is too informal, so replace the underlined words with *major drawback*, and use a more appropriate connector. *Going to be* is also too informal, so use a future passive structure with *located*.

5   Replace the first underlined phrase with one word and the second one with a more formal phrase, starting with *for those*, and ending with *transport* (as a noun). *Don't run very often* is informal, and can be replaced by an adjective.

6   Rewrite the whole sentence starting with *Should* ... Replace *didn't want to* with a suitable adjective, and the phrasal verb *think about* with a more formal verb.

5

1   Now write a report in answer to the following task.

> **TASK**
>
> You attended a meeting of the local Green Action Group recently, in which the main environmental problems facing your city were discussed as well as suggestions for making the urban environment 'greener'. As an assistant to the city mayor, you have been asked to write a report in which you summarise the problems faced by your city, the measures suggested at the meeting and making any appropriate recommendations or comments.
>
> (300–350 words)

2   Here are some of the ideas which were suggested in the meeting to help you.

• fining people who drop litter
• tree-planting programme and creation of parks
• recycling of rubbish
• imposing restrictions on traffic

> ### Exam Strategy
>
> • Read the task carefully and think about what points you want to include.
> • Write an outline of what each paragraph should contain, and its heading. You may find it appropriate to organise your report as follows:
> Background information
> Environmental problems
> Possible measures/solutions
> Comments/Recommendations
> • Think about the consequences of the measures suggested. What language will you use to connect the two? (For example, more trees → healthier atmosphere, city more attractive to tourists = *Were more trees to be planted, the atmosphere would ... and the city ...*)
> • When you make your comments or recommendations, you might want to mention anything which was **not** mentioned at the meeting, or any problems you foresee in implementing the proposals.
> • Check that your outline answers the task fully, and relevantly, **before you start writing**.

6   Exchange your report with another student if you can. Evaluate each other's work and suggest improvements.

8 A sporting chance

Language Focus: Grammar
Emphasis

> **Watch Out!** *so* and *such*
>
> - **articles**
>   *Such* only needs an indefinite article when used with a singular countable noun.
>   We've been enjoying such a good weather lately.
>   *So* can be used with an adjective, an article and a noun, often in preference to *such*, in formal situations.
>   He was such an adventurous climber, that ... ✔ =
>   He was so adventurous a climber, that ... ✔
>   He was a so adventurous climber, that ...
> - **inversions**
>   *Such* is not generally used in inversions which have an auxiliary verb. It can be replaced by *so* + adjective + article.
>   Such a good time did we have that we didn't want to leave. = *So* good *a* time did we have that we didn't want to leave. ✔
> - **conditionals and wishes**
>   *So* and *such* often appear in conditionals and wishes, meaning *as much as is/was true*.
>   If we hadn't received so much money, we wouldn't have ... (= *as much money as we did*) ✔
>   I wish my neighbours weren't so noisy! (= *as noisy as they are*) ✔

1

1 For each question below, complete the second sentence with three to eight words so that it has a similar meaning to the first sentence, using the word given. Do not change the word given.

1 It frightens me just to think about climbing that mountain.   **mere**
The ....
.... afraid.

2 Your winning the race doesn't surprise me at all.
                                                    least

I'm not ....
.... won the race.

3 Absolutely no-one in the team is a better player than Jack Carlton.   **exception**
Jack Carlton ....
.... player in the team.

4 He's the quickest learner I've ever met.   **so**
Never ....
.... learner.

5 I've told you on innumerable occasions not to do that.   **time**
I've told you ....
.... not to do that.

6 He's good at nothing except long distance running.
                                                      one

The ....
.... long distance running.

7 I'm afraid that a rematch is completely impossible.
                                                 whatsoever

I'm afraid that ....
.... a rematch.

8 They are a good team, but others are definitely better.   **means**
Although they are a good team, they ....
.... best.

2 When you have checked your answers, analyse any errors you made. Did you have to:

- use a particular expression?
- change a comparative to a superlative?
- invert the subject and verb?
- add an article?

2 Fill each of the gaps in the following sentences with a suitable word or phrase.

1 There .... indeed that doctors could do for her injury, and she had to retire from the race.
2 Why on .... me that you didn't want to take part?
3 We were forced to abandon the match, so .... weather.
4 Don't tell her, ... do – she'll be horrified if she finds out.
5 All the training he had done didn't seem to .... of difference to his performance.
6 I hadn't expected quite .... a wind. It blew us miles off-course.

3   Fill each of the gaps in the following text with **one** suitable word. Most, but not all, of the words you need are **emphatic words** or part of **emphatic expressions**. There is an example at the beginning (0).

Ice-fishing

Every weekend, hundreds of Russians trudge for miles across snow and ice to indulge in (0) ..*the*.... one thing which gives meaning to their often harsh lives: ice-fishing.

(1) .... finding a suitably desolate spot of (2) .... own, they drill a hole in the ice, dip in their line and wait for the fish to bite. With no company (3) ...., save that of the relentless howling of the wind, they sit for hours huddled over the frozen Moscow river, never exchanging more than the (4) .... of grunts or nods with a fellow fisherman, should one pass by. (5) .... the practitioners of this bizarre sport may say, the rewards of ice-fishing do not include the fish they hope to catch. To say the (6) ...., these are inedible. Could it be, then, that they do it (7) .... and simply for the challenge? Yet another case of man battling against the elements?

In fact, the majority of Russians do not understand why so large (8) .... number of their countrymen can waste the precious hours of winter daylight on what appears to be (9) .... a pointless activity. (10) .... all, why should anybody risk life and limb to catch fish which are usually thrown back into the river? For (11) .... ice-fishing may appear to be safe, it can be (12) .... dangerous indeed. In fact, (13) .... unpredictable can be the movement of an ice-flow, that every year lives are put (14) .... danger or lost altogether. Fishermen can find themselves swept away and stranded on sheets of ice, and, (15) .... rescued by helicopter within a few hours, will perish in the sub-zero temperatures.

Language Focus: Vocabulary

Phrasal verbs and expressions: *bring*

1   Rewrite the sentences using a phrasal verb with *bring*, making any necessary changes. Use a dictionary to help you if necessary.

1   Someone should have mentioned this matter at the meeting yesterday.
This .... yesterday.

2   It's unlikely that he'll manage to perform such a difficult dive in the competition tomorrow.
His chances .... slim.

3   Sponsorship is responsible for more than half of most athletes' earnings.
Sponsorship .... most athletes earn.

4   She regained consciousness when an old lady put some smelling salts under her nose.
An old .... putting some smelling salts under her nose.

5   There has been a huge change in smoking habits, as a result of this anti-smoking campaign.
This campaign .... people who smoke.

6   I'm sure we can convince him that our way of thinking is better.
I'm sure he .... thinking.

2   Rewrite each of the following sentences using an expression with *bring*. You have been given key parts of each expression in brackets.

1   It's unlikely that the adverse publicity will make her behave more sensibly in the future.
I doubt .... publicity. (*senses*)

2   His failure in the championships made him realise how important regular training was.
His .... training. (*home*)

3   This scandal will damage the reputation of the government.
The government .... scandal. (*disrepute*)

4   Nothing could have persuaded me to talk to him again after what he did.
After .... again. (*myself*)

5   The audience clapped and cheered ecstatically at the end of the performance last night.
The performance .... last night. (*house*)

Reading

▶ **Paper 1, Part 4**

1 Read the text quickly. What impression do you get of the voyage the *Stormchild* is about to make?

Stormchild sailed on the next tide, just after midnight. She slipped unseen down the river with her navigation lights softly blurred by the small rain. Instead of the champagne parting and the paper streamers there had only been David
5 and Betty calling their farewells from the pontoons, and once their voices had been lost in the night there were only the sounds of the big motor in *Stormchild's* belly, the splash of the water at her stern and the hiss of the wet wind. That wind was southerly, but the forecast promised it would change to
10 easterly by dawn and if the forecast held good then I could not hope for a better departure wind. It was blowing hard, but the big, heavily laden steel *Stormchild* needed a good wind to shift her ponderous weight.

I raised sail at the river's mouth, killed the engine, and
15 allowed the wind to take over. The wake from the boat foamed white into the blackness behind us as the coastal lights winked and faded in the rain that still pattered on the deck and dripped from the rigging. The green and red lights of the river's markers vanished, and soon the only mark to
20 guide *Stormchild* was the flickering gleam of the far Portland light. I had lost count of how many times I had begun voyages in just this manner: slipping off on a fast tide, making my way southerly to avoid the tidal rips that come off the great headlands of southern England, then letting my boat
25 tear westwards towards the open Atlantic. Yet however many times I had done it, there was always the same excitement.

'Gee, but it's cold,' Jackie Potten said sullenly.

'If you're going to moan all the way across the Atlantic,' I snapped, 'then I'll turn round now and drop you off.'

30 There was a stunned silence. I had surprised myself by the anger of my voice, which had clearly made Jackie intensely miserable. I felt sorry that I had snapped at her, though I also felt justified, for I was not at all sure that I wanted her on
35 board *Stormchild*, but the notion of Jackie coping on the boat had energised David and Betty with a vast amusement and they had overridden my objections with their joint enthusiasm. Betty had taken Jackie shopping, returning with a car-load of vegetarian supplies and armfuls of expensive foul-

weather gear that I had been forced to pay for. I had ventured 40 to ask the American girl whether she had any sailing experience at all, only to be told that she and her mother had once spent a week on a Miami-based cruise ship. 'But you can cook, can't you?' David had demanded.

'A bit.' Jackie had been confused by the question. 45

'Then you won't be entirely useless.' David's characteristic bluntness had left Jackie rather dazed.

Dazed or not, Jackie was now my sole companion on *Stormchild*, which meant that I had the inconvenience of sharing a boat with a complete novice. I could not let her take 50 a watch or even helm the ship until I had trained her in basic seamanship, and that training was going to slow me down. Worse, she might prove to be seasick or utterly incompetent. All in all, I was sourly thinking, it had been totally inconsiderate of David and Betty to have encouraged her to 55 join the ship.

There was also another and murkier reason for my unhappiness. I had felt an inexplicable allure towards this odd little stray girl, and I did not want that irrational feeling to be nurtured by the forced intimacy of a small boat. I told myself 60 I did not need the complication, and that this girl was too young, too naïve, too idealistic, too noisy and too pathetic. 'I thought you had a job to go home to,' I said nastily, as though, being reminded of her employment, Jackie might suddenly demand to be put ashore. 'Aren't you the 65 *Kalamazoo Gazette*'s star reporter?'

'I was fired,' she said miserably.

'What for? Talking too much?' I immediately regretted the jibe, and apologised.

'I do talk too much,' she said, 'I know I do. But that wasn't 70 why I was fired. I was fired because I insisted on going to Hamburg. I was supposed to be writing some articles about junior high schools, but I thought the Genesis Community was a better story, so I left the paper. And now I've got a chance to sail the Atlantic, so you see I was quite right. We 75 should always take our chances in life, or else we'll miss out on everything.'

2 Read the following questions and unfinished statements about the text. In each case, choose the answer (**A**, **B**, **C** or **D**) which you think fits best.

1 The writer implies that the departure of *Stormchild* was
   A an anticlimax.
   B very worrying.
   C a cause for celebration.
   D unexpected.

2 How did the writer view the weather conditions?
   A They were worse than he had expected.
   B They could have been better.
   C They would soon be ideal.
   D They were likely to improve slightly.

3 What was surprising about the writer's sense of excitement on setting sail?
   A There was no good reason for it.
   B He had set sail from England many times before.
   C The lack of navigational lights made conditions extremely dangerous.
   D He had a companion he disliked.

4 The writer lost his temper with Jackie Potten because he
   A hated people who complained.
   B wanted to be on his own.
   C disliked Americans.
   D resented her presence on the boat.

5 Why had David and Betty persuaded the writer to take Jackie Potten?
   A They thought she would make him laugh.
   B They didn't realise she knew nothing about sailing.
   C They wanted to play a trick on him.
   D They thought the situation would be funny.

6 What does the writer say about Jackie Potten's sailing experience?
   A She had never been on a yacht before.
   B She had once helped on a cruise ship.
   C She had undergone some basic training.
   D She knew practically nothing about sailing.

7 What was the writer afraid might happen during the trip?
   A He would begin to hate Jackie Potten.
   B Jackie Potten would demand to be put ashore.
   C He would fall in love with Jackie Potten.
   D Jackie Potten would talk continually.

3

1 Find the following words in the first and second paragraphs of the text, and try to deduce their meaning from the context. The sounds of some of the words can help you to understand their meanings.

1	slipped (line 2)	6	faded (line 17)
2	splash (line 7)	7	pattered (line 17)
3	hiss (line 8)	8	dripped (line 18)
4	shift (line 13)	9	flickering (line 20)
5	winked (line 17)	10	tear (line 25)

2 Make three lists in your notebook for words connected with movements, sounds and lights.

4 Use one of the words from Exercise 3, in the correct form, to complete each of the following sentences.

1 We listened to the rain as it .... on the roof of the caravan.

2 I don't understand how he managed .... away from the party unnoticed.

3 The fluorescent light started .... and then went out completely.

4 There was a long slow .... from the fire, as it started to rain and we abandoned the barbecue.

5 Sandra rushed out of the house and .... down the road towards the bus stop.

6 All we could see in the darkness were the lights of the houses as they .... at us in the distance.

7 Everyone laughed when David fell off the boat into the river with a huge ....

8 I had terrible problems trying .... the piano on my own, and eventually gave up – it was just too heavy.

9 The rainwater seeped through the ceiling and started .... onto the floor beneath.

10 As we drove away, the lights of the village gradually .... and then disappeared altogether.

Study Tip

Deducing the meaning of words from context is an important reading skill which you need to develop. It is probably the best way of building up your **passive vocabulary**: words that you can recognise and understand when listening or reading, but don't necessarily use (or even need to know) when you are speaking or writing. Look again at Unit 5, page 41 for guidance on techniques you can use to help you understand unknown words.

Listening

▶ **Paper 4, Part 1**

 You will hear four different extracts. For questions 1–8, choose the answer (**A, B** or **C**) which fits best according to what you hear. Listen to the recording twice.
(Remember that in the exam the extracts will **not** have a common theme.)

Extract One
You hear two friends discussing hang-gliding.
1 When Jenny says 'come on', she is
   A showing she understands Susan's point of view.
   B suggesting that Susan is exaggerating.
   C encouraging Susan to continue talking.
2 The speaker compares hang-gliding to driving a car to show that it
   A is quite safe after qualified instruction.
   B gives you the same sense of freedom.
   C requires a similar expenditure of money.

Extract Two
You hear a man talking about a sport he did at school.
3 The speaker felt that his teacher of kendo
   A had been unreasonably strict.
   B had always seemed to be in a bad mood.
   C had taken himself too seriously.
4 How did the speaker feel during the lessons?
   A proud
   B ridiculous
   C embarrassed

Extract Three
You hear part of a radio news broadcast.
5 The speaker says the crowd is enthusiastic despite
   A having had to wait for several hours.
   B the bad weather.
   C not being able to see the athletes.
6 Why does Steve feel lucky to have won a medal?
   A He was not completely fit.
   B He had to overcome a drug problem.
   C He almost fell over during the race.

Extract Four
You hear part of a talk on nineteenth-century social history.
7 Before the time of Edward Whymper's expedition
   A nobody took mountaineering seriously.
   B nobody had attempted to climb the Matterhorn.
   C only a privileged minority took part in sports.
8 Why does the speaker mention the founding of the Football Association?
   A It is a good example of changing attitudes to sport.
   B To show that there was a need for rules in sport.
   C To show that professional football dates from this time.

Language Focus: Vocabulary

Dependent prepositions and prepositional phrases

Fill each of the gaps in the following text with **one** appropriate preposition.

The hazards of extreme weather conditions discourage most walkers (1) .... venturing into the hills in winter. For those few adventurous souls who do insist (2) .... climbing in winter, however, a course in winter mountaineering skills lessens the dangers.

John White's Mountain School in Cumbria offers a short course which introduces beginners (3) .... winter climbing. Anyone is eligible (4) .... the Winter Walking Skills course, provided they are (5) .... good health. Those who participate (6) .... the sessions are taught basic navigation skills, winter skills (such as how to dig a snow hole), the use of ice-axes and crampons, and mountain first aid. This last subject, of course, is (7) .... particular importance. The necessity (8) .... learning how to recognise and deal (9) .... hypothermia and frostbite effectively, for example, is impressed (10) .... all the students who enrol (11) .... the course. By the end of the course, those determined to gamble (12) .... fate will have sampled their first proper ice-climbing route. Weather permitting, of course.

Use of English
▶ Paper 3, Part 3

> **Exam Strategy**
>
> Pay particular attention to any connectors (e.g. *although*, *so*, etc.) in sentences, as they will help you understand the meaning of the gapped phrase. It may then be easier to work out the missing word.

For the following six sets of sentences, think of **one** word only which can be used appropriately in all three sentences.

1   It's a very .... matter, so be extremely careful how you talk to her and what you say.
    Simon was a .... child and was always missing school for reasons of ill health.
    These roses give off a particularly .... scent that can only be appreciated by bringing the flowers very close to your nose.

2   Since Jones has not yet made a .... decision as to what he wants to do, we still have time to persuade him to join us.
    To check that a melon or pineapple is not overripe, squeeze it gently with the tips of your fingers to make sure that it is still ....
    If you are not .... with young children, they will become difficult and rude as adolescents.

3   What .... me when I first met her, was the penetrating look she gave me with those enormously intelligent eyes of hers.
    When Jack lit his cigar, he .... the match on the sole of his boot, instead of on the side of the matchbox.
    While I was waiting for the bus, I .... up a conversation with the woman who was standing next to me.

4   European governments are likely to .... sanctions, if that country breaks the treaty again.
    I don't wish to ...., but would you mind putting me up for the night?
    The new regulations .... a tremendous burden on the officials who have to go through all the paperwork involved.

5   The accident is thought to have been caused by a hairline .... in one of the plane's wings.
    I'm not really experienced enough to captain the team, but I'll have a .... at doing it if you want me to.
    There was a loud .... as one of the legs of the chair broke in two.

6   One of the wrestlers clearly indicated with a .... of the hand that he wanted the referee to stop the bout.
    The members of the committee voted on the .... that the forthcoming match should be postponed.
    The rocking .... of the boat made me feel rather sick.

Writing
▶ Paper 2, Part 1 (essay)

> **Exam Strategy**
>
> Always make a clear, organised outline of your essay. Make sure you have:
> a) an introduction – give some general information about the topic 'as it is today', and introduce the discussion; using a rhetorical question is one common way of doing this
> b) notes about the evidence you will use to support your points, and the connectors you will use to link them
> c) a genuine conclusion, which summarises your argument and, if possible, refers back to the essay title and your introduction.

1

1   Read the following writing task and underline the points to be covered in the essay.

> **TASK**
>
> You have read the following extract from a school prospectus, in which the school's policy towards team sports is clearly expressed. It has prompted you to write an essay for your tutor discussing the points raised and expressing your own views.
>
> (300–350 words)

SCHOOL SPORTS

We believe strongly in the value of competitive sports, and are proud of our traditions and achievements in that area. Who can possibly disagree with the view that such sports are the best way of developing in our children qualities such as a sense of discipline, a competitive spirit, and an ability to co-operate with others?

2 Decide:
- whether you agree or not with the views of the school.
- what evidence you could use to support your view.

Note down at least four or five points which you could use to support your ideas.

2

1 Read the following detailed outline written by a student preparing to answer the task. Are any of your ideas included?

Introduction
Opening comments: the situation as it is today.
1 Children encouraged to take part in team sports, in some cases forced.
2 Underlying philosophy of this participation = team sports good for the body, build character.
3 This may be true - true that it's the best way?

First supporting paragraph
Main idea: promoting focus and self-sacrifice.
Team sports involve lots of physical training.
1 Children train hard before inter-school matches - physically fit for 'big day'.
2 Such a rigorous programme demands self-sacrifice Other activities and non-team sports involve self-sacrifice/perseverance - tennis, chess.

Second supporting paragraph
Main idea: developing co-operation.
1 Team sports are character building - encourage co-operation.
Success of team depends on co-operation of individuals.
2 Valuable training for later life - but not only activities which encourage this. Plays and concerts encourage co-operation between children.

Third supporting paragraph
Main idea: criticising competitive attitudes.
1 Team sports are about winning - enhance the competitive spirit. Non-team sports do the same - whether this is character-building or not is open to question.
2 Many problems today - 'me-first' attitude.
3 Teach children there's more to life than winning?

Closing paragraph
1 Team sports one way of developing children's characters - wrong to consider them to be the best way.
2 Should encourage children to develop personalities in ways they think best.

2 Underline any parts of the student's outline which you think would be useful, but you didn't think of when making your own notes.

3 Look again at Unit 1, page 15 for guidance on common methods of organising information in paragraphs. Which method has been used in this outline?

3 Read the finished essay on page 71, and choose the best word or phrase from the list below to fill each of the gaps.

1 a) indeed
   b) whereas
2 a) on the one hand ...
      on the other hand
   b) not only ...
      but also
3 a) actually
   b) basically
4 a) of course
   b) however
5 a) as a result
   b) in order to
6 a) Without doubt
   b) Nevertheless
7 a) However
   b) Furthermore
8 a) Not to mention
   b) For instance
9 a) so as to
   b) in that they
10 a) As a matter of fact
   b) Obviously
11 a) of course
   b) similarly
12 a) for example
   b) such as
13 a) Although
   b) It goes without saying
14 a) however
   b) in fact
15 a) result in
   b) are the direct result of
16 a) Couldn't
   b) Shouldn't
17 a) In conclusion
   b) In the final analysis
18 a) Instead
   b) Naturally

In many schools in the world today children of all ages are encouraged, and (1) .... forced in some cases, to take part in team sports. The underlying philosophy is that team sports are (2) .... good for the body .... that they build a child's character. This may well be true, but is the suggestion that team sports are the best way of developing a child's character (3) .... true?

Participation in a team sport, (4) .... , usually involves a lot of physical training. Before important events children may have to train very hard (5) .... be well-prepared and physically fit for the 'big day'. (6) .... , such rigorous training demands dedication and self-sacrifice on the part of the child. (7) .... , there are other activities which also involve a high degree of perseverance. (8) .... , non-team sports such as tennis or even activities like chess require equal preparation and discipline.

Team sports are also considered to be character-building, (9) .... encourage co-operation between individual team members. (10) .... , the success or the failure of the team depends not so much on the individual skills of the players as on their ability to co-operate. This is valuable training for later life, (11) .... , but team sports are not the only activities which encourage children to do this. Plays and concerts, (12) .... , also encourage co-operation between children.

Teachers frequently point out that team sports are about winning. They enhance the 'competitive spirit' of the boys and girls who take part. (13) .... that non-team sports do the same. Whether this is character-building or not, (14) .... , is open to question. So many of the problems we face in society nowadays (15) .... the 'me-first' attitude found in so many people. (16) .... schools aim to teach children that there is much more to life than winning and being first?

(17) .... , clearly team sports are one way of developing children's characters, but it would be wrong to consider them to be the best way. (18) .... , we should encourage children to develop their characters and personalities in ways they themselves feel are best.

(355 words)

4 The language used in essays is usually objective and impersonal. Match each of the following phrases 1–10 with its function a)–c), below.

> ### Impersonal language for essays
> **1** the underlying philosophy is that …
> **2** … is/are often considered to be …
> **3** this may be due to …
> **4** according to recent research, …
> **5** it would be wrong to suggest/claim that …
> **6** … is/are frequently regarded as …
> **7** it is sometimes suggested/pointed out/ claimed that …
> **8** it seems unlikely that …
> **9** the idea behind this is that …
> **10** … this is open to question

a) explaining the reasons for something ....
b) reporting an opinion in an impersonal way ....
c) disagreeing with an opinion, or suggesting that it may not be well-founded ....

5 Now write an essay in answer to the following writing task.

> **TASK**
> You have read the following extract from a letter to a newspaper in which the writer criticises those who participate in dangerous sports. It has prompted you to write an essay for your tutor discussing the points raised and expressing your own views.
>
> (300–350 words)

> People who take part in dangerous sports are out of their minds. What can possibly be the attraction of hanging from a mountain ledge by your fingertips or flying through the air in some flimsy contraption or other? Such people endanger their own lives and the lives of those who might be called out to help them. What's more, the personal qualities these sports require and the achievements gained are overrated and of little value in everyday life.

6 Exchange your essay with another student if you can. Evaluate each other's work and suggest improvements.

The mind's eye

Language Focus: Grammar
Verb patterns (-ing and infinitive)

> **Watch Out!** *problem areas*
>
> - **verb + *to* infinitive or *-ing* form**
>   Several verbs have one meaning when they are followed by a *to* infinitive and a different meaning when followed by an *-ing* form.
>   I *tried to cut up* the chicken, but without success. (= *attempted*) ✔
>   You ought to *try cutting up* the chicken with a cleaver. (= *to see if it works*) ✔
>   We *regret to tell* you that your application has been turned down. (= *we know this is unfortunate*) ✔
>   I really *regret not telling* him what I was planning to do. (= *I made a mistake*) ✔
>   After describing the work of his colleagues, he *went on to talk* about his own research. (= *he changed the subject*) ✔
>   She *went on talking* even when the meeting had finished. (= *she continued*) ✔
> - ***begin* and *start***
>   These can both be followed by a *to* infinitive or an *-ing* form, with little change in meaning. A *to* infinitive must be used, however, when the form is *beginning* or *starting*.
>   Oh dear! It's beginning ~~raining~~ ˄ *to rain*.
> - **preposition + *-ing* form**
>   Prepositions should be followed by an *-ing* form.
>   She congratulated me *on passing/having passed* my driving test. ✔
>   After some verbs, *to* is a preposition and therefore must be followed by an *-ing* form.
>   She objected to ~~have~~ ˄ *having* to get up so early in the morning.
>   (also *be/get used to, look forward to, confess to*)
> - **infinitives: continuous/passive/perfect**
>   I expect *to be working/to be promoted/to have finished* by next week. ✔

For each question below, complete the second sentence with three to eight words so that it has a similar meaning to the first sentence, using the word given. Do not change the word given.

1 Perhaps finding someone to replace her is proving difficult for him. **difficulty**
   He appears ....
   .... replace her.

2 I can't wait for the new theatre to be completed. **forward**
   I'm ....
   .... the new theatre.

3 I really wish I'd paid more attention to his warnings. **little**
   I bitterly ....
   .... to his warnings.

4 They are going to send us the tickets next week. **sent**
   I've arranged ....
   .... next week.

5 'I forgot to postpone the appointment,' Robert admitted. **put**
   Robert confessed to ....
   .... the appointment.

6 He said it was absolutely untrue that someone had lent him the money. **having**
   He categorically ....
   .... the money.

7 It's not normal for me to have to start so early. **make**
   I'm not used ....
   .... start.

8 The workmen think that it will take them until the end of the day to demolish the wall. **finished**
   The workmen hope to ....
   .... down by the end of the day.

9 I really don't like it when they make us work overtime. **made**
   I strongly ....
   .... work overtime.

10 Did it really slip your mind to contact us when you arrived there? **touch**
   Did you honestly ....
   .... when you arrived there?

Language Focus: Vocabulary
Verb + noun collocation

In the following sentences, only one of the nouns in italics collocates with the verb **and** fits the meaning of the sentence. Underline the correct noun in each case.

1   She gave him a sharp *hit/slap/punch* across the face and walked away.

2   She made several *gestures/faces/waves* to gain the attention of the waiter.

3   Yesterday, the management took an important *conclusion/decision/plan* regarding payment of part-time staff.

4   This pizza's new – would you like to give it a *try/chew/bite*?

5   Could you have a quick *glimpse/read/glance* at this letter I've written?

6   Do you have any *memory/recollection/thought* at all of what he said to you?

7   After the operation, he made a remarkable *recovery/improvement/progress*.

8   Realising I was late, I took a quick *suck/gulp/drink* of my drink and left.

9   He made me a(n) *offer/suggestion/plan* I couldn't refuse.

10 What *influence/effect/consequence* do you think his resignation will have on the company?

11 As soon as he saw me, he gave me a big *grimace/smile/frown* and waved the tickets triumphantly in the air.

12 I can't decide now – I need to have a *reflection/thought/think*.

13 When he saw the body, he gave a heart-rending *gasp/cry/murmur* and sank to his knees.

14 She has no *intention/aim/plan* of giving you back the money you lent her.

Study Tip

Record collocations on separate pages of your notebook, so that you can add to them when you meet new ones. Be careful! Some of the nouns may be wrong in the context of a particular sentence but still collocate correctly with the verb. Use a good English–English dictionary to help you check appropriate contexts for using your vocabulary.

Dependent prepositions and prepositional phrases

Fill the gaps in the following text with the correct prepositions.

The power of the unconscious mind

Suddenly you find that you have lost all awareness (1) .... what you were going to say next, though a moment ago the thought was perfectly clear. Or perhaps you were (2) .... the verge of introducing a friend, and his name escaped you, as you were about to utter it. You may say you cannot remember. (3) .... all probability, though, the thought has become unconscious, or (4) .... least momentarily separated from consciousness. We find the same phenomenon (5) .... our senses. If we concentrate hard (6) .... a continuous note, which is (7) .... the edge of audibility, the sound seems to stop (8) .... regular intervals and then start again. Such oscillations are the result of a periodic decrease and increase (9) .... our attention, not due to any variation (10) .... the note.

But when we are unconscious (11) .... something it does not cease to exist, any more than a car that has disappeared round a corner has vanished into thin air. It is simply (12) .... of sight. Just as we may later see the car again, so we come across thoughts that were temporarily lost (13) .... us.

Thus, part of the unconscious consists of a multitude of temporarily obscured thoughts, impressions, and images that, in spite of being lost, continue to have an influence (14) .... our conscious minds. A man who is distracted or 'absent-minded' will walk across the room (15) .... search of something. He stops, in a quandary – he has forgotten what he was (16) .... His hands grope (17) .... the objects on the table as if he were sleepwalking or (18) .... hypnosis; he is oblivious (19) .... his original purpose, yet he is unconsciously guided by it. (20) .... the end, he realises what it is that he wants. His unconscious has prompted him.

Reading

▶ **Paper 1, Part 1**

Read the three texts below and choose the word or phrase (**A, B, C** or **D**) which best fits each gap. (Remember that in the Proficiency exam, the texts will be from different sources and will not have a common theme.)

An experiment in hypnosis

What is particularly interesting about hypnosis is that it is capable of activating what the (1) .... psychologist Carl Jung called the 'creative imagination'. I was fortunate enough to witness this phenomenon several years ago in an experiment which was (2) .... by a fellow doctor, who wanted to confirm whether or not a subject could be made to see a 'ghost'. The volunteer was hypnotised and told that when she awakened she would first hear a bell ring, and then she would see the (3) .... of a seventeenth-century clergyman passing the window; his appearance was described in detail. No sooner had the doctor (4) .... his fingers and brought her out of the trance, than a bell rang in the distance. The woman looked at the window and uttered a cry. 'Who is that man? Where did he come from?' she screamed, evidently deeply disturbed by what she had (5) .... No amount of explaining on the (6) .... of the doctor could convince her that she had not seen a ghost.

1	**A** grandiose	**B** notorious	**C** eminent	**D** prestigious
2	**A** made out	**B** carried out	**C** put out	**D** taken out
3	**A** figure	**B** character	**C** picture	**D** icon
4	**A** slapped	**B** snapped	**C** nudged	**D** poked
5	**A** glanced	**B** peered	**C** glimpsed	**D** gazed
6	**A** side	**B** part	**C** half	**D** behalf

Sandra's dreams

Sandra remembered (7) .... the circumstances under which the nightmares had begun. In hospital, following the birth of her second child, she had been deliriously happy, and those around her had been especially supportive, (8) .... to her every whim and going out of their way to be nice to her. She (9) .... the thought of sitting in the newly decorated nursery, rocking the baby in her arms and watching his little face as he (10) .... to sleep. But her contentment had been (11) .... on her first night back at home. (12) .... retrospect, that first awful dream had probably been the worst. It had been so unexpected; so alien somehow.

7	**A** utterly	**B** distinctly	**C** fully
	D totally		
8	**A** indulging	**B** pampering	**C** catering
	D providing		
9	**A** relished	**B** appreciated	**C** gloated
	D basked		
10	**A** drifted off	**B** carried off	**C** slipped off
	D popped off		
11	**A** smashed	**B** cracked	**C** slashed
	D shattered		
12	**A** At	**B** In	**C** To
	D On		

Help with phobias

Do you suffer from illogical phobias? Do you wake up in the morning and dread leaving the house? Or do you (13) .... a cold sweat every time you see a spider? If you do, you can (14) .... comfort from the fact that you are not alone – thousands of people suffer from such irrational fears. There is nothing 'strange' about you! Nor should you despair of ever getting (15) .... grips with the fears that seem to (16) .... you day and night. Help is at hand. Hundreds of people have visited our clinic over the years and found that the expert help and advice they have received has given them a new (17) .... of life. Our team of doctors and psychologists – by far and (18) .... the most qualified in this field – use a variety of techniques, including 'virtual reality' simulations, to help people overcome their worst fears. So don't hesitate!

Give us a call on 455 655 – before you have second thoughts!

13	**A** give off	**B** break into	**C** turn on
	D set up		
14	**A** extract	**B** dig	**C** draw
	D accept		
15	**A** at	**B** in	**C** on
	D to		
16	**A** hound	**B** victimise	**C** bully
	D persecute		
17	**A** extension	**B** period	**C** lease
	D length		
18	**A** away	**B** more	**C** over
	D above		

Use of English

▶ **Paper 3, Part 5**

1 Why do you think children's games might play an important role in their development as individuals? Make a note of your thoughts. Now read the following texts quickly, to see if any of your ideas are mentioned.

2 Read each text carefully and answer questions 1–4.

In child development there is an important phenomenon that shows very clearly the process of preparation for the future:
5 play. Contrary to popular belief, its importance should never be underestimated. Games are not the haphazard creations of parents or
10 educators. They should be seen as educational aids and as stimuli for the child's psyche, imagination and life skills. Every game is a
15 preparation for the future. The manner in which children approach a game, their choice of game and the importance they place upon it, show their
20 attitude and relationship to their environment and how they relate to their fellow human beings. Whether they . are hostile or whether they are
25 friendly, and particularly whether they show leadership qualities, are evident in their play. In observing children at play we can see their whole attitude towards life; play is of 30 the utmost importance to every child.

But play is more than preparation for life. Games are above all communal exercises 35 that enable children to develop their social feeling. Children who avoid games and play are always open to the suspicion that they have not adjusted 40 satisfactorily to life. These children gladly withdraw from all games, or when they are sent to the playground with other children usually spoil 45 the pleasure of others. Pride, lack of self-esteem and the consequent fear of 'getting it wrong' are the main reasons for this behaviour. In general, 50 by watching children at play, we can determine with great certainty the extent and quality of their social feeling.

1 Explain in your own words what **two** features of children's games are implied by the writer when he says that they are 'not the haphazard creations of parents or educators'. (lines 8–10)

2 Explain in your own words why some children might worry about 'getting it wrong' (lines 48–49) when playing games.

It is easy to see why psychologists find children's games so fascinating. Which game, for example, does not
5 prepare children in some way for later life or help them to develop important social skills? In fact, psychologists have been able to identify a
10 number of factors involved when children get down to the serious business of playing with their friends. One of these, according to
15 researcher Dr John Davies at the University of Manchester, is what he refers to as children's 'striving for dominance' within the play
20 group. 'The goal of superiority is commonly revealed in play and betrays itself in the child's tendency to be the leader and
25 organiser. We can discover this tendency by watching how children push themselves forward when they play,' he claims.
30 As most parents realise, of course, children can also give vent to their emotions when they play with their friends. Dr Davies sees this as being of prime importance. 'Children must express themselves. Play is first and foremost an opportunity for children to do this, and it is not a trivial matter to disturb them when they are engaged in play. When they are left to their own devices, what they do and how they behave is stimulated by their interaction with other children. There are lots of games that emphasise their natural creativity. In preparation for their future profession, those games giving children the opportunity to exercise their creative spirit are especially important. I've heard of fashion designers, for example, whose favourite game when they were children was making clothes for their dolls; engineers who, as toddlers, played for hours with building blocks.'

Dr Davies is adamant about one thing: play is never a waste of time. 'Play is a serious matter!' he says with a disconcertingly childlike smile.

3 What does the writer imply about the goal of superiority when he says that it 'betrays itself'? (lines 22–23)

4 Which word in paragraph 2 echoes the popular misconception mentioned in the first text that children's play is unimportant?

3 Now read the summary question below. Underline the relevant information in the texts, make a list of points, and then write the first draft of your summary. Remember to use connectors and try not to use the same grammatical structures in each sentence.

> In a paragraph of between **50 and 70** words, summarise, **in your own words as far as possible**, the reasons given in the texts for why games are important in a child's development.

4 Check and edit your summary. Look again at Unit 2, page 21, for guidance on methods of summary editing. Make sure you check for spelling, punctuation and grammar mistakes.

Language Focus: Grammar
Emphasis (cleft sentences)

Very often, the **way** we speak reinforces the meaning of the grammatical structures we are using. In Exercises 1 and 2 below, the **intonation** and **stress** used by the speakers are as important as the actual words they say.

1

1 For each of the following sentence endings, 1–6, you will hear two possible **beginnings**, **A** or **B**. These beginnings have slightly different **stress** and **intonation**, which affects the meaning. Listen and write the letter of correct beginning, **A** or **B**, in the spaces provided. The first one has been done for you as an example.

1 1 ..*A*.. not important, so it seems.
   2 ..*B*.. how on earth did they do it?
2 1 .... she did.
   2 .... to fix the car.
3 1 .... is why he didn't ask her to marry him.
   2 .... is this problem on page 66.
4 1 .... at the cinema.
   2 .... not a thriller.
5 1 .... doesn't concern you at all.
   2 .... is that more and more people are breaking the law.
6 1 .... I suddenly broke out in a cold sweat.
   2 .... was when he didn't come to work on time.

2 Now listen again to check your answers.

2

1 For each of the following statements you will hear a reply. Tick which statement, **A** or **B**, the reply refers to.

1 **A** Wasn't it that meeting that Peter was late for?
   B I think it was Peter who waltzed in over an hour late for the meeting.
2 **A** It was his dishonesty which amazed me more than anything else.
   B I was really taken aback by his dishonesty.
3 **A** All he ever does is moan about how much studying he has to do.
   B He always seems to have his head buried in a book.
4 **A** What he really wanted to do was go abroad to study.
   B It was Paris that he had his heart set on visiting.
5 **A** Anna's the one who can't make it to the party tomorrow night.
   B I think it's tomorrow night that Anna can't come to the party.

6 **A** What's new is that this test is being done on a human subject.
   B This is the drug being tested for the first time on humans.

2 Now listen again to check your answers.

3 Cleft sentences are common in both written and spoken English. For each of the following extracts, 1–5, rewrite the sentence in italics in a way which makes it more emphatic or persuasive.

1 People's lifestyles are changing. The majority of people are no longer concerned just about making money, or about moving on in their careers – they are beginning to pay attention to the way they live. *More and more people are leaving big cities to go and live in small towns and villages. This is particularly interesting.*
   What ....

2 I like going out with friends – you know, to cafés and fast food restaurants and I'm keen on music ... um ... but *I really like going to parties!*
   What ....

3 I'm sick to death of my husband! *He just complains about the weather!*
   All ....

4 I have wonderful memories of my childhood. Long summer days spent out on the veranda with my brothers and sisters, the excitement of Christmas or going on holiday, the magic of birthday parties spent with all my friends ... *I remember my father playing the piano in the evenings most, though.*
   What ....

5 You know, I can hardly remember a thing about the operation I had yesterday. It seemed to be over before I knew what had happened. *I can remember the doctor giving me the injection though.*
   The only ....

4 Rewrite each of the following sentences beginning with the words given and using a cleft sentence structure.

1 Janice is in America, so you probably saw her twin sister in town yesterday.
   Janice is in America, so it ....

2 I can't understand why you didn't telephone me when you heard the results.
   What ....

3 What I find particularly offensive is his arrogant attitude.
   It's ....

4   Going out to parties is the only
    thing you think about.
    All ....
    ....

5   I'm baffled by his lack of enthusiasm
    for the project.
    What ....
    ....

6   I'm more concerned about the state
    of your health than about your
    finishing the job.
    It's not ....
    ....

7   I am not interested in what they
    have decided to do.
    What ....
    ....

8   They will ask you to attend an
    interview.
    What ....
    ....

9   You should complain to the
    manager.
    The person ....
    ....

10 I first realised that something was
    wrong when one of the cheques
    bounced.
    The first ....
    ....

Listening
▶ Paper 4, Part 2

Look again at Unit 2, page 18 for guidance on the best way to approach sentence completion exercises.

You will hear part of a radio show in which a psychologist talks about what makes people lucky or unlucky. Read the prompt sentences before listening, and try to predict what kind of information you will need to listen out for. When you have done this, complete each sentence with a word or short phrase. Listen to the recording twice.

A recent study in Iowa suggests that there is a
[_____1] for good and bad luck.

The study involved the choice of cards which awarded
[_____2] to the participant.

Researchers concluded that the 'intuition part' of
some people's brains was not [_____3]

Not only are some people rich and healthy, but
[_____4] also go in their favour.

People who believe that good things
[_____5] find their expectations
fulfilled.

Lucky and unlucky people also [_____6]
in different ways.

Many individuals gain [_____7] being
particularly lucky or unlucky.

Some people possess [_____8]
which brings good things to them.

Lucky people often say that [_____9]
is responsible for their good fortune.

Writing

▶ Paper 2, Part 2 (proposal)

1

1 Read the following writing task.

TASK

You are a junior manager in a company where the staff are expected to work hard and produce results. Recently, it has been observed that many employees are falling sick as a result of the stressful working environment. The senior managers of the company are obviously very concerned about this situation. As part of your job, you send them a formal proposal in which you outline measures which could be taken to reduce stress at work, explaining how these measures would be effective.

(300–350 words)

2 Underline the main points to be covered in your proposal.

3 Now read the following outline which was written in answer to the task. Note how the student who wrote it made choices about the verb forms and vocabulary he wanted to use **at the planning stage**.

Introduction
Description of problem – stress common nowadays.
In our company – 2/3 employees each week take time off work.
Senior management concerned – will allocate money to deal with problem.

Main problems
As result of stress, employees:
not able to sleep – tired so make mistakes
suffer from headaches/migraine
catch colds/flu more easily because 'run down'
become irritable/have frequent disagreements.

Recommendations
(1) Create 'relaxation room' – employees go there 30 mins/day
Furnishing/lighting important – total ban on smoking, etc.
Effective because people need time during day to relax, etc.
(2) Company should employ therapist/psychologist – would keep an eye on employees + give seminars about relaxation and meditation techniques.
Effective because will enable people to make the most of their time in 'relaxation room'.
(3) Encourage employees to attend local gym.
Effective because regular exercise reduces stress + would appeal to those not willing to try relaxation/meditation techniques.

Conclusion
Above measures will entail financial outlay.
However – long term benefits to company + individuals.

4 Which set of details are **not required** and should therefore be omitted? Cross them out on the outline above.

2 Read the following proposal which was written using the outline in Exercise 1. Check to see if you were correct about which set of details were not required.

Introduction

Stress-related illnesses are particularly common nowadays. In our company alone, it is not unusual for two or three employees each week to take time off work because they are suffering from the effects of overwork and stress. The senior management of the company would like to help employees deal with the problem and has generously offered to allocate a sum of money for this purpose. Below are some recommendations as to how the situation might be improved.

Recommendations

It is essential for employees to spend some time each day relaxing and concentrating on something other than work. We need to ensure that there is a place where they can do this, so I would suggest that we convert one of the offices into a special 'relaxation room' and encourage staff to spend half an hour there every day. Obviously, the furnishing and lighting of this room would be of particular importance, as would any background music we provided. It would also be beneficial for there to be a total ban on smoking, drinking, reading and talking in this area.

Another idea for dealing with the problem of stress is for the company to employ a therapist or psychologist to keep an eye on employees, and to give regular talks on subjects such as relaxation techniques, stress control and meditation. This would also enable people to make the most of the time they spent in the 'relaxation room'.

Finally, I suggest that employees should be encouraged to attend a local gym two or three times a week. Regular exercise is known to reduce levels of stress and anxiety, and also, of course, promotes general fitness and health. Working out at a gym might appeal to those employees who are unwilling to experiment with the relaxation techniques mentioned above.

Conclusion

The measures for combatting stress suggested here would entail some financial outlay. However, the long-term benefits of implementing some or all of these measures would be quite considerable – both to individual members of staff and to the company as a whole.

(341 words)

3

1   Read the following extract from a proposal written by a student in answer to the same task. The style and register of **the extract** is **inappropriate**.
Would this extract be more appropriate in an essay or in an informal letter to a colleague?

> The company should allow employees to work at home if they want to do so. Maybe this won't work for some jobs, where it is important for people to talk things over together, but it should be possible for many activities which have traditionally been carried out at the office. If we took this step, efficiency and quality of work would probably improve, and there would be much less stress.

2   Now rewrite the extract in the correct style and register for a proposal by filling in the gaps in the paragraph below.

> I suggest that employees .... wish to do so. This .... feasible for some jobs, where collaboration ...., but it should be possible for many activities which have traditionally been carried out at the office. Were ...., efficiency and quality of work would probably improve, and levels of ....

4   Plan and write a proposal in answer to the following writing task.

TASK

You work for a holiday company which provides organised holidays for groups of people visiting your country. Your boss is thinking of organising holidays which would cater for elderly tourists who feel a need to restore and improve their mental and physical well-being. She has asked you to write a proposal outlining activities which could be organised for these people and to explain how you feel they would benefit those taking part.

(300–350 words)

5   Exchange your proposal with another student if you can. Evaluate each other's work and suggest improvements.

10 The world of work

Language Focus: Vocabulary
Adjectives

> **Watch Out!** *problem areas*
>
> • **gradable and limit adjectives**
>   Gradable adjectives, which can exist in different degrees, can be modified with a range of adverbs.
>   She is a(n) very/extremely/fairly *friendly* person, isn't she? ✔
>   Limit adjectives, which have strong meanings and cannot exist in different degrees, can only be modified by adverbs with very strong meanings.
>   That meal was ~~very~~ ₍absolutely₎ delicious!
>   We were ~~extremely~~ ₍utterly₎ exhausted when we arrived.
>   *Really* can be used with both gradable and limit adjectives.
>   I think he's really *intelligent/brilliant*. ✔
>   She's a really *good/wonderful* teacher! ✔
>
> • ***almost, nearly, virtually* and *practically***
>   These intensifiers can only be used with ungradable adjectives which have a **fixed meaning**.
>   This bottle of wine is *almost* empty. ✔
>   The book she is writing is *nearly* complete. ✔
>   The building was ~~virtually~~ ₍absolutely₎ enormous.
>
> • ***quite***
>   *Quite* has two different meanings.
>   The film was *quite interesting*, I suppose. (= *reasonably*) ✔
>   His contributions to science have been *quite remarkable*. (= *absolutely*. We stress *quite* when we use it with this meaning.) ✔

1 Look at the following sentences and decide which answer (**A, B, C** or **D**) best fits each gap.

1 We were .... amazed that nobody had thought of the idea before us.
  A virtually **B** almost **C** quite **D** extremely

2 They were .... devastated by the news of his death.
  A extremely **B** very **C** really **D** rather

3 Unlike you, I find him .... friendly.
  A slightly **B** virtually **C** practically **D** fairly

4 Apparently, they need someone for the job whose French is .... fluent.
  A rather **B** practically **C** somewhat **D** slightly

5 I found the assistants in the shop .... rude and unhelpful.
  A somewhat **B** virtually **C** absolutely **D** almost

6 He has lived in Paris for so long that he is .... French.
  A quite **B** fairly **C** almost **D** rather

2 Rewrite each of the following sentences, using the word in brackets.

1 Hardly anyone turned up to watch the football match. (*nobody*)
  ....

2 I know you can produce good work when you put your mind to it. (*capable*)
  ....

3 Meeting the professor tonight will be a real honour for me. (*proud*)
  ....

4 He only wants to join the project because he thinks he'll make some money out of it. (*sole*)
  ....

5 The chances of our finding someone to replace Mr Jones are incredibly slight. (*virtually*)
  ....

6 I cannot understand why you are unwilling to give Max a job. (*baffled*)
  ....

7 In some countries people under the age of sixteen are not allowed to buy tobacco. (*restricted*)
  ....

8 There were a few tiny mistakes in Harry's homework. (*quite*)
  ....

Determiners and pronouns

> **Watch Out!** *problem areas*

- **use of the definite article**

  Many ~~of the~~ people don't agree with the changes which have been made. (= *people in general*)

  Many (of the) people I have spoken to would like to have a greater say in matters. (= *a specific group*) ✔

  ~~All the people want~~ ∧*Everyone wants* better working conditions.

  I managed to read ~~all the~~ ∧*the whole* report in a day.

- ***each* and *every***

  When we use *each* we look at people or things separately or 'one at a time'. *Every*, on the other hand, puts people or things into groups (like *all*).

  Each/every manager we get seems to want to make us work harder. ✔

  She had a child on *each/either* side of her. ✔ (= *only two sides*)

  There were enemy soldiers on *every* side. ✔ (= *many sides*)

  Each/Every one of the customers who came into the shop was given a questionnaire ✔ = they were ~~every~~ ∧*each* given a questionnaire.

- ***neither* and *none***

  Neither applicant who applied for the job was successful. ✔ = Of the two applicants who applied for the job, *neither* was successful. ✔

  None of the applicants who applied for the post was accepted. ✔ = Of the many applicants who applied for the post, *none* was accepted. ✔

Fill each of the gaps in the following sentences with a suitable word or phrase

1 How dare you interfere! What I do in my private life is .... yours!
2 No .... you say to him, he never listens.
3 You have every .... angry about how you were treated.
4 Although neither sister was a high flyer, ... them managed to pass their exams.
5 The help desk should be .... who has a problem with their computer.
6 There's no .... a fuss – things will only get worse if you do.
7 I asked two colleagues, but found .... could help.
8 I got lots of feedback, ... unfortunately turned out to be useful.

Use of English

▶ **Paper 3, Part 4**

> ### About the exam
>
> Remember: **Never change the key word** you are given and **never write more than eight words.** If you find that you have used more than eight words, you have made a mistake. Go back and check!

For each question below, complete the second sentence with three to eight words so that it has a similar meaning to the first sentence, using the word given. Do not change the word given.

1 The fact that Charles has lost his job does not surprise me.   **comes**

   It ....
   .... that Charles has lost his job.

2 It appears that nobody disagrees with the new plans.   **along**

   Everybody appears ....
   .... the new plans.

3 The staff bitterly resent the remarks he made recently.   **rise**

   His recent remarks ....
   .... among the staff.

4 The total collapse of the company is inevitable.   **conclusion**

   It is ....
   .... collapse.

5 There is a rumour that the manager has been accepting bribes.   **alleged**

   The manager ....
   .... bribes.

6 The result of the election is not at all easy to predict.   **means**

   It is ....
   .... the result of the election.

7 No matter what happens, you must not try to contact me.   **circumstances**

   Under ....
   .... to contact me.

8 Without his help, we would have gone over the deadline.   **met**

   But ....
   .... the deadline.

Reading

▶ Paper 1, Part 4

1 Read the following text about the construction of a traditional wooden building in southwest England and answer the questions on page 83.

Where do you think the text was taken from?

- an encyclopaedia
- a magazine
- a school textbook
- a newspaper
- a poster

The Great Oak Hall at Westonbirt

Many people would quail at the idea of having to construct an open-plan building 70ft long and 24ft wide out of freshly cut oak, using nothing but their hands and traditional tools. But to a master-craftsman like Henry Russell, the task of creating the Great Oak Hall at Westonbirt, the Forestry Commission's arboretum, or botanical tree garden, in southwest England, is no more than an agreeable challenge. A tousle-haired beanpole of 32, Henry is a versatile fellow, and for the past few years has been at the forefront of the revival in green woodworking. For years he has dreamt of building a big hall at Westonbirt, and now he has his chance.

Even though many of the materials have been given, and much of the work will be done by trainees, the building will cost over £300,000. So that work can start at once, a third of this sum has been underwritten by the charity Friends of Westonbirt Arboretum, and a fund-raising campaign will open later this year. When the project was launched at a reception in a marquee by the site of the hall, a number of oaks, contributed by local woodland owners, already lay on the ground outside, and 50 more mature oaks had been felled in the Silk Wood, one area of the arboretum. In a celebratory speech, the chairman of the Forestry Commission emphasised that nobody should see the cutting-down of ancient trees as an act of destruction or vandalism. On the contrary, he said: the harvesting was merely the latest move in centuries of careful woodland management, and the flora and fauna were already responding to the light which the felling of the trees had let in.

His words were very much to the point, but he rather gave away his own lack of practical skills when Henry Russell, handing him a sledge-hammer and wedges, invited him to split a round of oak as a token start. For Henry, in contrast, cutting, splitting and shaping green wood is second nature. He has waited a long time to begin work on the hall, and one of his first tasks will be to select trees which, by their natural bend, lend themselves to forming the curved beams that will support the roof.

He is well capable of tackling an entire oak on his own, cutting it to size with handsaws and axes. In this case, volunteer workers, many of whom are novices, will be taken on for the initial preparation of the trunks, using mechanical tools to save time. Thereafter, hand-tools will be the order of the day. One of the smaller but most time-consuming tasks will be to split and shape the 500 oak pegs which will lock the beams in position.

Starting on 29th May, five week-long courses to train the volunteers will be held under the supervision of Gudrun Leitz, another pioneer of the green wood revival. Taught by her and Henry, students will learn the techniques of cutting and shaping the wood. All they need bring with them, she says, is energy, enthusiasm, suitable clothes, and a pair of boots with steel toecaps. If they behave like most latter-day woodworkers, they will live on site in tents or homemade shelters. They will also need to be fairly impervious to scrutiny, for the site is in a commanding position, near the entrance, and visitors to the arboretum – around 300,000 a year – will doubtless flock round. Everyone who takes part will be invited to a 'grand raising party' when all the components are ready and the building finally goes up at the end of August.

From models and drawings, it looks as though the hall, which will act as meeting point, conference centre and lecture theatre, will be a striking blend of ancient and modern. Like all its main members, the furniture will be made of oak, but the windows will be of high-tech glass. As to which will last longer – the wood in the building, or the oaks growing outside it – no one can say; but there is no doubt that the hall will be the most striking innovation at Westonbirt since the arboretum was founded in 1829.

2   Look at the following questions and unfinished statements about the text. In each case, choose the answer (**A**, **B**, **C** or **D**) which fits best, according to the text.

Look again at Unit 3, page 27 for guidance on how distractors operate, and of the best way to approach this type of question.

1   What does the writer imply about the technique of green woodworking in the first paragraph?
   A   It is often used to build traditional houses.
   B   It was neglected as a building technique until recently.
   C   It has been developed in recent years.
   D   It requires master-craftsmen like Henry Russell.

2   The writer suggests that the felling of trees for this project
   A   occurred at the site of the building.
   B   was essential for the other life on the forest floor.
   C   was seen as controversial by some.
   D   was funded entirely by the Friends of Westonbirt Arboretum.

3   The chairman of the Forestry Commission
   A   wanted more traditional woodland management.
   B   initiated the project with a public speech.
   C   had very pointed things to say about the project.
   D   was better at public speaking than at woodworking.

4   The beams which support the roof will be made from trees which
   A   have the right shape.
   B   are particularly straight and tall.
   C   can be cut, split and shaped easily.
   D   have been grown especially for that purpose.

5   The writer says that the volunteer workers will
   A   have to construct their own accommodation.
   B   be using hand-tools wherever feasible.
   C   stay on the site for over a month.
   D   be expected to have some previous experience.

6   What will the workers on the project have to get used to?
   A   being looked at closely by visitors
   B   meeting vast numbers of tourists
   C   being made to live in tents on site
   D   supervising visitors to the site

7   The Great Oak Hall at Westonbirt will
   A   be something new and original that will attract attention.
   B   use fashionable hi-tech materials.
   C   be unusual, because built entirely of wood.
   D   be more durable than most modern buildings.

Use of English
▶ Paper 3, Part 1

Fill each gap in the following text with one suitable word. You may need to look again at Unit 1, pages 12–13, for guidance on the best way to approach this task.

Big Brother is watching you

Big Brother could soon be (0) *keeping* an eye on the staff. Several international companies are consulting scientists on ways of developing microchip implants for their workers in (1) .... to measure their timekeeping and whereabouts.

The technology, (2) .... has already been successfully tested (3) .... pets and human volunteers, would (4) .... it possible for firms to track staff around a building. The data could enable them to draw (5) .... estimates of workers' efficiency and productivity.

British scientist Kevin Warwick hit the headlines recently when he (6) .... a silicon chip implanted in his forearm. He was subsequently (7) .... to show how a computer could monitor (8) .... every move, using detectors that were located around the building (9) .... he worked.

In his experiment, Warwick showed how the system could also (10) .... of benefit to workers by programming (11) .... to switch on lights, computers and heating systems (12) .... he entered a room.

It seems highly (13) .... that the technology will (14) .... an appeal to companies with high labour costs, and (15) .... which small increases in productivity can have an immediate impact on profits. At just a few pounds per employee, it is also relatively cheap.

Language Focus: Vocabulary
Adverb + adjective collocation

1 Match the adverbs in box A to the adjectives in box B. The first one has been done for you.

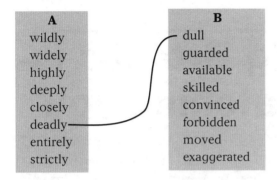

A	B
wildly	dull
widely	guarded
highly	available
deeply	skilled
closely	convinced
deadly	forbidden
entirely	moved
strictly	exaggerated

2 Complete each of the following sentences with the appropriate adverb + adjective combination from Exercise 1.

1 The lecture was .... and I almost went to sleep.
2 The gameplan of the winning team remained a .... secret.
3 She was .... by all the letters of support she received.
4 The report was published last week and is now .... in all leading bookshops.
5 Smoking in the work area is ....
6 Osborne quickly gained the reputation of being a .... negotiator.
7 The details of the scandal have been ....
8 I am not .... that we need to make so many workers redundant.

Study Tip

Watch out for collocations like these when you are reading. Read with a pencil in your hand, mark interesting language that you come across, and transfer it to your notebook.

Few students learn and use adverbs really effectively; successful use of collocations like these in **Paper 2** essays and **Paper 5** speaking will impress your examiner.

Phrasal verbs and expressions: *work*

1 Fill the gaps in the following sentences with the correct form of the phrasal verbs *work up* or *work out*. Make any necessary changes to complete each sentence. Use a dictionary to help you if necessary.

1 I can't .... he left so suddenly without telling anybody. It really baffles me.
2 Here's a calculator – can you .... much money we owe the part-time staff, please?
3 I'm afraid it's just not .... me and my new boss. We've had three rows already.
4 I can't .... enthusiasm for his plan. It just seems to me like a real waste of time and money.
5 Come on, calm down. It's not worth getting yourself all .... such a small issue.
6 Sarah .... the gym three times a week. I don't know where she finds the energy.
7 I haven't told Alex I don't want to go to the party yet – I'm .... it. He'll be so upset when I do tell him.
8 It's better for you to travel to work by train, I think. Using your car will .... too expensive.
9 If you want to .... appetite before dinner, why don't you go and chop up some wood for the stove?
10 You've got it .... , haven't you? You know exactly what you have to do in order to get promoted, don't you?

2 Choose the correct alternative to complete each of the following sentences.

1 The assessment wasn't much of a challenge to Sarah, and she made *short/small* work of it, finishing the whole thing in a matter of hours.
2 You'll have your work *cut/pulled* out to change the filing system here. I don't see how on earth you can do it.
3 I see that the firemen are working to *regulation/rule* again. I know they deserve a pay rise but I don't think this is the way to get it.
4 I'm working my fingers to the *skin/bone* trying to make enough money to live on. I don't think I can carry on like this.
5 Calm down! Don't work yourself into a *frenzy/fuss*, simply because you think you may lose your job!
6 I'm trying to work up the *courage/bravery* to go and tell my boss what happened.
7 Try rubbing the tablecloth with salt. Salt works *wonders/surprises* with wine stains.
8 I need to keep myself in good shape. In my *category/line* of work, accidents can happen if you aren't one hundred per cent fit.
9 He tried to persuade me to steal the computer disk for him, but I told him to do his own *immoral/dirty* work.
10 I'm so tired of always being given the *donkey/mule* work to do that I'm thinking of looking for another job.

Language Focus: Grammar
Future forms

Watch Out! *problem areas*

- ***will** and **going to***
  Going to is frequently over-used where *will* would be more appropriate.
  I'll help you with your suitcase, if you like. ✔
  I'm going to help you with your suitcase.
  (= *sounds aggressive*)
  Will/Would you help me with this? ✔
  Are you going to help me with this?
  (= *sounds angry/sarcastic*)

- **intentions and predictions**
  The present continuous should only be used for arrangements. It cannot be used for intentions or predictions.
  I'm getting *going to get* really angry with you soon! (= *intention*)
  He's having *He'll have/He's going to have* an accident one of these days if he's not careful.
  (= *prediction*)

- **future continuous**
  This future form is commonly used when we want to ask a favour of someone. Here, *will* or *going to* would appear too direct.
  Will you be going to the bank? Could you give them this letter, please? (= *are you planning to do this anyway?*) ✔

- **other future forms**
  Modal verbs can be used to refer to the future, as can structures such as *likely to*, *bound to*, etc. These tend to add something to the meaning.
  The plane *is due to/should* leave in half an hour.
  (= *it is expected to leave*) ✔
  She was *on the verge of* tears when I arrived.
  (= *very close to tears*) ✔
  The Prime Minister *is to* visit Spain next week.
  (= *formal engagement*) ✔
  We're *about to* go – are you ready? (= *we'll go in a few minutes*) ✔

1

1 Choose the appropriate ending, a) or b) for each sentence. Indicate your choice in the spaces provided.

1 I'm playing tennis with Roger tomorrow, ...
   a) if the weather is good.
   b) so I'm afraid I can't come with you on the picnic.

2 Are you going to marry me, ...
   a) if I promise to give you whatever you want?
   b) or do I have to wait for another five years?

3 The train is due to arrive at six o'clock this evening, ...
   a) but I expect it'll be late.
   b) owing to the bad weather conditions.

4 He is on the verge of resigning, ...
   a) by the end of this month, I'm sure.
   b) though I don't think he's told the boss yet.

5 That tree's going to fall down, ...
   a) so get away from it quickly!
   b) by the time we return.

6 I'll be wearing a red pullover, ...
   a) if you'd prefer that.
   b) so I'll be easy to spot.

7 I'll be going to the supermarket later, ...
   a) so if you want something, let me know.
   b) if you can't be bothered to.

8 You'll be working overtime every day next week, ...
   a) because three members of staff are ill.
   b) if you don't listen to what I'm telling you!

2 Now rewrite the stems 1–8 above, so that they are appropriate for the **other** ending.

EXAMPLE:

I'll play tennis with Roger tomorrow if the weather is good.

2

2 For each question below, complete the second sentence with three to eight words so that it has a similar meaning to the first sentence, using the word given. Do not change the word given.

1 He'll be getting promoted soon. **long**
   It won't .... promoted.

2 He doesn't stand a very good chance of winning the race on Saturday. **unlikely**
   In the race on Saturday, he ....
   .... first.

3 When he refuses to work overtime, I'm certain there'll be problems. **bound**
   His .... create problems.

4 Scientists are very close to discovering a cure for cancer. **verge**
   Scientists .... a cure for cancer.

5 I have to renew my licence next month. **due**
   My licence .... next month.

6 Everyone thinks the sale of the house will be complete by the end of the week. **expected**
   The house ....
   .... by the end of the week.

Writing

▶ Paper 2, Part 2 (report)

1 Exercises 1 and 2 focus on the differences between a report and an essay.

1 Read the following two extracts from student compositions. One comes from an essay and the other comes from a report. Tick the one which comes from a report.

1 ☐

Income and status

The majority of students thought that income and status were inseparable. Interestingly enough, however, only about 40% of those present expressed a wish to become doctors or lawyers – careers which offer both a high income and high social status. Money was thought to be important, but not the most important factor in choosing a career.

Job satisfaction

Most students regarded job satisfaction as the most important factor in their future careers. The opinion was expressed by a number of participants that since work comprised a large part of most people's lives, it was essential that this area should bring fulfilment. Job satisfaction was seen to include other factors such as prospects of promotion and ...

2 ☐

It is interesting that large numbers of people nowadays have become disillusioned with the system whereby career status and income are seen as the most important aspects of a person's life. There has even been a tendency among young people in recent years to reject the values of materialism altogether and to embrace alternative lifestyles. The fact that the 1960s are viewed with nostalgia by many today, and that the songs of the Beatles and Bob Dylan are once more in vogue, shows that young people have not lost their idealism. In fact they are probably just as idealistic as their fathers and mothers were when they were young. How exactly does this idealism express itself today however?

What is certain is that students and young people have grown just as tired of politics as they have with the values of materialism. They find politicians difficult to take seriously and prefer to become involved in ecological or 'green' issues, such as campaigning against the destruction of the rainforests or modern farming methods, or even ...

2 Put a cross (X) next to the items in the following list which you would be **unlikely** to find in a report.
a) direct speech
b) phrases like 'it is interesting that ...', 'significantly, ...'
c) rhetorical questions
d) examples to support ideas
e) a general or abstract discussion of a topic
f) use of the passive voice

2

1 Extract 1 in Exercise 1 was written in answer to the following task.

TASK

You attended a conference at your school or college recently in which students discussed the factors they considered to be important in their future careers. Income, prospects, job satisfaction and social life were among some of the points covered.

Using these points or others you consider to be appropriate, write a report summarising their views and comment on what they reveal about the hopes and aspirations of young people in your country.

(300–350 words)

2 Read extract 1 again, and the alternative conclusions below. Decide:

- which conclusion is most appropriate for the task, and extract 1
- which conclusion is most appropriate for an essay.

A ☐

The conference was a great success. Those who participated benefited enormously from the opportunity it presented to exchange opinions and to discuss issues of importance to young people today. I would recommend that further conferences be held in the future on subjects such as the attitude of European countries towards poverty, the problem of environmental pollution or the place of music and art in a modern society.

B ☐

In conclusion, it is clear that young people demand much more from a job than just money or status. Even though there is little job security these days, the youth of today is looking for something more than just 'landing a better job' or buying a bigger house. Should we not consider changing the education system to bring it more in line with these hopes and aspirations? A system which encouraged creativity and social awareness would be more valuable than the one we have at present, which appears to actively encourage only selfishness and greed.

C ☐

The conference was extremely worthwhile and gave young people an opportunity to express their feelings about a number of issues relevant to the world of work. It is particularly significant that income is no longer considered to be the most important factor in a career. This seems to suggest that young people today are less materialistic than the previous generation. It is also significant that most young people do not see their social life as being a priority – something which would indicate that older people have seriously misunderstood the younger generation.

3

1 Write a report in answer to the following writing task.

TASK

You work as librarian in a school or college library. Recently, you attended a meeting of regular users of the library, where complaints were made about the unavailability of certain books, the lack of space and photocopying facilities, and various other services. Write a report to the Finance Director, outlining the most serious problems mentioned by students at the meeting and suggesting what should be done to improve the situation.

(300–350 words)

2 Plan your report, deciding which problems you intend to include, and the headings you will use for your paragraphs.

3 Now write your report, making sure that the language you use is formal and impersonal.

Useful expressions for report writing

this report will describe …
the aim of this report is to …
it has been mentioned/pointed
    out/suggested that …
the opinion has been expressed
    (by many students) that …
is/are seen to be …
it is apparent that …
I (would) recommend/suggest that …
    be done …
I feel (strongly) that …

4 When you have finished, check your report carefully for errors.

4 Exchange your report with another student if you can. Evaluate each other's work and suggest improvements.

The monster in the machine

Language Focus: Grammar
Reflexive pronouns

> **Watch Out!** *problem areas*
>
> - **verbs followed by *to***
>   Several verbs take the dependent preposition *to* after a reflexive pronoun. This means that they are followed either by a noun or by the *-ing* form of a verb.
>   She has *dedicated herself to* (fight**ing** for) the rights of animals. ✔
>   This book doesn't *lend itself to* (be**ing** adapted for) television. ✔
>
> - **nouns which become verbs**
>   When a noun becomes a verb, there is usually also a change of preposition.
>   I maintained a certain distance *between* myself and my mother. = I distanced myself *from* my mother. ✔
>   She takes pride *in* her cooking. = She prides herself *on* her cooking. ✔
>
> - ***enjoy* and *entertain***
>   These verbs always need an object.
>   I *enjoyed* the film very much. ✔
>   I didn't *enjoy myself* very much at the party last night. ✔
>   A magician *entertained* the children for over an hour. ✔
>   I'm afraid I have to go out on urgent business. Can you *entertain yourselves*? ✔

1 For each question below, complete the second sentence with three to eight words so that it has a similar meaning to the first sentence, using the word given. Do not change the word given.

1 Anne is proud that she is able to speak five languages fluently.   **prides**
Anne ....
.... to speak five languages fluently.

2 She does not want to be involved in the scandal caused by her husband's remarks.   **distance**
She wants ....
.... the scandal caused by her husband's remarks.

3 It would be easy to make a film adaptation of Danielle Steel's latest novel.   **lends**
Danielle Steel's latest novel ....
.... into a film.

4 You need not make a final decision now about whether to support the proposal.   **commit**
You do ....
.... the proposal now.

5 She knew she couldn't cope with the temptation to eat the bar of chocolate.   **trust**
She knew she ....
.... the bar of chocolate.

6 He reluctantly accepted that he would have to travel alone.   **resigned**
He ....
.... own.

2 Fill each of the gaps in the following sentences with a suitable word or short phrase. In this exercise some, but not all, of the sentences require a **reflexive pronoun**.

1 I know you're nervous about the exam, but you really .... together before it starts!

2 Take a rest! You'll .... out if you continue to work as hard as this.

3 I was distracted by the noise outside to such an extent that I .... on what I was doing.

4 Unless you .... a bit more, the boss will treat you like a doormat, you know.

5 He didn't mean to steal the money. He just .... himself.

Use of English
▶ **Paper 3, Part 5**

1 Read the following texts about voice-controlled computers. Do the writers think that natural conversation with a computer is a real possibility for the future?

2 Read each text carefully and answer the comprehension questions 1–4.

One of the shared assumptions in computer research is that talking to computers is a very good idea. Such a good idea that speech is regarded as the natural interface between human and computer. 5

Each company with enough money to spare and enough egotism to believe that it can shape everyone's future now has a 'natural language' research group. Films and TV series set in the future use computers with voice 10 interfaces to show how far technology has advanced from our own primitive day and age. The unwritten assumption is that talking to your computer will in the end be as natural as shouting at your relatives. 15

The roots of this shared delusion lie in the genuine naturalness of spoken communication between humans. Meaning is transferred from person to person so effortlessly that it must be the best way of 20 transferring information from a human to another object.

This view is totally misguided. Computers do not experience life as people do – it is shared human experience which enables 25 people to understand each other precisely in a conversation where a transcript would make very little sense. Unfinished sentences, in-jokes, catchphrases, hesitation markers like 'er' and 'you know', and words whose 30 meaning is only clear in the context of that one conversation are no bar to human understanding, but baffled early attempts at computer speech recognition.

It is true that recent advances in linguistic 35 research and artificial intelligence address this problem, but they address it only in part. The problem essentially remains.

1 Explain in your own words what the phrase 'this shared delusion' (line 16) describes.

2 What point is the writer making in paragraph 4 when he mentions 'in-jokes, catchphrases, hesitation markers' and other features of language?

I've never understood the belief that talking to your computer is a Good Thing. It seems to me to be totally misguided. In fact, so-called 'natural communication' with a computer would appear to be about as unnatural as you can get. People and computers inhabit different worlds. Even if you succeed in ordering your computer about, it'll never laugh at your jokes, make sarcastic comments, tell you the latest gossip or do any of the other things that make real human conversation such fun.

Then there's that awful prospect of an office full of people talking to their machines. Quite apart from the noise generated, most people are bound to feel pretty ridiculous talking to something so obviously non-human.

I doubt very much, though, whether people in modern society are capable of speaking clearly and unambiguously enough to a computer. Most of us don't have servants to boss around any more, and changes in the way we work mean that office managers are no longer used to giving crisp orders and expecting them to be obeyed.

There's no doubt that controlling a computer by speaking to it only works if you imitate an army drill sergeant. You have to avoid all those 'could you's' and 'would you mind's' that most of us use when we're trying to get someone to do something they don't really want to do. Since this will be nigh on impossible for most of us, we'll end up with machines never doing what we really want and making all manner of mistakes in the process. We'll probably even be unable to pull the plug out when we've given up trying.

3 What phrase in paragraph 1 echoes the lack of shared experience between computers and people mentioned in the first text?

4 What attitude does the writer imply must be overcome by users of voice-controlled computers?

3

1 Read the following summary task.

> In a paragraph of between **50 and 70** words, summarise, **in your own words as far as possible**, the problems involved in using computers to react to human orders.

2 Underline the relevant information in the texts, make a list of points, and then write the first draft of your summary. Check and edit your summary, remembering to correct any spelling, punctuation or grammar mistakes you may have made.

Reading

You are going to read four extracts which are all connected in some way with modern technology. For questions 1–8 choose the answer (**A**, **B**, **C** or **D**) which you think fits best according to the text.

Electronic literature

It's Wednesday, late afternoon, in Seattle, and I'm writing about classical composers – Bach, Beethoven, Mozart and so on, 30 of them for a multimedia product on European history. It's an odd assignment. I've never written about music or studied the people who make it. 5
My speciality before I started writing for CD-Rom companies, was environmental journalism, and what I know about classical composers is, basically, *Amadeus*. But ignorance, in the new electronic literature, isn't always an obstacle. The irony of the so-called information 10
revolution is that consumers neither like nor expect long, densely written texts on their computer screens.

Long texts addle the eyes; they slow the rapid-fire 'interactive' process; steal precious screen space from the animation, video and multimedia's other, more remarkable 15
gewgaws. So we writers needn't be experts so much as filters whose task is to absorb and compress great gobs of information into small, easily digestible, on-screen chunks. Brevity and blandness: these are the elements of the next literary style. Of roughly 1,000 'essays' I've 20
'written' for CD-Rom companies here in Seattle over the last year and a half, fewer than 40 ran longer than 200 words – about the length of the paragraph you're reading now – and most were much, much shorter.

1 What does the writer imply about the term 'information revolution'? (lines 10–11)
   A It accurately summarises the present situation.
   B It wrongly suggests that information is important.
   C It reflects the way people view the changes.
   D It would be more appropriate for literature.

2 What is the attitude of the writer towards the texts he writes?
   A He is dismissive of them.
   B He feels they are useful.
   C He thinks they are well written.
   D He likes their brevity.

The Stone Age brain we have inherited

The human brain achieved its modern form and size between 50,000 and 100,000 years ago, equipping our Stone Age ancestors with a mental toolbox which they used to master rocks, tools, plants, animals, and one another. Since then, nothing much has changed. The same mental toolbox provides us with the intuitions which enable us to handle the most complex concepts of science and mathematics.

This intuitive way of looking at the world gradually grew into the formal sciences that we know today. The conviction that living things have some kind of inner essence, for example, is what impelled the first professional biologists to try to understand the nature of plants and animals by cutting them open and putting bits of them under a microscope.

But modern science also forces us to make some changes in our thinking. Our intuitions may sometimes turn out to be unhelpful, or may need to be directed away from what they usually apply to. For example, like monkeys and apes, we are visual animals. Seeing things is important to us. So we invented graphs and charts in order to do mathematics. These allow difficult ideas to present themselves to our mind's eye as familiar shapes. To do chemistry, we stretch our intuitions about the physical world and treat the essence of a natural substance as a collection of tiny, bouncy, sticky balls.

3 The writer says that modern science is the product of
   A a brain which has evolved substantially from the Stone Age.
   B man's constant search for abstract truth and meaning.
   C early investigations into the nature of living matter.
   D the way our brains have worked for thousands of years.

4 The writer mentions mathematics and chemistry to show how
   A severely limited our view of the world is.
   B our natural capacities determine the way we understand the world.
   C our understanding of the world has developed since the Stone Age.
   D skilled we are at thinking intelligently and logically.

A buyer's guide to digital cameras

A buyer's guide to digital cameras

Forget fragile negatives, red-eyed relatives and endless waiting for your snaps to come back from the developer. Photography has entered the digital age. A cable connection transfers images directly from your camera to your desktop computer, allowing you to view and edit images quickly and easily, and print out your snaps on photo-quality paper.

Alan Mayhew, our senior photographer, gives us his comments about two state-of-the-art models (by Canon and Olympus), which he tried out last week.

- The Canon (full details opposite) sits comfortably in the hand; but while not quite credit-card sized, as Canon claims, it is smaller than a packet of cigarettes. Getting out and about with your digital camera is now a practical proposition. Picture quality is equally attractive. This is a high class camera, and the quality is reflected in the price.

- The Olympus (full details opposite) incorporates no trendy gimmicks: it is very much a photographer's camera. You will need to have a good knowledge of current jargon in order to make sense of all the available options. The image quality is a step above the cheaper cameras available, and only slightly less defined than the most expensive models. The only real qualm is with the resolution, which is more than adequate for use on your computer, but is not ideal for printing.

Modern technology – the pace of change

In case you hadn't realised it, the digital revolution is drastically changing and improving our lives. As electronics companies find new ways to cram more data onto microchips, so the ⁵ sophistication of their goods continues to grow and grow. Implicit in the marketing of such technology is the assumption that our lives will become better and brighter thanks to such ¹⁰ products. For instance, open the pages of *Computer World* magazine, the journal established to track and cheer on current advances in technology, and you will find breathless editorials echoing just this ¹⁵ motion. Not since the 1950s has there been such whole-hearted faith in technology.

Yet while the advocates of an electronic golden age have their eyes ²⁰ firmly set on the future, the rest of us are living in the imperfect present. Rather than making our lives better and simpler, technology tends to make them more complicated. Office workers stay late at ²⁵ night wading through tides of e-mail. Half a dozen people in a restaurant reach for their breast pocket or bag at the anonymous trilling of a mobile phone.

Once upon a time, it was machines ³⁰ which became obsolete. Now, in the information age, we are running to keep pace with the rate of change, and fearing it is us – not technology – that will end up on the scrap heap. ³⁵

5 What does the writer imply about early models of digital cameras?
A They were large and cumbersome.
B They were extremely expensive.
C They were inferior to traditional cameras.
D They were only available to a few people.

6 The Olympus camera would be suitable for
A younger members of the family.
B experienced photographers.
C travellers with little space to spare.
D perfectionists.

7 What does the writer say about *Computer World* magazine?
A It is a magazine written for computer experts.
B It is aimed at those who market hi-tech goods.
C It is very enthusiastic about technological advances.
D It dates from the 1950s.

8 Which of these phrases is used without sarcasm by the writer?
A digital revolution (lines 1–2)
B advances in technology (line 14)
C golden age (line 20)
D imperfect present (line 22)

Reading

▶ Paper 1, Part 3

You are going to read an extract from a novel. Seven paragraphs have been removed from the extract. Choose from the paragraphs **A–H** the one which fits each gap (**1–7**). There is one extra paragraph which you do not need to use.

Mother had gone to town on the bus, leaving Liza alone in the morning room at Shrove House. She had obviously thought that her daughter wanted to be there instead of the library because it was much lighter and from the windows you could see the trains go by. But that was not the reason. After Liza had looked out of the window and had seen a train going south and had studied once more the wedding photograph of Mr Tobias in a sleek dark suit and Mrs Tobias in a large hat and spotted dress, she drew aside a curtain to reveal the stepladder. It was just as she had left it.

1 ....

It was still there. Liza came down the ladder, unlocked the door and opened it. She stood in front of the box thing with the window on the front and studied it. There were knobs and switches underneath the window, rather like the knobs and switches on Mother's electric stove. Liza pressed or turned them one after another but nothing happened.

2 ....

When she turned the largest knob nothing happened, but when she pushed it in, a buzzing sound came out of the box and, to her extreme astonishment, a point of light appeared in the window. The light expanded, shivering, and gradually a picture began to form, grey and white and dark grey, the colours of the etchings on the morning room walls, but recognisably a picture.

3 ....

Briefly she was afraid. The people moved, they danced, they threw their legs in the air, they were manifestly real, yet not real. She had taken a step backwards, then another, but now she came closer. The children continued to dance. One girl came to the centre of the stage and danced alone, spinning round with one leg held out behind her. Liza looked round the back of the box. It was just a box, black with ridges and holes and more switches.

4 ....

But that feeling gradually passed. She was afraid, she was filled with wonder, then she was pleased, gratified, she began to enjoy it. She sat down cross-legged on the floor and gazed, enraptured. A woman was teaching another woman to cook something. They mixed things up in a bowl, eggs and sugar and flour and butter, and no more than two minutes later, when the first woman opened the oven door, she lifted out the baked cake, all dark and shiny and risen high. It was magic. It was the magic Liza had read about in fairy stories.

5 ....

Most reluctantly, she turned off the set by pulling towards her the knob she had pushed in and switched off the plug at the point. She locked the door and climbed up the steps to put the key back on the top of the picture frame. It was just as well she started when she did. Carrying the steps back to hide them behind the curtains, she saw through the window Mother coming up the drive towards the house and Bruno Drummond with her.

6 ....

There was nobody to ask. Why was it bad for her to see. Would it hurt her? Her eyes, her ears? They felt all right. It was strange to think of Mother knowing all about this magic and never saying, to think of Bruno Drummond knowing too, very probably having one of his own at home over the greengrocer's shop.

7 ....

After she had gone to bed, she heard them go out of the front door. She got up and looked out of the window at them. Without knowing why, she didn't like Bruno Drummond much.

A

She understood about electricity. Their old heater wouldn't work unless it was plugged into the point and the switch pressed down. Here the plug was in but the point not switched on. She pressed the switch down. Still nothing. Try the routine of pressing or turning all those knobs and switches.

B

She carried it across the room and set it up close beside the picture of the flowers and the Death's Head moth. She took great care to press down the top step which would make it safe. It was possible of course that the key was no longer there. Mother had been in this room many times since Liza had seen her place it on top of the picture frame and it was a wonder she had never come upon the hidden steps. Climb up and find out.

C

They were early because he had brought Mother back in his car. Liza wasn't much interested in him that evening. Her head was full of what she had seen on, or through, or by means of, the window on that box. She wondered what it was, how it did what it did and if there was only one like it in the world, the one at Shrove, or if there were others.

D

It was not still, as an etching was, but moving and happening, like life. There were people, of about her own age, not speaking but dancing to music. Liza had heard the music before, she could even have said what it was, something called Swan Lake, by Tchaikovsky.

E

Why didn't they have one in the gate-house? There was no-one she could ask. She was so quiet that evening, hardly saying a word throughout the meal – which Bruno stayed for – that Mother asked her if she was feeling all right.

F

He disliked her being there, she could sense that, she could sense waves of coldness coming at her. Bruno looked so sweet and gentle, he looked kind, but she guessed he wasn't really like that. People might not always be the way their faces proclaimed them to be.

G

A lot of print, white on black and grey, came up on the window, then a face, then – most alarming of all – a voice. The first words Liza ever heard come out of a television set she could never remember. She was too over-awed by the very idea of a person being in there and speaking. She was very nearly stunned.

H

She watched for an hour. There was a dog driving sheep about on a hillside, then a man with a lot of glass bottles and tubes and a chart on the wall. She went to look at the clock. If it had been possible, she could have watched all night. But if Mother came back and caught her she would never be able to watch it again.

Writing
▶ Paper 2, Part 1 (essay)

About the exam

In the essay in **Paper 2, Part 1** you may have to present only one side of an argument.

Exam Strategy

- You should not discuss alternative points of view, but instead you should provide evidence which either supports or disproves the statement given in the writing task.
- You may want to evaluate the statement briefly in your introduction or conclusion, but be relevant and concise. Try to echo or mirror the words of the title or introduction in your conclusion.

1

1   Read the following paragraph, which is from an essay about the Internet. Ignore the underlining for the moment. Is the tone of the paragraph:

1   too indecisive?
2   too blunt and direct?
3   more appropriate for a report than an essay?

Large numbers of people use the Internet these days at home and in the office. (1) This trend will continue as people become aware of the ease with which they can send and receive information in any format and communicate with others around the world by means of e-mail. Although the benefits of this new technology are apparent, the negative aspects of the Internet (2) have been ignored. (3) People dismiss any view that is even mildly critical as being alarmist or perhaps uninformed. (4) It is sad, for example, that many parents (5) do not worry about the amount of time their children spend 'surfing the net'. Even though doctors and psychologists have warned about the possibility of Internet addiction, few parents take these warnings seriously.

2 The writing is rather blunt in tone. We often use expressions which 'tone down' statements, to avoid appearing aggressive. Rewrite the underlined parts of the introduction on page 93, using the words or phrases from the box below. More than one answer is possible.

> to a large extent/largely   rather
> in all probability/there is every likelihood/
> it is likely that   seem to/appear to
> is/are apt to/tend to   there is a tendency for

2

1 Read the following writing task.

> **TASK**
>
> Your tutor has asked you to write an essay about how improvements in information technology may result in people becoming isolated from one another, and outlining ways of dealing with the problem. The following extract from a popular newspaper gave you some ideas. Write your essay, covering the areas mentioned in the extract and adding details to support your arguments.
>
> (300–350 words)

The Information Age: Ten Causes for Concern!

- People talk to their friends for hours on their mobile phones. Whatever happened to meeting for coffee?

- Mobile phones have a habit of going off when you're trying to talk to someone. Why can't people just turn them off?

- Everyone is always going on about the Internet, shopping on-line or sending e-mails. Perhaps because it all saves you the bother of actually having to meet and be nice to real people.

- So many of our young people have become computer nerds. They spend their whole lives in cyberspace, it seems. What are their parents doing?

2 Read the following list of features which could be included in the introduction of an essay. Which would you include if you were writing an introduction to an essay answering the task above?

1 A sentence quoting the words of a famous person.
2 A brief outline of the situation today.
3 The aspects of technology which will be discussed.
4 A detailed discussion of the benefits of improved communications technology.
5 A sentence which echoes the negative aspect of technology mentioned in the task.

3 Now read the following introduction, which was written in answer to the task. Which of the features from the list above does it contain?

> Recent technological advances have meant that people nowadays are generally able to communicate much more easily and effectively than ever before. This may, of course, have benefited many people, but it has also resulted in a situation where people have perhaps become more isolated from their immediate surroundings. Two good examples of this negative trend can be seen in the way large numbers of people seem to have become dependent on mobile telephones and the Internet as means of communication.

3 Read the three following supporting paragraphs, which make up the body of the essay. The gaps indicate places where ideas or connecting phrases have been omitted. Choose the phrase or sentence, a), b) or c) opposite, which best fits each of these gaps. Remember that you need to consider the text **as a whole**, to do this effectively.

> Increasing numbers of people are using mobile telephones to communicate with friends, family and colleagues. Wherever they may be, (1) .... To a large extent, this has resulted in less meaningful face-to-face contact between people. It has also brought about a situation where meal times, social occasions and even (2) .... , are apt to be interrupted by the bleeping of a mobile phone. Needless to say, (3) ....
> The Internet has likewise (4) .... Since it is possible to send and to receive almost any information you want over the Internet, the need to interact socially simply does not exist for some people anymore. In fact, the appeal of the Internet for many may be that they can work and play from home (5) ....
> Clearly, we need to be rather more aware of the effect this new technology is having on our lives and find ways to limit the damage. Mobile telephones, of course, can be turned off or left at home. It is unlikely to prove disastrous (6) .... , and messages can always be left on an answerphone. Similarly, the use of the Internet can, and possibly should, be regulated. Parents in particular need to keep an eye on their children in order to prevent 'Internet addiction' from developing. As with most things, common sense is what is needed most.

1 a) they can contact whoever they
      want easily and reasonably cheaply
   b) mobile telephones are both cheap
      and easy to use
   c) it will be possible to talk to
      whoever they want to
2 a) other important occasions
   b) when driving to work
   c) the Christmas dinner
3 a) it has been known for people to
      be woken up in the middle of
      the night
   b) this is both annoying and has a
      detrimental effect on relationships
   c) people nowadays are simply not
      allowed to be 'unavailable'
4 a) affected people's social skills
   b) had a more disastrous effect on our
      relationships
   c) grown over the past few years
5 a) and spend very little money in
      the process
   b) without ever having to get involved
      in human relationships
   c) and make many new friends in
      the process
6 a) unless a call is answered
   b) if a call is left unanswered
   c) provided a call is left unanswered

4   Which of these conclusions is more
appropriate?

A
In summing up, I feel that it
would be wrong to pretend that
the advantages of improved
communications technology are
insignificant. Nevertheless, it
is true to say that there are
negative aspects of this new
technology and increased social
isolation is perhaps the most
important of these. This is
something which most definitely
should not be ignored.

B
In conclusion, it is obvious
that this new technology is
slowly destroying the fabric
of society. It may even be
detrimental to our health.
There have been reports, for
example, that mobile
telephones cause cancer.
We should take action now –
before it is too late.

5   The following two methods of organising the information would
both be acceptable for the task we have been examining. Which method
was used to write the essay above?

A
```
Para. 1 - introduction
Para. 2 - mobile telephones - how they cause
          isolation
        - what could be done to deal with the
          problem
Para. 3 - Internet - how it causes isolation
        - what could be done to deal with the
          problem
Para. 4 - conclusion
```

B
```
Para. 1 - introduction
Para. 2 - mobile telephones - how they cause
          isolation
Para. 3 - Internet - how it causes isolation
Para. 4 - what could be done to deal with
          these problems
Para. 5 - conclusion
```

6   Read the following writing task.

> **TASK**
>
> Your tutor has asked you to write an essay on the benefits of
> space exploration in the areas suggested by the pictures below.
> Write your essay, covering three of the areas illustrated and
> adding details to support your argument.
>
> (300–350 words)

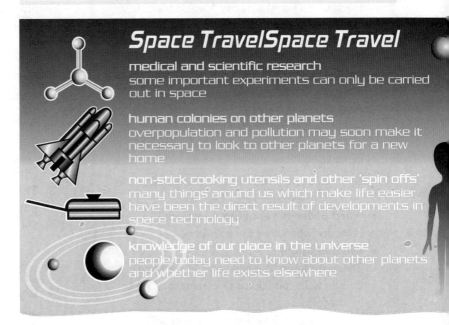

7   Exchange your essay with another student if you can.
Evaluate each other's work and suggest improvements.

12 The last frontier

Language Focus: Grammar

Indirect speech

> **Watch Out!** *problem areas*
>
> - **reporting general meaning**
>   The structure you use depends on the reporting verb.
>   'It's your fault that the accident happened,' she said. = She *blamed me* for the accident. ✔
>   'Don't go and see that film – it's awful,' he said. = He *warned me not to go* and see the film (because it was awful). ✔
>
> - **sequence of tenses: modal verbs**
>   Modal verbs such as *might*, *could*, *would* and *should* don't usually change in reported speech.
>   'I *might* go back home,' he said. ✔ = He said that he might ~~have gone~~ ∧*go* back home.
>   'I *could* fly tomorrow,' she said. ✔ = She said she could ~~have flown~~ ∧*fly* the next day.
>
> - **sequence of tenses: conditional sentences**
>   Depending on the meaning, conditional sentences may or may not change in reported speech.
>   He said, 'If I had the money, I would travel first class.' →
>   He said that if he *had had* the money, he *would have travelled* first class. (= *referring to a specific occasion*) ✔
>   He said that if he had the money he would (always) travel first class. (= *a general statement*) ✔
>   She said, 'If I *left* tomorrow, I *would miss* my flight'. ✔
>   = She said that if she ~~had~~ ∧*left* the next day, she ∧*would* ~~have missed~~ ∧*miss* her flight.
>
> - **word order in reported questions**
>   I wonder when ~~does~~ the train leave∧s.
>
> - ***whether* and *if***
>   These are interchangeable only in reported questions. In conditional-type sentences *if* must be used.
>   I would be grateful ~~whether~~ ∧*if* you could help me.

1 Rewrite each of the following sentences using an appropriate reporting verb from the box below. There are some verbs you don't need to use.

order	demand	accuse	recommend	promise
warn	thank	plead	deny	enquire	direct
blame	urge	threaten	compliment	advise

1 'It's your fault that we missed the train, Sandra!' said her mother.
Sandra's mother ....

2 'If I were you, I wouldn't say anything about this to the manager,' she said.
She ....

3 'If you don't behave yourselves, I won't give you your pocket money!' our mother told us.
Our mother ....

4 'I won't ever tell anyone about the money you've given me,' she said.
She ....

5 'I didn't steal the money,' he said.
He ....

6 'Please don't pay any attention to their silly comments,' she said.
She ....

7 'You've done an excellent job here,' he told us.
He ....

2 Fill each of the gaps in the following sentences with a suitable word or short phrase.

1 Although I hadn't been in his room, he accused .... his wallet.

2 They warned .... trying to make contact with her mother.

3 The misunderstanding was your fault! Don't try to put .... me!

4 She admitted that the plane .... off by the time they arrived at the airport.

5 We suggested .... an eye on their luggage while waiting for their train.

6 When we told them we had nowhere to stay, they offered .... up for the night.

Use of English
▶ **Paper 3, Part 2**

1   Fill in the gaps in the following
sentences with the correct form of the
word in capitals. Use your dictionary if
you are unsure of the spelling.

1   Scientists have been perplexed
by the frequent .... of storms
in the area. OCCUR

2   This substance is highly ....
so treat it with extreme care.
EXPLODE

3   Unfortunately, the houses in this
part of town are .... to all but
a few people. AFFORD

4   You will need to send your
.... to the company before
you go for an interview. REFER

5   This sports car doesn't really suit
our needs; we'd be better off
having a smaller car with better
.... MILE

6   Complete .... of the factory
will cost a huge amount of
money. MODERN

7   What I find irritating is his
.... that he should work
alone on the matter. INSIST

8   The amount of .... involved
in the process is far too high.
WASTE

9   This book will be .... to all
but a few experts on the subject.
COMPREHEND

10   The .... army received an
ecstatic welcome from the
citizens of Paris. TRIUMPH

2   Read through the following text quickly to get a general idea of what
it is about. Then use the word given in capitals at the end of some of the
lines to form a word that fits in the space in the same line. There is an
example at the beginning (0).

Mass tourism

One of the (0) ..*ensuing*.. benefits of   ENSUE
increased wealth which has (1) .... changed   QUESTION
the character of much of the world today is the
phenomenon of mass tourism. All over Europe
countries brace themselves for the annual
(2) .... of tourists, rather as their ancestors   INVADE
awaited the arrival of the barbarians; and the effects
of the onslaught are often just as (3) ....   DESTROY

Mass tourism has degraded all it has come in
contact with. It encourages shabby (4) .... and   PRETEND
false traditionalism. It frequently reduces the beauties
of nature and the ageless (5) .... of cathedrals   NOBLE
and palaces to the level of gimmicks. Furthermore,
commercialism promotes greed and often leads to
tourists feeling they have been (6) .... for   CHARGE
services or 'had' in other ways.

Perhaps the outlook need not be so gloomy
though. The (7) .... that tourism needs to be   REALISE
carefully regulated if it is to be (8) .... has   BENEFIT
prompted several countries recently to introduce
legislation curbing development in particular areas.

(9) ...., the tide is now turning. Tourist   MERCY
facilities now have to blend in with their surroundings.

Mass tourism should not be something to be
feared. It does, after all, offer (10) ....   BOUND
opportunities for local employment and brings
about greater understanding between peoples from
different races.

Reading

Read the three texts below and choose the word or phrase (**A**, **B**, **C** or **D**) which best fits each gap. (In the exam these texts will be unconnected in theme.)

Tourist threat to the pyramids

Visiting the pyramids of Giza in Egypt is set to become much more difficult as the Egyptian government has pledged to (1) .... on the numbers of sightseers to protect the ancient site from being loved to death.

Current restrictions limit tourist numbers to 300 a day, but the regulation is (2) .... disregarded – particularly during peak months when there are at least three times as many holiday-makers within the mile-square site. The main concern is that most turn a blind (3) .... to the warning to stay off the monuments. Indeed, some tourists are encouraged by their guides to (4) .... over the pyramids for photo opportunities; others have (5) .... graffiti into the exposed rock. The antiquities are also suffering from deterioration caused by visitors' breath and lipstick from women who kiss the stones.

Now, the government is planning to cordon off the area with fences, keep a (6) .... rein on the number of visitors and discourage the use of tour buses, whose exhaust emissions also cause damage.

1	**A** clamp down	**B** push down	**C** put down	**D** weigh down
2	**A** brazenly	**B** blatantly	**C** strongly	**D** overtly
3	**A** gaze	**B** look	**C** eye	**D** glance
4	**A** scuttle	**B** scramble	**C** slither	**D** stagger
5	**A** engraved	**B** etched	**C** inscribed	**D** carved
6	**A** tight	**B** strong	**C** rigid	**D** hard

The Grosvenor Hotel

THE GROSVENOR HOTEL

A weekend at the Grosvenor Hotel will (7) .... you back £400 or so, but you'll come away feeling – as we did – that it is worth every penny of it. A little off the beaten (8) .... for some visitors perhaps, the hotel is situated on a rocky promontory just north of the town, within easy walking distance of some of the most stunning (9) .... of unspoilt beach in the country. (10) .... for the odd seal, you'll come across little else as you explore the mysterious caves and rock pools that await you at low tide. You'll certainly see none of the tourist traffic that (11) .... so many other beautiful places these days. Excellent food, friendly staff, idyllic surroundings – that's what the Grosvenor offers its guests. (12) .... many other hotels in this part of Ireland, we feel it represents exceptionally good value for money.

7	**A** put	**B** set	**C** take	**D** carry
8	**A** path	**B** road	**C** track	**D** way
9	**A** ribbons	**B** corridors	**C** zones	**D** stretches
10	**A** Apart	**B** Except	**C** Excepting	**D** Bar
11	**A** tarnishes	**B** taints	**C** impairs	**D** mars
12	**A** Compared to	**B** At the expense of	**C** With regard to	**D** Contrary to

Trekking in Greece

The Greek backcountry offers something – solitude – which has (13) .... vanished from trails in the rest of Europe, the Americas and the Himalayas. This neglect is the result of (14) .... information, not lack of intrinsic merit. Whoever has ventured inland to the vastness of a truly enchanted kingdom can only greet with a sceptical smile the (15) .... of woe from those who have fallen prey to the tourist industry at the beaches or antiquities. Slowly but (16) .... the word is getting out as a handful of the intrepid dust the beach sand off themselves and (17) .... for the hills, sometimes in an organised expedition, but more (18) .... than not as solo travellers.

13	**A** all too	**B** all but	**C** all along	**D** all told
14	**A** thin	**B** slight	**C** rare	**D** scant
15	**A** tales	**B** stories	**C** histories	**D** recitals
16	**A** certainly	**B** definitely	**C** surely	**D** steadily
17	**A** march	**B** set	**C** go	**D** make
18	**A** often	**B** regularly	**C** frequently	**D** common

Use of English
▶ **Paper 3, Part 3**

For questions 1–6, think of **one** word only which can be used appropriately in all three sentences.

1   Only when his pension fund .... in ten years' time, will he be allowed access to the money.
A teenager .... quickly on leaving the security and comfort of home.
This cheese .... much more slowly than other types of cheese, so don't attempt to eat it yet.

2   The police attempted to .... order, but the crowd seemed determined to vent their feelings of anger and dissatisfaction.
How long do you think it will take them to .... the Queen Anne Theatre?
Surgeons feel that the operation to .... my father's hearing will be successful.

3   She looked so .... at the party, I wondered whether she was going down with the flu.
I think the .... blue curtains we bought will be ideal for this room.
Experts agree that this copy of the painting is a .... imitation of the original work.

4   Suddenly the door .... open and Simon rushed into the room.
'I don't believe a word you're saying!' she .... out, fixing him with an angry stare.
Several water pipes .... last winter, causing untold damage to carpets and furniture.

5   She's obviously very upset after the accident, so just allow her to .... her feelings out.
If you don't .... the tea more carefully, I'll ask someone else to do it.
No sooner were the doors opened than customers began to .... into the shop.

6   You'll never .... the dispute with Mr Baxter unless you agree to compromise.
Should you decide to .... in America, you must make sure that you have all the necessary documents.
I think that butterfly will .... on your arm, as long as you don't make any sudden movements.

Language Focus: Grammar
Impersonal passive constructions

> **Watch Out!** *problem areas*
>
> - **use of continuous/passive/perfect infinitives**
>   He is thought to ~~make~~ ∧*be making* his way to the coast at this moment.
>   This painting is believed to be stolen. ✔
>   She was reported to ~~steal~~ ∧*have stolen* the money yesterday.
>   Five terrorists were said to ~~be arrested~~ ∧*have been arrested* by the police yesterday.
> - **negative sentences**
>   It is thought that he didn't commit the crime.
>   = He is thought not to have committed the crime. ✔
>   = He is not thought to have committed the crime. ✔
>   It is feared that he hasn't responded to treatment.
>   = He is ~~not feared~~ ∧*feared not* to have responded to treatment.

Rewrite each of the following sentences beginning with the words given and using an impersonal passive construction.

1 It is alleged that he had no knowledge of the situation.
  He ....

2 It is thought that he will be arriving later in the day.
  He ....

3 According to reports, the police have already arrested a man.
  The police ....

4 She was believed to have been using a false passport to enter the country.
  It ....

5 She is not thought to have been involved in the scandal.
  It ....

6 It was said that he hadn't been aware of the gravity of the situation.
  He ....

7 It is claimed that he knew exactly what was happening.
  He ....

8 There were rumours about her having married a rich film star.
  She ....

Listening
▶ Paper 4, Part 3

You will hear an interview with Sarah Chapman, who describes her experiences on the Inca Trail in Peru. Her destination was the Inca city of Machu Picchu. For each of the following questions, tick which of the alternatives (**A**, **B**, **C** or **D**) is the most appropriate response. Listen to the recording twice.

1 What made climbing particularly difficult for Sarah as she approached Dead Woman's Pass?
  A A wall had been built across the path.
  B She felt physically sick.
  C The steps she was climbing up were very steep.
  D the lack of oxygen in the air

2 On the group's first night in tents in this part of the holiday
  A the temperature was not excessively low.
  B the water froze in their water bottles.
  C all their belongings were covered in a layer of ice.
  D their sleeping bags did not keep out the cold.

3 Sarah didn't want to sit down at the top of Dead Woman's Pass until
  A she had taken photographs of Conrad.
  B she felt sure she could relax.
  C the whole of the group was reunited.
  D the lunch was prepared.

4 How did Sarah feel when she arrived at Machu Picchu?
  A disappointed
  B overwhelmed
  C confused
  D nostalgic

5 According to Sarah, the climbing group
  A contained real professional explorers.
  B took a very professional approach to the challenge of the climb.
  C was exactly the right size.
  D contained very adventurous people.

Language Focus: Vocabulary

Dependent prepositions and prepositional phrases

Rewrite each of the following sentences, using the word in brackets together with a dependent preposition or as part of a prepositional phrase.

1   How do you regard people who exploit the vulnerability of tourists? *(attitude)*
    What is ....
    .... advantage of the vulnerability of tourists?

2   At least they'll look after her well at the clinic. *(hands)*
    At least she will ....
    .... at the clinic.

3   The building urgently needs to be completely renovated. *(need)*
    The building ....
    .... renovation.

4   Dr Jenkins has not kept up with recent technological developments. *(touch)*
    Dr Jenkins is ....
    .... technology.

5   I don't mind working hard on occasions. *(averse)*
    I .... hard work.

6   The standard of her homework is no longer acceptable. *(scratch)*
    Her homework ....
    .... recently.

7   If we don't make changes, there will be problems in the future. *(long)*
    There will be problems in ....
    .... we make changes.

8   In southern England, the police still haven't caught the escaped prisoner. *(large)*
    The escaped prisoner is ....
    .... of England.

9   At first we were not too sure whether to employ Alan or not. *(doubtful)*
    At first we ....
    .... Alan.

10 Mussels always make her ill, so don't give her any to eat. *(allergic)*
    Don't give her any mussels to eat ....
    .... them.

Language Focus: Grammar

Future modals

> **Watch Out!** *problem areas*
>
> - **the importance of context**
>   Sometimes only the context (and not the verb form itself) tells us that a sentence refers to the future.
>   In the future, robots *might be used* to do a number of household chores. ✓
>   If the weather doesn't improve, we *could be spending* next week sheltering from the rain. ✓
> - **modal perfects**
>   Modal verb + *have* + past participle can be used to refer to the future *or* the past. Check the context.
>   By the year 2050, we *might have reached* Mars.
>   = *perhaps we will have reached* … (= *future*) ✓
>   The plane *should have landed* by eight o'clock.
>   = I *expect it will have landed* … (= *future*) ✓
>   The robber *might have cut* his hand when he broke the window. = *perhaps he cut* his hand …
>   (= *past*) ✓

Rewrite each of the following sentences, using the word in brackets.

1   It is possible that plastic will be used for the bodies of cars in the future. *(made)*
    The bodies of cars ....
    .... in the future.

2   There's a possibility the meeting will still be on when you arrive. *(finished)*
    The meeting ....
    .... time you arrive.

3   I don't expect you to be working on that report any more tomorrow. *(completed)*
    You ....
    .... by tomorrow.

4   Your involvement in this matter would be unwise. *(get)*
    You ....
    .... in this matter.

5   It is possible that there will be Moon colonies in fifty years' time. *(living)*
    In fifty years' time, people ....
    .... on the Moon.

Writing

▶ **Paper 2, Part 2 (article)**

Exam Strategy

- Read the question carefully. Make sure you understand clearly what you have to describe and explain. You will lose marks if you only answer one part of the question! Plan your answer before you start writing.
- Use a range of descriptive verbs, adjectives and adverbs.
- Use direct speech where appropriate – but don't over-use it.

1 Read the following writing task. Note down the place you would write about, and two other things you would try to include in your introduction.

TASK

A monthly travel magazine has invited readers to contribute an article to a special edition entitled *Memorable Places*. Write an article describing a visit to a place which made a great impression on you and explaining why it affected you so much.

(300–350 words)

2

1 Now read the following two introductions, which were written in answer to the task. Tick the one which has a more appropriate style for an article, and makes more of an impact on the reader.

1 ☐

Cracow, the ancient capital of Poland. Just the name of the place is enough to bring back a flood of happy memories. It was around Christmas time, a few years back, when I first visited this city with a group of friends.

2 ☐

The architecture of a city is of supreme importance. So many of our cities today have been ruined by poorly-designed buildings and a lack of planning. It is a sad fact, however, that many people do not appear to recognise the role the urban environment plays in our lives. Cracow is a city I visited a few years ago with some friends. It shows clearly what a great city should be like.

2 Read the rest of the article, ignoring the gaps and underlining for the moment. Has it answered the task fully?

We arrived in Cracow at around midnight. I remember that it was <u>very cold</u> and there was a lot of snow about. Our hotel <u>had no lights on</u> when we arrived, but fortunately the receptionist was still on duty. (1) ....

Our first few days in Cracow were spent looking around, exploring <u>the streets</u> and castle, and <u>looking at</u> the statues and monuments which seemed <u>to be in</u> every public square we came across. <u>The old buildings lining the streets were mysterious</u> and (2) ....

The snow continued to fall constantly, (3) .... Everywhere was covered in <u>a layer</u> of snow, which had the effect of <u>softening</u> the sound of cars and passing trams. (4) .... <u>I will never forget New Year's Eve</u>. An enormous crowd had gathered in the main square of the city, and most people were dancing. (5) ....

My time in Cracow was a truly unforgettable experience.

3   Use the words in the box to rewrite the parts of the article which are underlined.

> narrow, cobbled   to grace
> gazing up in awe   at
> shrouded in darkness   a thick blanket
> was particularly memorable   bitterly
> there was an air of mystery about   muffling

3   The article fails to deal with how the place has affected the writer. Match one of the sentences or phrases from the following list a)–g) to each of the gaps in the article, adding any necessary punctuation. There are two letters you don't need to use.

a) throughout our stay in the city, we were frequently overwhelmed by the sense that we had somehow walked back into a magical kingdom belonging to another age

b) what amazed us was how friendly and hospitable she was, even though it was late and she was obviously tired

c) the fact that everyone seemed so happy and well-behaved – and intent on enjoying themselves – made an enormous impression on us

d) which made me feel small and insignificant

e) reminding me of scenes from novels I had read by Tolstoy and other Russian and Polish writers

f) it also made us feel like travellers in some mysterious, silent land, far away from the noise and bustle of modern city life

g) what struck me was how incredibly beautiful it all was

4   The conclusion of the article is very weak. The writer does not **reflect** at all on his experiences in Cracow or say what overall effect it had on him. Write a more appropriate conclusion from the following notes.

- will never forget week in Cracow
- have been back several times since
- each time – struck by friendliness/openness of inhabitants
- Cracow – one of those places which reminds us of splendour lost/destroyed in many cities today

5   Plan and write an article in answer to the following writing task.

> **TASK**
>
> Your school or college magazine has invited students to contribute an article to a special edition entitled *Awful Journeys*. Write an article describing a journey where everything seemed to go wrong and your reactions to the problems you encountered.
>
> (300–350 words)

Remember to include in your article:

- an introduction with impact
- vivid language
- a reflective conclusion.

Use the phrases in the box below to help you incorporate your personal reactions into your description.

> ### Phrases to introduce personal reactions
>
> I was overwhelmed by …
> I was amazed at how/what amazed me was how …
> the fact that … made a great impression on me
> it made me feel …
> what struck me was how …
> it reminded me of …
> I felt as if …

6   Exchange your article with another student if you can. Evaluate each other's work and suggest improvements.

> ### Study Tip
>
> Group vocabulary for articles together in your vocabulary notebook. You could, for example, group words and phrases:
>
> - according to the type of thing described, e.g.
>   old buildings → dilapidated, haunted, tumbledown, austere, cosy …
>   facial expressions → (positive) beaming, glowing … (negative) gloomy, downcast …
>
> - according to the feelings associated with them, e.g.
>
>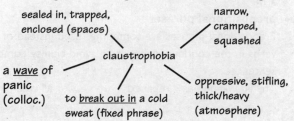

13 The price of success

Language Focus: Grammar
Continuous aspect

┌───

Watch Out! *problem areas* ◄

The continuous aspect refers to **temporary** states or actions which are **unfinished**. It is usually used when we are especially interested in the nature of the activity, its duration or the experience of the person performing it, rather than its results or consequences.

- **past continuous**
  The past continuous is used to refer to an activity or repeated action continuing up to or around a time in the past. It is *not* used to refer to a past habit or state.
  When I was a child, I ~~was going~~ ˄*used to go* fishing with my grandfather every weekend.
  We ~~were living~~ ˄*used to live* in a large house in the country.

- **stative verbs**
  Stative verbs are not usually used in the continuous form. If they are used, a change in meaning is often involved.
  I ~~think~~ ˄*am thinking* of changing my job.
  You aren't ˄*being* very honest with him about this matter.
  Why ~~do you smell~~ ˄*are you smelling* the milk? It can't have gone off already!
  You can't have seen Jack yesterday – you must ~~imagine~~ ˄*be imagining* things.

- *always/constantly/forever* + **present (or past) continuous**
  This structure is used to refer to the frequency of people's habits, often ones which we find irritating.
  It can also be used to refer to things which happen frequently, and probably unexpectedly or by accident. (*Never* cannot be used in the same way!)
  ~~He's never tidying up his room!~~ *He's forever leaving his room in a terrible mess!*
  He *is always turning up* with a bottle of wine under his arm. ✔

- **prepositional phrases**
  Prepositional phrases are sometimes used instead of verbs in the continuous aspect, to avoid clumsy complex sentences.
  The lift will be ~~being repaired~~ ˄*under repair* all week.

└───

1 Read the following pairs of sentences and answer the questions below. The first one has been done for you.

1 1 I've come to see Dr Hawkins.
   2 I've been coming to see Dr Hawkins for weeks.
   Which sentence:
   a) focuses on the purpose of the visit? ...*1*...
   b) focuses on the frequency of the visits? ....

2 1 He's chopped up the wood for the fire.
   2 He's been chopping up wood for the fire all morning.
   Which sentence:
   a) suggests that he may now be feeling tired? ....
   b) suggests that the wood is now ready for use? ....
   c) suggests that he may not have finished? ....

3 1 He's been working on the car all day to fix the ignition.
   2 He was working on the car to fix the ignition until five o'clock.
   Which sentence:
   a) suggests that he is now doing something different? ....
   b) suggests that the work may or may not be finished? ....

4 1 She'll probably be studying for her exams all afternoon.
   2 She'll probably study medicine at university.
   Which sentence:
   a) focuses on how busy she is? ....
   b) focuses on her future plans? ....

5 1 I'll go to the post office later, if that letter needs posting.
   2 I'll be going to the post office later, if that letter needs posting.
   Which sentence:
   a) suggests I was already planning this? ....
   b) is a spontaneous offer of help? ....
   c) is the more indirect way of making an offer? ....

6 1   I saw her slap him.
   2   I saw her slapping him.
   Which sentence:
   a) suggests that she slapped him several
       times? ....
   b) suggests that the slapping started before I arrived?
       ....

2   Rewrite each of the following sentences beginning with the words given.

1   Negotiations for a settlement have been in progress for over two months now.
    They ....
    ....

2   Journalists have attacked the minister's policies several times.
    The minister's policies have ....
    ....

3   His sarcasm was plainly obvious to all but a few people in the room.
    The fact that ....
    ....

4   Political talks are already underway to bring peace to the region.
    Politicians have ....
    ....

5   Shortly before his eighteenth birthday he left home to go to university.
    By the ....
    ....

6   That house has been up for sale for over a year now.
    They ....
    ....

3   Fill each of the gaps in the following sentences with a suitable word or phrase.

1   I know I should trust him, but I can't .... he's cheating us.
2   From these inconsistencies, I'd say your accountant .... records up to date lately.
3   He thinks .... point by arriving late, but everyone in the office just thinks he's lazy.
4   I've .... over, and I'm afraid I'll have to reject your offer.
5   They were drinking lots of champagne, so they .... a celebration.
6   Is it midday already? I can't believe I've spent the whole .... dishes.
7   I'm afraid he .... up debts of over £20,000 already this year!
8   I can't believe she .... me lies all this time!

Language Focus: Vocabulary
Phrasal verbs and expressions: stand

1   Rewrite each of the following sentences using a phrasal verb with *stand*, and making any other necessary changes. Use a dictionary to help you if necessary.

1   Whatever the outcome of the trial, we must be supportive and remain loyal to him.
    We must .... the outcome of the trial.
2   What do the letters REM represent in this sentence?
    What do the letters .... sentence?
3   We find such behaviour quite unacceptable!
    We won't .... behaviour!
4   It will be easier for people to see the sign at night if we use neon lights.
    Neon lights will .... at night.
5   It's a pity nobody defended him when they started making their accusations.
    I wish somebody .... their accusations.
6   Make it clear you don't accept his unfair treatment of you, otherwise he'll never change.
    He'll continue to treat .... him.
7   Of all the singers, Carol is by far the best.
    Carol .... the singers.
8   Would you mind doing Robin's job while he's away?
    Would you mind .... he's away?

2   Rewrite each of the sentences below, using the word in brackets. Use an expression with *stand* in the sentence you write.

1   They will try Abrams for murder at the High Court next week. (*trial*)
    ....
2   After such a long time together they are still happily married. (*test*)
    ....
3   How do our sales compare with those of other firms? (*relation*)
    ....
4   He is unlikely to win the competition. (*chance*)
    ....
5   I'm not going to prevent you from leaving, if that's what you really want. (*way*)
    ....
6   It's obvious that hard work and determination lead to success. (*reason*)
    ....

Use of English

1 Do you think school and university exams indicate how successful someone will be in later life? Why/Why not? Write down your ideas briefly in your notebook.

2 Now read the following texts and see if any of your thoughts are mentioned by the writer. When you have done this, answer the comprehension questions.

Every year fresh cohorts of young people pour out of the trenches to do battle with school and university examinations. The emotional casualty rate is grievously high. It is no exaggeration to say that the great majority emerge from this ordeal feeling like failures, with lowered self-esteem. And just as the generals in the First World War failed to question the purpose of the carnage, so it is with modern-day educationists. They will not ask themselves the fundamental question: what is the point of exams?

Of course, all children need to emerge from school knowing how to read and write, and it is a definite advantage nowadays for children to know a second language. But this does not justify the fiercely competitive exams at ever younger ages.

Schoolchildren are cudgelled into studying by the threat that exams are critical to their occupational future. In reality, the evidence clearly shows that teachers and parents who scare children with the idea that exams are essential for success are perpetuating a myth.

There are only a few, mostly technical, occupations in which a good school or university exam results are an important determinant, even of initial acceptance. It is a fable that good exam results help survivors of the educational system to get a good job on leaving. In fact, many large retail companies now rely on their own assessment systems and regard exam results as an unhelpful guide.

While that old saying 'First in School, Last in Life' may not be true, doing well at school certainly does not determine success later on. When I surveyed captains of industry, they were unanimous in declaring university degrees irrelevant to long-term success. Charles Reynolds, Managing Director of a large multi-national electronics company, was adamant: 'Studies show that among top business people school failure is actually the norm.'

It is staggering, then, when you consider that parents and teachers consistently exhort children to 'do well at school for your future', that there is no scientific evidence that school or university exam results predict success throughout life. There is even evidence suggesting the opposite.

Professor Liam Hudson has published a number of studies which shatter the myth that high grades at university are an essential prerequisite for carrying out leading scientific research. 'Given what it takes to get a first class degree at university,' he told me, 'this should not be surprising. To achieve high grades, you need to please your teachers, enjoy being supervised closely and, ultimately, please the examiners. You must ignore what you think and concentrate on what they want. To do important scientific research you need the opposite: to think originally and be highly self-motivated rather than craving constant praise, and to be able to work alone for long periods.'

I suspect that it is a myth that those who achieve first class degrees are of superior originality. They work hard and they are ambitious to do well in exams, but that does not prepare them for success in their subsequent careers.

1 Explain why the writer has chosen to compare modern educationists to First World War generals in the first paragraph.

2 What does the phrase 'cudgelled into studying' (line 17) imply about the students taking exams?

3 Explain in your own words why the opinions of 'captains of industry' (line 4) might be sought.

4 Explain in your own words what 'this' refers to in line 22.

3 Do the following summary task.

In a paragraph of between **50** and **70** words, summarise **in your own words as far as possible**, the negative aspects of school and university examinations.

Use of English

▶ Paper 3, Part 1

Read the text below and think of the word which best fits each space. Use only **one** word in each space. There is an example at the beginning (0).

Sports and success

Schools and colleges around the world have long
(0) ..*been*... aware of the connection (1) .... sports
and leadership. But in (2) .... years the power of sports
to influence business success has become increasingly
acknowledged. Management consultants have, for instance,
(3) .... extensive use of sporting metaphors as a
(4) .... of focusing executives' thinking. Accordingly, terms
(5) .... as 'run with the ball', 'player' and 'team' now
pepper the business lexicon in much the (6) .... way as
military references do.

The increased attention (7) .... to leadership qualities
nowadays has, if (8) ...., only heightened this interest.
(9) .... managers being told that they should inspire and
coach rather than give orders, the sports connection has
(10) .... looked more tempting.

It is with this (11) .... mind, that organisations are
beginning to invite famous athletes to talk to (12) .... staff
about the secrets of success. They show how directors can
improve their own leadership skills to bring (13) .... better
levels of performance throughout the company. Using a
(14) .... of coaching techniques, they are (15) .... to
help their listeners identify leadership qualities, while creating
a better working environment generally.

Language Focus: Vocabulary

Verb + noun collocation

Complete the following sentences with a verb in the correct form from the box below. You may need to use some of the verbs more than once.

take	set	seize	handle
achieve	get	jump	make

1   I know it's difficult to know what to do, but I think you should .... a chance and apply for the position.
2   You've certainly .... your mark as director of the company. Things are running much more smoothly now than they ever have before.
3   She seems to have .... the crisis very well. She should be congratulated.
4   Let's not .... to conclusions – we don't know for sure that Robert is responsible for this mistake.
5   We need to .... a more realistic target. How about aiming for a 30% increase in production by the end of the year?
6   When he was given the new position, he .... the opportunity to make a number of radical changes.
7   He may be an unpleasant man to deal with, but he does .... results.
8   In order for us to .... our aim, we all need to work a lot harder.
9   The organisation is expanding too quickly. We ought to .... certain limits to growth, I think.
10 I can't believe I .... such a mess of that interview!
11 I hope you won't .... offence if I say that I think you are wasting your talent in your present job.
12 Dwindling numbers of tourists have meant that our new hotel has .... a considerable financial loss this year.

Dependent prepositions and prepositional phrases

Complete the following sentences with one or more suitable prepositions.

1 Mrs Summers is unable to attend the meeting, so I'm going to speak .... her behalf.
2 He's currently .... threat of legal action.
3 .... my knowledge, there have been two break-ins there already this year.
4 This building is being converted .... a restaurant soon.
5 He stared at her intently, but could say nothing .... response to her offer.
6 He scanned the morning paper quickly .... stories of interest.

Use of English
▶ Paper 3, Part 4

For each question below, complete the second sentence with three to eight words so that it has a similar meaning to the first sentence, using the word given. Do not change the word given.

1 Although Maria hasn't said so, we can be sure that she will want to come to the party. **read**
We can ....
Maria will want to come to the party.

2 Shall we split the cost of a taxi into town? **halves**
Why ....
.... a taxi into town?

3 It wasn't until I started college that I knew I wasn't suited to being a lawyer. **cut**
I only knew that ....
.... a lawyer when I went to college.

4 Trying to get Roger to come with us is an utter waste of time. **whatsoever**
There ....
.... to get Roger to come with us.

5 He doesn't realise the damage the changes will cause. **damaging**
Little ....
.... the changes will be.

6 We will only let you take the final exams if you pass this test. **allowed**
Failing this test will result ....
.... take the final exams.

7 Pensions have not increased at the same rate as inflation. **pace**
Pensions have failed ....
.... inflation.

8 James has had a cold since Christmas. **over**
James ....
.... at Christmas.

Listening
▶ Paper 4, Part 4

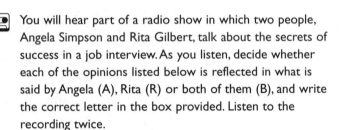

You will hear part of a radio show in which two people, Angela Simpson and Rita Gilbert, talk about the secrets of success in a job interview. As you listen, decide whether each of the opinions listed below is reflected in what is said by Angela (A), Rita (R) or both of them (B), and write the correct letter in the box provided. Listen to the recording twice.

1 It is important to check up on an employer before the interview ☐
2 Many candidates need to believe in themselves more. ☐
3 Candidates should emphasise useful skills to the employer. ☐
4 It is best to be truthful about areas of weakness. ☐
5 It is important not to be too general when talking about achievements. ☐
6 Many interviewers may try to catch out candidates with unexpected questions. ☐

Language Focus: Vocabulary

Dependent prepositions and prepositional phrases

Read the following text and fill the gaps with appropriate prepositions.

The writing is on the wall for the brilliant but bullying boss. Driving ambition and a high IQ might give you a head start in the race for the top, but a lack of 'emotional intelligence' will be a hindrance (1) .... achieving medium- to long-term success.

Senior managers have long been convinced (2) .... the value of interpersonal skills in the workplace. The concept that emotional intelligence can account (3) .... the difference (4) .... outstanding and average performance, however, is comparatively new. But what exactly is emotional intelligence? One psychologist defined it (5) .... the ability to regulate your behaviour so that there is a balance (6) .... personal feelings, emotions and drives, and the feelings and needs of others. It is about being able to resolve the conflict that may arise (7) .... high motivation and conscientiousness and integrity. People with low emotional intelligence don't get promoted because others object (8) .... working with them.

In the workplace, there is a great need (9) .... sensitivity in relationships, and people in managerial jobs should focus more (10) .... understanding people's feelings (11) .... change and their fears (12) .... redundancy. An organisation which attaches importance (13) .... the emotions of the employees is more likely to be an effective organisation. If a manager regularly compliments his staff (14) .... their work, and sympathises (15) .... them when they have problems, the profits of the company will increase (16) .... a greater rate. And people will enjoy working with each other.

Getting in touch with your own feelings has benefits which extend (17) .... the workplace. If you are only working with your brain, you won't see the emotional cost to yourself. Making a move that is beneficial (18) .... your career but means travelling all the time could result (19) .... the destruction of your relationship with your partner and children. Without emotional intelligence, (20) .... the medium- to long-term, you will have a less balanced personal life and make a lot of enemies.

Writing

▶ Paper 2, Part 2 (review)

About the exam

In **Paper 2, Part 2** you may have to write a **review** for a magazine or newspaper. A review is often about a book or film, but it may also be about a restaurant, hotel or other place. Whatever type of review you are asked to write in the exam, the examiner will expect to see evidence of appropriate register, suitability for the intended reader, and thorough coverage of all the requirements set out in the task. This means that it is extremely important that you spend time on planning and careful organisation.

Exam Strategy

When planning your review, focus on these questions.

What kind of review do I have to write?

- Make sure you are clear about what you have to review. If you are asked to write a review of a film, for example, you will lose marks if you write about a play!
- Think about the tone (e.g. light, persuasive, friendly) you should adopt, and how formal your language needs to be.

What do I need to include?

- Look carefully at what you have to include in your review, and whether you are asked to incorporate your own ideas. Good marks depend on including all the points mentioned in the task appropriately.
- Information about plot and character forms the basis of most film and book reviews. For a review of a place you will probably need to include details about the building itself, the facilities offered and the standard of service.
- A review needs to start with an impact. Try to conclude your piece too with a reflective comment which reinforces your purpose for writing.
- Many reviews include reported speech or ideas. Use a variety of methods of reporting to maintain interest, and show your own views of the opinions expressed.

1

1 Reported speech is often used in reviews of places. A careful choice of reporting expressions can convey your own feelings, as well as those of the person whose ideas are being reported. Read the following statements. Are there any differences in **tone** between them?

1 I inferred from what he said that business was booming. ....
2 He implied that business was booming. ....
3 I was given to understand that business would soon be booming. ....
4 He claimed that business was booming. ....
5 He acknowledged that business was booming. ....
6 I detected in him a sense of pride that business was booming. ....

2 Now match each of the statements above with one of the 'attitudes', a)–f), below.

a) The manager admitted that this was true.
b) The manager said that this was true, but the writer has his doubts.
c) The manager didn't actually say this, but it was the opinion formed by the writer.
d) This was the impression which the writer got, but we can't be sure how he came to believe this.
e) The manager found this quite hard to conceal.
f) The manager suggested this, without actually saying so.

2 As in all writing tasks for the exam, the vocabulary you use in a review should be varied and rich. Rewrite the following sentences, which come from a review of a restaurant. Use the words given in brackets and start your sentences with the words provided.

1 You won't believe how amazing the place is if you don't go and see for yourself. (*seen*)
The place has to ....

2 The first thing that makes an impression on you as you enter is the sheer size of the place. (*strikes*)
The first ....

3 The restaurant is more like a warehouse than a place for eating and drinking in style. (*wining*)
The restaurant is ....

4 It extends in all directions for a very long distance. (*eye*)
The restaurant extends as far ....

5 The place is now making a lot of money. (*handsome*)
The place is ....

3 Read the following writing task and the review which has been written in answer to it. Ignore the gaps for the moment. Check your answers to Exercise 2.

TASK

You have been asked to write a review for a local magazine of a new restaurant in your town which has proved extremely popular. Write your review, giving your personal perspective, and suggesting the reasons for its success.

(300–350 words)

When I visited the new seafood restaurant 'Taste of the Atlantic' last week I wasn't expecting any surprises. But surprised I was — for the place has to be seen to be believed.

The first thing that strikes you as you enter is the sheer size of place. The restaurant is more like a warehouse than a place for wining and dining, covering three floors and extending in all directions as far as the eye can see. In fact, first impressions are not so misleading, for 'Taste of the Atlantic' is housed in an old fabrics warehouse. (1) .... was just what he had been looking for.

Mr Childes, who showed me around, (2) .... of the old warehouse and (3) .... he had been willing to pay any price for a place with 'real atmosphere'. (4) .... money spent on restoring the warehouse and transforming it into a restaurant has already been recovered, and the place is now making a handsome profit.

On every floor of the restaurant there must be at least twenty to thirty small tables, some hidden away in snug alcoves, and the only lighting comes from the hundreds of candles fixed into the stone walls. Waiters rush from table to table, taking orders or bringing food, and the pleasant buzz of conversation is accompanied by the tinkling of a fountain on the ground floor.

The unusual layout and décor of 'Taste of the Atlantic' — the combination of old and new, spaciousness and privacy — has obviously contributed to the restaurant's spectacular success. The prices and the quality of service would also take some beating. What about the food though? I spoke to one or two of the customers at the restaurant, and (5) .... (6) .... is as delightful as the surroundings. So why not go there and see for yourself?

4   Now choose the phrase, a) b) or c), which best fits each of the gaps in the review. Think carefully about the writer's **attitude** and what suits the **style** of the article best.

1 a) According to the manager, Mr Frank Childes, this
   b) I inferred from the manager, Mr Frank Childes, that this
   c) The manager, Mr Frank Childes, acknowledged that this
2 a) lamented the 'discovery'
   b) enthused over the 'discovery'
   c) decried the 'discovery'
3 a) gave me to understand that
   b) denied that
   c) claimed that
4 a) If Mr Childes is to be believed, the
   b) I was somewhat hesitant to believe his claim that the
   c) I was rather cynical about Mr Childes's assertion that the
5 a) they were all highly favourable
   b) they were all very positive
   c) they all spoke with relish
6 a) The food, it seems, is
   b) The food, I was made to understand, is
   c) The food, I detected, is

5   The conclusion of the review is rather abrupt. Which two additional sentences **A** or **B**, 'round off' the review in a more appropriate way? Remember that the conclusion of such a review should:

- take the reader back to the writer's sentiments or comments in the introduction
- clarify the purpose of the whole review
- suit the style of the review (in this case, quite personal and light-hearted).

A

I'm going this weekend, at the invitation of the manager. Since I'll know what to expect this time, I won't be distracted from what's most important — eating!

B

You are bound to like the food and the décor. In all probability you will want to take your friends there in the future too.

6   Now write a review in answer to the following writing task.

> **TASK**
>
> You have been asked to write a review for a student magazine of a sports centre which has just opened in your town and is proving to be a great success. Mention the factors which have contributed to the success of the sports centre, and detail the reasons why you recommend it to all local students.
>
> (300–350 words)

Use the Exam Strategy box and exercises on these pages to help you plan your review, to use appropriate language, and to write an introduction and conclusion which create impact.

7   Exchange your review with another student if you can. Evaluate each other's work and suggest improvements.

> **Study Tip**
>
> **Style** and **register** are particularly important in reviews and articles from newspapers and magazines. Collect as many examples of such types of writing as you can from English newspapers and magazines and compare them:
>
> - with each other – can you find any differences in style, vocabulary, structures and layout?
> - with newspapers and magazines in your own language – look for features which are typical, and check how these differ in English publications.
>
> Try rewriting a variety of reviews and articles from your own language in English, and vice versa, to help you discover the types of expression you need to learn.

14 Revision unit

This unit contains strategy advice to help you approach the various tasks in the Proficiency exam in a structured and confident way. The practice tasks revise some important items of vocabulary which you will need a good knowledge of in order to **maximise your exam success**.

Reading

▶ Paper 1, Part 1

Exam Strategy

- Read the text carefully and try to fill the gaps without looking at the four options. Only then should you look at the options and make your choice.
- When deciding, think about:
  a) the grammatical patterns which are associated with words in the options (e.g. dependent prepositions, verbs followed by an infinitive/-ing form, etc.)
  b) collocations, fixed phrases and idioms.
- If you are not sure, always guess, as you lose no marks for incorrect guesses. When you finish, read through the text again to make sure it makes sense.
- The multiple-choice questions in **Paper 1, Part 1** are designed to test **passive** vocabulary (the words you recognise and understand, but might not be able to use), and so very often your instincts about the answer may be correct.

For questions **1–18**, read the three texts and decide which answer (**A, B, C** or **D**) best fits each gap.

Another Angry Scene

'How could you have lost all your library books?' Charles asked his wife, (1) .... her angrily from across the kitchen table. 'I suppose we'll have to pay for them now.'

Katherine took a (2) .... breath and tried to avoid his fierce gaze. It was better to (3) .... her tongue and remain silent, she reminded herself; otherwise it would end up in another row. (4) .... his own forgetfulness, his accusations struck her as being grossly unfair. Only yesterday, he had left the front window wide open all afternoon, when neither of them had been at home, and then (5) .... into a rage when she had mentioned it to him later. It was no (6) .... getting upset about it though. Shaking her head, she sighed and looked up at her husband. 'I'm sorry, darling,' she said meekly.

1	**A** staring	**B** eyeing	**C** seeing	**D** monitoring
2	**A** broad	**B** profound	**C** deep	**D** heavy
3	**A** bite	**B** eat	**C** swallow	**D** chew
4	**A** Regarding	**B** Despite	**C** Providing	**D** Given
5	**A** shot	**B** leapt	**C** broken	**D** flown
6	**A** worth	**B** need	**C** point	**D** good

Fantastic Stories   by Terry Jones

The publisher (7) .... these stories by Terry Jones for eight to eleven-year-olds, but this is one children's audio book production that could entertain the whole family on a tedious car journey. In the fourteen short stories, interspersed with jolly (8) .... of music, Jones mixes the traditional imagery and settings of fairy tales with some (9) .... of fancy of his own devising, including a dinosaur in the garden shed and a baby made of snow. The humour varies from the schoolboy belly (10) .... to the strainingly facetious. He (11) .... his stories with some bracingly realistic (one might even say cynical) observations about life – don't (12) .... the bidding of patently ridiculous people just because of their rank is one helpful life-lesson.

7	**A** suggests	**B** advises	**C** recommends	**D** proposes
8	**A** snatches	**B** snippets	**C** extracts	**D** portions
9	**A** journeys	**B** jumps	**C** flights	**D** springs
10	**A** chuckle	**B** laugh	**C** giggle	**D** snigger
11	**A** does up	**B** sets down	**C** takes off	**D** tops off
12	**A** do	**B** obey	**C** enact	**D** hear

Taking Good Photographs

Good photographs are all around us. The secret is to spot them and to have enough technical skill to take the photographs without (13) .... worrying about how to handle the camera. Advances in the manufacture of films and cameras have (14) .... people to produce excellent pictures without (15) .... knowledge of photographic technicalities. However, to acquire the freedom of knowing that most of your photographs will (16) .... satisfactorily, you do need to practise such basic skills as focusing and setting shutter speeds until these become second (17) .... While you are mastering this side of photography, you should also be developing an awareness of why you are taking the picture at all. Without this sense of purpose, your photographs are liable to be dull, (18) .... how technically correct they may be.

13	**A** largely	**B** frantically	**C** utterly	**D** hugely
14	**A** facilitated	**B** empowered	**C** enabled	**D** authorised
15	**A** an extensive	**B** a total	**C** an absolute	**D** a keen
16	**A** turn out	**B** get out	**C** make out	**D** work out
17	**A** thought	**B** mind	**C** nature	**D** self
18	**A** no doubt	**B** no longer	**C** no matter	**D** no less

Reading

▶ Paper 1, Parts 2 & 4

Exam Strategy

- Read the instructions carefully to see what the text or texts are about. For Part 2, look at the title and opening sentences of all four texts to get a general idea of their content, style and register.
- Skim through the first text of Part 2 (or the one long text of Part 4) for a broad understanding of the information it contains and the author's attitude or tone. Don't worry about unknown words.
- Look at each question or unfinished stem and try to find the information you need in the text **without** reading the four options.
- Then consider the options and choose the one which most closely resembles your answer from the text. Watch out for options which:
  a) contain words which appear to be similar to those in the text
  b) have negative expressions in them
  c) only answer half the question
  d) seem to answer the question logically, but are not actually what is said in the text
  e) look very similar to each other. Try to distinguish the difference between them and go back to the text to double-check.

Language Focus: Vocabulary

Phrasal verbs (revision)

Complete each of the sentences below, **using a suitable phrasal verb** derived from the verb in brackets. Make sure you use the correct form of the verb.

1 I can't understand why you didn't .... (*keep*) the agreement we made. If you had, none of this would have happened.

2 Thieves broke into the gallery last night and .... (*make*) paintings worth £50,000. The police have no idea of their present whereabouts.

3 The children are very quiet, aren't they? Do you think they might .... (*get*) something? Last week they spilt paint all over the bedroom carpet!

4 The publicity his novels received .... (*bring*) a change in the way people viewed his work.

5 I want you to leave. I'm not prepared to .... (*put*) your bad behaviour any longer.

6 I hadn't expected James to react so violently. I was quite .... (take) by the strength of his opposition to the proposals.

7 I don't think he gave a good impression during the interview. In fact, I feel he .... (*come*) as being rather arrogant.

8 You'll have to cut back on spending while you're at college. You .... (*run*) huge debts this semester.

9 Will you tell me exactly what you mean? I really don't understand what you .... (*get*)! I hope you're not implying I'm incompetent!

10 He's been stealing money from the company for years without anyone suspecting. It baffles me how he .... (*get*) it for so long.

Reading

▶ **Paper 1, Part 3**

You are going to read an extract from a novel. Seven paragraphs have been removed from the extract. Choose from the paragraphs **A–H** the one which fits each gap (**1–7**). There is one extra paragraph which you do not need to use.

Once in the air over Khartoum, the pilot of our plane wisely put it at once into a steep climb. Even an amateur like myself could see that it was not the sort of day for hovering close to the ground, and the sooner we got into steadier air the better. For a while I was able, despite the wind and dust below, to distinguish a few landmarks in that featureless country, but very soon, as we steadily gained height, the land lost all character and coherence.

1 ....

One of the older women in the plane suddenly went very white, started to moan to herself, and had to be given oxygen. The plane flattened out and the engines got back to their more comforting deep-throated roar. We had stopped climbing, but even at that height the air, although not so agitated as it had been the night before, was far from steady. The element of the unpredictable in the external circumstances of our flight now seemed to enter into the minds of the passengers. They began to do things which they would not normally have done.

2 ....

The Army nurse said later: 'I don't know what happened. I seemed to have a black-out and then came round to find myself sitting next to a strange man, drinking a large whisky.' The plumber, I am sure, did not usually have so much beer at that hour, nor did he normally chain-smoke in that manner. On solid earth the businessman would certainly not have stared so at strangers, particularly not through horn-rimmed spectacles placed, in such a precarious and unmilitary fashion, on the tip of his nose.

3 ....

I noticed that the dust had gone and that a world of level, white cloud had appeared beneath us. Far to the east a peak or two of the formidable Abyssinian escarpments pierced through the cloud. I could not identify them from my map. The maps of Africa betray how young and incomplete is our knowledge of the continent. Beyond the peaks on the horizon to which we were heading, and above the white, level world of cloud below us, I saw a tremendous array of curling, twisting, and turning cumulus cloud, stretching as far as the eye could see.

4 ....

They were very like the great monsoon clouds that sweep down from Burma and Northern Malaya over the Bay of Bengal. Once on an occasion like this, a pilot of a flying-boat I was in refused to fly into them because he had known a flight of five planes attempt it once, and only one had emerged intact on the other side.

5 ....

Morning tea, that abiding, almost fanatical ritual of Southern Africa, was observed elaborately on the plane with trays full of cakes and half a dozen varieties of sandwiches, with fresh fruits and, of course, with cups of Nile-red tea. Just after all this had been consumed, at about noon, the clouds below us were suddenly parted and Lake Victoria appeared.

6 ....

The range of cumulus came up dead in front of us. The pilot clearly intended to fly underneath it, now that he knew precisely where he was. The green hills and the green valleys, the well-watered succulent vegetation of this part of Africa lay there for our desert-worn and cloud-dazed senses to enjoy. But not for long. Wherever one looked, the horizon was black, purple-silver and pearl-grey with cloud. The far hills were already grey with rain and mist.

7 ....

I said goodbye to my companions at the aerodrome. From now on our ways divided. I had to spend the night in Nairobi and then take a smaller plane on towards my destination, early the following morning.

A

For a while something unexplained and irrational appeared to dominate the actions of all of us. My own reaction was to concentrate more than ever on what I would see of the world outside. With my maps handy on my knees, I continued to look down with fierce concentration as if I expected the haze and dust to vanish at any moment and a promised land to appear. After an hour or two I had my reward.

B

Shortly afterwards I realized that the pilot of this aircraft must have reached a similar conclusion, for suddenly we changed course. Nevertheless, without a split or a break appearing anywhere in its formation, it pushed steadily towards us. The atmosphere grew slowly darker, chillier, and more ominous because if its grim encroaching presence.

C

Little more than a mild, yellow, unrelieved glare stared back at me from the earth. Soon we had again the sharp sting of air in our nostrils that we had had the night before.

D

I exchanged addresses with the businessman. We shook one another warmly by the hand and promised, without fail, to meet again. At the barrier his motor car was waiting. The business man pointed to his chauffeur who was grinning with delight, his eyes shining with excitement: 'Send me a telegram, any time. Doesn't matter how far, I'll send him to meet you,' he said.

E

Up the valleys and down the plains, over mountain-tops and across rivers, the storms came striding towards us. Bumping and driving hard through heavy rain, we hardly saw land again until some hours later we climbed with relief out of the plane at Nairobi airport.

F

It was a most beautiful and impressive sight, but at that hour it made me fear for this lap of our journey. In our kind of plane, with the load we carried, I could not see how we could possibly fly over those far-flung, those dense electric Himalayas of cloud, and through them we could hardly attempt to go with any degree of safety.

G

Kampala was almost exactly underneath us; a long way down, the blue waters of the greatest of the African lakes, unrippled and serene, stretched away as far as we could see. One could, at the same time, almost hear the relief which filled the cockpit at that moment. The aircraft, losing no time, immediately put its nose into a long decline.

H

The men suddenly started drinking. One of the commercial travellers, while drinking a double brandy, began pulling letters and documents out of a case and tearing them to bits. I heard him say afterwards that he did not know what possessed him for he had destroyed several important papers.

Language Focus: Vocabulary

Dependent prepositions and prepositional phrases (revision)

Fill each of the gaps in the following sentences with the appropriate preposition.

1 I'm not accustomed .... having to justify all the decisions I make .... the office.
2 Unfortunately, I've not been .... good terms with my neighbour ever since my dog trampled his flowers.
3 You can't accuse her .... negligence just like that – you have no evidence.
4 I understand that you are interested .... showing our visitors something of the town's nightlife. What exactly did you have .... mind?
5 You can't go out in that old coat – it's quite .... the question!
6 I had some difficulty .... finding Monty this morning. I looked everywhere for him. .... the end, I discovered him asleep under the kitchen table.
7 The government appears to be .... the verge of building an airport in an area of outstanding natural beauty. This is bound to have a huge impact .... the wildlife of the area.
8 I think that we should get rid .... this old washing machine. It's not just .... date – it should be in a museum!
9 There will be several changes .... the way we run this department. All staff will be monitored .... regular intervals to ensure that standards are being maintained.

Use of English
▶ **Paper 3, Part 1**

Read the text below and think of the word which best fits each space. There is an example at the beginning (0).

The Artist's Perspective

It is the job of the artist to encourage people to look at the world afresh. In a great (0) ..*deal*. of art, colours and forms may vary from what people are used (1) .... For this (2) ...., many people, some of (3) .... consider themselves to be experts on art, react (4) .... indignation when they see that an artist has painted the sky red or made (5) .... a person from geometrical shapes.

(6) .... these people do not understand, (7) ...., is that their prejudices are preventing them from seeing the world (8) .... a new and exciting way. Unless we approach a painting with an open mind, we will be (9) .... to discover anything of value in ourselves or in the world (10) .... us. We will remain in the darkness of our pre-conceived ideas (11) .... the time when we are prepared to open our eyes and ignore our intellects.

People of (12) .... ages, it seems, want the things in the 'outside world' to be familiar. However, hardly (13) .... claiming to be a 'real' artist would subscribe to (14) .... comfortable an outlook on life. Seeing everything from a different perspective, such people are like beings from (15) .... planet.

Use of English
▶ **Paper 3, Part 2**

For questions **1–10**, read the text below. Use the word given in **capitals** at the end of some of the lines to form a word that fits in the space in the same line. There is an example at the beginning (0).

Musical Greatness

Like all artists, musicians are often astonishingly precocious. It is well known, for example, that Mozart's first public (0) ..*performance*.. took place when he was only six. Chopin, a skilled concert (1) .... as well as composer, wrote his first work for piano when he was seven. In both cases, of course, indications of (2) .... musical skill were recognised during childhood and encouraged. Had their talents gone (3) ...., however, they would not have had the opportunity to utilise their skill and would never have developed their greatness. It is a (4) .... thought that thousands of potentially (5) .... artists may have lived and died without ever knowing that they had an inherent ability to become great.

For a reason which is (6) .... associated with the unusual development of a special part of the brain, brilliant artists frequently possess an awareness of their own importance and a (7) .... of purpose lacking in most other people. They may also feel a tremendous (8) .... to utilise their gifts to the full, (9) .... of the consequences to them or to anyone else. Beethoven, who died from illness and exhaustion, was said to have been (10) .... to give up work until lying on his deathbed. 'I shall hear music in heaven' were his final words.

PERFORM

PIANO

ORDINARY

NOTICE

SOBER
STAND

DOUBT

CLEAR

COMPEL
REGARD

WILL

Use of English

▶ **Paper 3, Part 3**

For questions **1–6**, think of **one** word only which can be used appropriately in all three sentences.

1   Given your difficult circumstances, there are probably a number of benefits you could .... from the state.

The renewed wave of unrest and violence in the capital seems likely to .... yet more lives.

If the police ask him where he was on the night of the murder, he is bound to .... that he was with friends.

2   If that country wants to .... its position as a leader among nations, it will be forced to reform its economy.

In order to .... the equipment in the workshop, the company needs to put aside at least £10,000 annually.

How can you .... such a large family on the salary you earn?

3   With all the upsets I've had at home recently, I feel totally unable to .... even the smallest of difficulties at the moment.

As many of the Chinese vases on display are extremely fragile, visitors to the museum are asked not to .... them.

Since it's illegal to .... stolen goods, you would be mad even to think about buying those paintings.

4   It was only when we came to a .... bend in the road that we realised we had taken a wrong turning.

When the doctor asked me to move my arm, I felt a .... pain in my back.

When David Swanson interviews politicians on television, he conceals an incredibly .... mind behind what appears to be an easy-going, friendly manner.

5   The latest .... to curb increasing crime on the streets is unlikely to be much of a success.

Members of the public will suffer unless there is some .... of cooperation between the two bus companies.

School and university exams may not be the best .... of a student's abilities.

6   There will be much less chance of a similar situation developing again, since the new regulations will .... policy-makers of the future.

Doctors had to .... both the arms and legs of the patient so that he couldn't move while they examined him.

The cake won't turn out well unless you add a fresh egg to the other ingredients in order to .... the mixture together.

Use of English

▶ **Paper 3, Part 4**

For each question below, complete the second sentence so that it has a similar meaning to the first sentence, using the word given. **Do not change the word given.** You must use between **three** and **eight** words, including the word given.

1 They say that someone has been giving her large bribes. **alleged**
She ....
.... large bribes.

2 People have criticised the government heavily over its immigration policy. **come**
The government ....
.... over its immigration policy.

3 It is unlikely that they will terminate his employment. **likelihood**
There is ....
.... the sack.

4 I'm sure Charles was deceived by all the lies she told. **bound**
Charles ....
.... in by all the lies she told.

5 Sarah is determined to win first prize for English. **heart**
Sarah has ....
.... first prize for English.

6 She didn't try very hard to have friendly relations with her colleagues. **little**
She made ....
.... along with her colleagues.

7 We should not continue the experiments, because we have encountered serious problems. **against**
Since we have ....
.... a halt to the experiments.

8 It was difficult not to smile when he reprimanded us for such a minor mistake. **keep**
It was difficult to ....
.... off about such a minor mistake.

9 It's impossible for us to agree to their terms. **question**
There ....
.... to their terms.

10 She doesn't seem to be willing to allow them to leave the building. **intent**
She seems ....
.... in the building.

11 The fact that you contributed enabled me to complete my research. **contribution**
Had ....
.............................., I would not have been able to complete my research.

12 Her participation in the discussion was entirely voluntary. **obligation**
She was ....
.... part in the discussion.

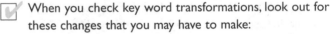

When you check key word transformations, look out for these changes that you may have to make:

- a word/phrase to a set phrase or expression (e.g. *it's likely that* → *in all likelihood*)
- a word/phrase to a phrasal verb (e.g. *continue* → *carry on*)
- a word/phrase to a synonym or antonym
- the word order
- the verb form (e.g. active → passive, past simple → modal perfect)
- a part of speech (e.g. adjective → adverb)
- an adjective/adverb/noun to a noun or *-ing* form because it follows a preposition (e.g. *happy to be here* → *delight in being here*)
- a verb in a particular tense to the appropriate infinitive form (e.g. → *to use, to be used, to have used, to be using*, etc.)
- a comparative to a superlative form, or vice versa
- a negative word/phrase to a positive, or vice versa
- adding a verb/noun/adjective/adverb which collocates with a particular word (e.g. *start* → *make a start*).

Use of English
▶ Paper 3, Part 5

In Paper 3, Part 5 you have to answer four comprehension questions on two texts and summarise certain aspects of the writers' arguments in a paragraph of between 50 and 70 words.

Look again at Unit 6, page 50, for guidance on the best way to approach the comprehension questions.

> ### Exam Strategy
>
> - Read the summary question carefully and decide what information you need to answer it.
> - Find and underline the parts of each text that contain the information you want.
> - Make brief notes of the main points, using your own words as far as you can. If the same point is made in both texts, only note it once. You usually need **four or five points** for a Proficiency summary.
> - Expand the points you have jotted down into a connected paragraph.
> - When you have finished, count the number of words you have used – it should be between **50 and 70 words**. If your paragraph is too long, decide how you can shorten it, using the techniques outlined below. Also look back at the question to check that all your points are relevant.
> - Rewrite your summary. The examiner will give you marks for two things:
>   a) Identification of points
>   Are the points you have found all relevant?
>   b) Use of language
>   Is your paragraph well-written and concise?
>   Have you used your own words?
>   Have you organised the points logically and used connectors?

Read the following summary task and the following notes.

> In a paragraph of between **50 and 70** words summarise, **in your own words as far as possible**, the advantages of ordering books from an Internet bookshop.

Notes

1 books – less expensive than from traditional bookshop
2 find almost any book in print
3 ordering – quick and easy
4 many Internet bookshops – information about other books/same author, related subject
5 reviews by other readers

Now read the first draft of the summary made from these points. What's wrong with it?

It is very often much less expensive to buy books from an Internet bookshop than to buy them from a conventional bookshop. For example, some Internet bookshops sell books at half the price they would be in a normal bookshop. In addition to this, it is possible to find almost any book which is in print and to order it over the Internet both quickly and easily. As well as providing a lot of useful and interesting information about books by the same author or books on a related subject, a large number of Internet bookshops also encourage readers to send in reviews of books they have read and would recommend to other readers. These reviews enable readers to order books they know are good.

(125 words)

 Use this checklist to guide you in editing the first draft of the summary to the correct length. Always remember to:

- check that every sentence makes a new point or points
- check that you haven't made the same point twice in different ways
- remove supporting examples
- remove unnecessary adjectives and adverbs
- replace phrases with single words
- replace full clauses with participle clauses.

Writing: all tasks

In this section, there is further practice for each type of writing task. For reasons of space, only **one** writing task for Part 1 is provided. (In the exam there are a number of different types of writing you could be asked to produce in Part 1.)

1 Essay (Part 1)

Whenever you write an essay, make sure you:

- write a clear introduction, in which you outline the situation as it is today, or has been recently. Perhaps use a rhetorical question to lead into the main body of your essay.
- divide the essay into clear paragraphs, each covering a particular point in your argument or aspect of the subject.
- identify whether the task demands a 'balanced' or 'one-sided' approach. If the essay is one-sided, don't develop points which contradict the overall aim of your writing: mention the alternative view briefly in your introduction or conclusion.
- support your ideas with brief examples.
- use connectors and adverbial phrases to link your sentences and ideas.
- write a conclusion which 'echoes' your introductory paragraph.

TASK

You have read the following extract from a magazine article in which the writer expresses his feelings about the usefulness of advertising. It has prompted you to write an essay for your tutor discussing the points raised and expressing your own views.

(300–350 words)

Does advertising serve a useful purpose in a modern, democratic society? The answer to this question must surely be no. The sooner we face up to the fact that advertising only confuses people and distorts the truth, the better. It is something we would all be better without. When was the last time you saw an advertisement that gave you some useful, accurate information about a product? How often have you felt dissatisfied with what you already have simply because an advertisement tells you that it is old-fashioned or of poor quality? Advertisements are at best irritating and at worst extremely offensive.

2 Article (Part 1, Part 2)

Whenever you write an article, make sure you:

- understand what kind of article you have to write (e.g. for a newspaper, magazine, journal or newsletter) and who your readers will be. This will affect the style and register of the language you use.
- use a range of descriptive verbs, adjectives and adverbs to make events more interesting. If writing an article for Part 1, you will also have to include a reasoned discussion of particular issues.
- write an introduction which will make an impact on your readers.
- use direct speech only where appropriate.

TASK

Your school or college magazine has invited students to contribute an article to a special edition entitled *My Home Town*. Write an article describing what you like most about your home town or village and explain how you feel about any changes which might be occurring there at present.

(300–350 words)

3 Formal letter (Part 1, Part 2)

Whenever you write a letter, make sure you:

- think carefully about what the purpose of your letter is and who your reader(s) will be. A letter to a newspaper, for example, will aim to give an opinion and make a point about some matter; a letter of complaint will give details about an event or situation that has not lived up to expectations.
- make sure your register and style are appropriate.
- refer to the situation or events you are describing in an unemotional, reasonable way. If writing a letter for Part 1, respond to points raised in the input you have been given and make sure you support your arguments or point of view.
- organise your letter carefully. A standard method of paragraphing is:
  1 your reason for writing
  2 detailing your concerns or views
  3 supplying further information
  4 concluding remarks/suggestions/requests.
- only include details which are strictly relevant.

TASK

You were recently one of a group of delegates at a student conference and found the arrangements for lectures, accommodation and travel to be inadequate. Write a letter of complaint to the conference organiser, detailing how you expect arrangements to improve before next year's conference, which you are also planning to attend.

(300–350 words)

4   Proposal (Part 1, Part 2)

Whenever you write a proposal, make sure you:

- are clear about the purpose of a proposal. A proposal is different from a report in that it is mostly devoted to making recommendations for a future project or course of action.
- organise it for your reader. Use headings for each of the sections, and group your ideas together very clearly. The most important section will obviously be the 'Recommendations' section in the middle.
- bear in mind the person who will read it so that the style and register are appropriate.
- only include details which are strictly relevant.

TASK

You are employed as an advisor by a large city hospital. Your manager has asked you to write a proposal on how the hospital could be made more attractive and be of greater benefit to its patients. Within your proposal you should include ideas on how to improve the hospital environment and facilities, as well as patient care and well-being.

(300–350 words)

5   Review (Part 2)

Whenever you write a review, make sure you:

- know what you have to write about and who you are writing for.
- have the appropriate vocabulary to describe a film or book.
- know what tone (e.g. light, persuasive, friendly) to adopt. Use descriptive adjectives, verbs and adverbs to make it more interesting.
- write an introduction which will make an immediate impact on your readers.
- conclude your review with a reflective comment which reinforces your purpose for writing.

- include the reported views of people you have spoken to (if appropriate).

TASK

You have been asked to write a review for your college magazine of a hotel you recently stayed at. Write your review, and say what factors you think are important in the running of a good hotel.

(300–350 words)

6   Report (Part 2)

Whenever you write a report, make sure you:

- are clear about the purpose of a report. A report usually involves an account of something which has happened (e.g. a meeting, a visit, a survey of opinion) and the presentation and interpretation of information deriving from this.
- organise your report carefully. Use headings for each section, and group your ideas clearly and logically. A standard organisation of a report is:
  1 introduction/background information
  2 main body of the report in headed sections
  3 comments/recommendations.
- use an impersonal style and register.
- only include details which are strictly relevant.

TASK

As local tourist officer, you have been asked by your regional manager to prepare a report on the standard of facilities for visitors to your town. Comment on the reactions of visitors to these facilities, and suggest ways to improve them.

(300–350 words)

7   Set book (Part 2)

In Question 5 of Part 2, you have the option of writing about a book you have studied and prepared beforehand. You may be asked to write an article, an essay, a letter, a review or a report about this book.

If you decide to attempt this question, make sure you:

- feel confident writing about the structure and plot, the main characters and important events.
- use the appropriate format for the task.
- use language which is appropriate in style and register.
- support your ideas with evidence from the text.

Practice exam

PAPER 1 – READING   (1 hour 30 minutes)

PART 1

For questions **1–18**, read the three texts below and decide which answer (**A**, **B**, **C** or **D**) best fits each gap. Mark your answers **on the separate answer sheet**.

MONKEYS IN SPACE

Later this week, a meeting will take place of a group of American and British scientists to (**1**) .... two astronauts from a shortlist of twelve candidates. Aboard the spacecraft *Odyssey*, the two astronauts will then be (**2**) .... into space on a 14-day mission, the aim of which is to investigate the (**3**) .... effects of weightlessness on bones, muscles and nerves. The mission would normally attract very little publicity. But not this time. The *Odyssey* space mission has given (**4**) .... to violent opposition from around the world. Every day, the US senate is (**5**) .... with complaints, thousands of leaflets are handed out to people on the streets of America, and TV chat shows threaten to get out of hand. Why such hysteria? The public (**6**) .... would seem to be a mystery – until you learn the nature of the *Odyssey* crew. The two astronauts are to be rhesus monkeys.

1	**A** take up	**B** make up	**C** figure out	**D** pick out
2	**A** thrown	**B** tossed	**C** hurled	**D** chucked
3	**A** long-gone	**B** long-term	**C** long-range	**D** long-time
4	**A** rise	**B** start	**C** motive	**D** cause
5	**A** crowded	**B** flooded	**C** drenched	**D** infested
6	**A** exclamation	**B** scuffle	**C** disturbance	**D** outcry

---

JAMES TURNBULL'S DEPARTURE

It was with a sense of disbelief that I read in your newspaper yesterday of the forthcoming departure of Mr James Turnbull. After only six months as headmaster of the troubled Pinewood Secondary School in east London, Mr Turnbull has (**7**) .... fit to resign and move on to another – no doubt less problematical – school. According to your report, he has felt unable since taking up the post to (**8**) .... the varied needs and expectations of the children of the school, their parents and the board of governors. This is a tremendous shame for all concerned, and I cannot pretend to be other than disappointed. I (**9**) .... believed that he would be the one to (**10**) .... change and improve both the standard of teaching there and the (**11**) .... inadequacy of the school's facilities; that he would be able to deal effectively with the many problems which beset Pinewood School, (**12**) .... the indifference of the local authorities. It seems I was mistaken in this belief.

7	**A** considered	**B** seen	**C** viewed	**D** looked
8	**A** achieve	**B** purchase	**C** meet	**D** gain
9	**A** firmly	**B** totally	**C** utterly	**D** greatly
10	**A** bring off	**B** bring up	**C** bring to	**D** bring about
11	**A** unhappy	**B** woeful	**C** solid	**D** grim
12	**A** not least	**B** as regards	**C** contrary to	**D** at most

THE PIANO COMPETITION

A few years ago, my best friend (13) .... me to enter a piano competition that was to be held at a well-known London school of music, and foolishly I agreed. Colin – that was my friend's name – must have known that my musical ability was not (14) .... with that of the other competitors, but he certainly didn't let on if he did. When the big day arrived, I sat down in the packed auditorium and awaited my fate. The first pianist played a very difficult piece by Bach and her performance was virtually (15) .... . The others were just as good – or so it seemed to me. When my own turn came, I was (16) .... aware of my own inadequacy and it was about as much as I could do to get to the piano and sit down. Needless to (17) .... , my performance was awful. I couldn't have played worse if I had tried. People were very nice about it afterwards, but nobody was able to (18) .... me. Especially not Colin. It was months before I could bring myself to talk to him again.

13	**A** suggested	**B** urged	**C** insisted	**D** pleaded
14	**A** compared	**B** in league	**C** on a par	**D** consistent
15	**A** marvellous	**B** excellent	**C** perfect	**D** complete
16	**A** sharply	**B** steadily	**C** acutely	**D** powerfully
17	**A** say	**B** mention	**C** speak	**D** tell
18	**A** relieve	**B** brighten	**C** console	**D** alleviate

PART 2

You are going to read four extracts which are all concerned in some way with the natural environment. For questions **19–26**, choose the answer (**A**, **B**, **C** or **D**) which you think fits best according to the text. Mark your answers **on the separate answer sheet**.

The Aims of Conservation

Between wildlife and humanity, there is a subconscious connection stretching back to the origins of man. Many people sense that wildlife and humans are part of the same living scene and that man should therefore strive to see that the other actors have at least a walk-on part.

For the majority, conservation was initially thought of as only being relevant to endangered species. Their plight could be readily understood, and saving them was the focus point for both moral and public support. Now it is recognised that conservation must also be applied to the environment in which both wildlife and humans live. In the wealthier nations, the realisation that it is as important to protect the whole environment, including the oceans and the atmosphere, as it is to conserve flora and fauna, affects many people's entire lifestyle. It influences what they eat and drink, what they buy and wear, and for whom they vote.

Protecting wildlife, however, is still the bedrock of conservation. Common to each operation aimed at saving wildlife is the fact that man's requirements have clashed with and taken precedence over the needs of wild animals and plants. This situation is sometimes justifiable from a human standpoint. Under-privileged people may have to make a precarious living from land that is occupied by wildlife. If those people's welfare, let alone their survival, is at stake, then these must take priority. Occasionally a compromise can be found but, in a world in which over-population is a major cause of starvation and 'land hunger', this is increasingly hard to bring about.

19 The writer says that awareness of conservation issues has

    A historically been man's responsibility.

    B changed the entire lifestyle of the majority of people.

    C expanded from initially focusing primarily on animals.

    D gained general moral and material support.

20 The writer thinks that the wish to protect wildlife cannot be justified if

    A people's lives are therefore imperilled.

    B some people continue to starve.

    C impoverished people hunt the animals to live.

    D the population of the world continues to grow.

Basking Sharks

I do not think that any of the Hebridean fishermen with whom I talked could tell me the food of the shark. Even now, after all the publicity which the press accorded my shark-fishing venture, daily papers in the Scottish Hebrides still report plagues of Basking Sharks 'in pursuit of herring shoals', and there are many fishermen who believe this to be true. In fact, the shark feeds upon the same food as the herring: small organisms in the water which in aggregate are called 'plankton'. The word embraces all minute free-swimming organisms in the sea, as distinct from those which are attached to, or crawl upon, the bottom.

To the herring fishermen the sharks were a menace, to be avoided at all costs. They destroyed their nets, passing through them as an elephant would pass through a stretched sheet of muslin, and when the nets were mended the tear would reopen like a recurrently festering wound, rotted by the black, glue-like slime from the shark's fins and back. To a small boat the sharks were dangerous, and also apparently inquisitive; a fisherman putting out lines for mackerel from a dinghy would pull with all his strength for the shore when the black sail surfaced nearby.

21   What does the writer imply about local opinion regarding the sharks' eating habits?
   A   It is based on the experiences of the herring fishermen.
   B   It is uniformly the same throughout the Scottish Hebrides.
   C   It is surprisingly inaccurate.
   D   It reflects the fishermen's fears.

22   The writer says that the sharks were avoided by fishermen because they
   A   could make a hole in a fishing boat very easily.
   B   would cause irreparable damage to their fishing nets.
   C   were known to have attacked people.
   D   were attracted by the sail of a nearby fishing boat.

Newspaper Advertisement

The world may be small but it's all we've got. The way that some people treat it, you would think there is somewhere else to go once the Earth's resources have been exhausted. You know there isn't. Our small planet is being ravaged and its limited resources are fast disappearing.

As a non-profit organisation supported by memberships and donations, we are among the few trying to protect our fragile planet. By applying international direct action with scientific research and political pressure, we have had many notable successes:

• The atmospheric testing of nuclear weapons in the Pacific has been stopped.
• Commercial whaling is in the process of being stopped.
• Dumping of radioactive waste in the ocean has been stopped.
• The large-scale slaughter of baby harp seals has been stopped.
• Incineration at sea of dangerous toxic chemicals is in the process of being stopped.

We don't want to stop everything though. What we have started is a general raising of awareness of the environment across the globe. There is still a long way to go. Deforestation and the depletion of the ozone layer are just two of the problems we are aiming to overcome; there are countless others.

To find out what part you can play in all this, fill out the coupon below and mail it today.

23 The aim of the advertisement is to
 A inform the public of serious environmental problems.
 B encourage people to form action groups.
 C ask people to send in donations.
 D recruit people who are willing to help.

24 The tone of the writer's opening remarks is
 A ironic.
 B humorous.
 C resigned.
 D bitter.

Environmental Scares

Is it not a good thing to exaggerate the potential problems the world faces rather than underplay them? Not necessarily. A new book, *Lie of the Land,* edited by Melissa Leach and Robin Mearns, documents just how damaging the myth of deforestation has been in parts of the Sahel region of Africa, where Westerners have forced inappropriate measures on puzzled local inhabitants in order to meet activists' preconceived ideas about environmental change. The ill-conceived notion that oil and gas will imminently run out, together with worries about the greenhouse effect, is responsible for the despoliation of wild landscapes in Wales and Denmark by ugly wind farms. School textbooks are counsels of despair and guilt, which offer no hope of winning the war against famine, disease and pollution, thereby inducing fatalism rather than determination.

You can be in favour of the environment without being a pessimist. There should be room in the environmental movement for those who think that technology and economic freedom will make the world cleaner and also take the pressure off endangered species. But at the moment such optimists are distinctly unwelcome among environmentalists. They are quick to accuse their opponents of vested interests, but their own incomes, advancement and fame can depend on supporting the most alarming versions of every environmental scare.

---

25 The writer mentions the wind farms of Wales and Denmark as an example of
 A an effective response to the discovery of the greenhouse effect.
 B the way activists can cause damage to the environment.
 C what needs to be done if fossil fuels are to be conserved.
 D the current fatalistic view of environmental problems.

26 What does the writer say about the attitude of environmentalists?
 A They do not care sufficiently about environmental problems.
 B They regard technology as their main enemy.
 C They may allow self-interest to guide their actions and opinions.
 D They are mainly concerned about attacking their opponents.

You are going to read an extract from a novel. Seven paragraphs have been removed from the extract. Choose from the paragraphs **A–H** the one which fits each gap (**27–33**). There is one extra paragraph which you do not need to use. Mark your answers **on the separate answer sheet**.

'Mogul Trust House Forte,' my father muttered, his open-necked shirt hanging out of his baggy and creased cotton trousers, as he insisted, to everyone's embarrassment, on carrying his suitcase for himself instead of leaving it to one of the horde of sleek boys, in red uniforms picked out with gold braid, who crowded the concourse.

27

Mr Singh, whose complexion was the beautiful colour of an ivory cigarette holder faintly tinged with nicotine and who wore a shimmering grey silk jacket buttoned up to the neck, had a disconcerting way of letting his melancholy eyes wander to what appeared to be someone standing just behind me, a little to my right. But when eventually I looked over my shoulder to see who kept attracting his attention, there was no one there.

28

'I'm very sorry, sir. Very sorry.' Mr Singh did indeed look very sorry, long, upcurling eyelashes lowered over those melancholy eyes. 'You may see for yourself, sir. I am not kidding you.' He turned the ledger round to me. 'You will see for yourself that we have no such booking entered.' It was, in fact, impossible to see for myself, so quickly did he jerk the ledger back again.

29

'Well?' Kirsti asked. She knew that I hated these confrontations. But she also knew that, since I had accepted this role of courier imposed on me by my father, it would be useless for her, so much better equipped for it by temperament, to offer to take it over now. She listened in silence now as I told her that there was no record of any reservation. The girl in the hotel in Bombay unfortunately never given us any kind of written confirmation.

30

'Since the same group owns both hotels, I never thought ...' Then I lowered my head to him and whispered, even though Mr Singh was too far

away and too busy with another customer to hear even my normal voice. 'Perhaps a present might help?' He shook his head vigorously, and I realised that it was foolish of me to have said it. When, three days before, I had made the similar suggestion of a 'present' after it had become clear that we were not going to get a seat on the plane, my father had given way to one of his rare attacks of anger. He considered such actions to be morally wrong. As to what we were supposed to do in the present situation, I didn't have a clue.

31

I returned to the reception desk, where Mr Singh looked up from the English-language newspaper now spread out before him. 'Yes, sir?' We might never before have spoken to each other. He stared steadily at me as I repeated my request for a room, but already I knew the futility of my pleading.

32

Hoping that my father was not watching me, I furtively drew a note out of my pocket and pushed it across the counter. Mr Singh looked down at it as though it were one of the cockroaches that are ubiquitous in Indian hotels even as new and as clean as this one. 'Do you think you could telephone the Lantern Hotel for us?' I asked.

33

The Lantern was also full, with another party of Western tourists, this time French. Mr Singh was clearly not prepared to telephone anywhere else, since two luxury coaches had by now drawn up outside the hotel, to disgorge a number of middle-aged men and women all seeming to wear exactly the same kinds of sun hats and dark glasses. The boys were officiously crowding around them, some of them even struggling to relieve the new arrivals of handbags or camera cases which they were fiercely determined not to give up.

A It was my father who invariably decided our itineraries, as was perhaps only right since he was paying for both Kirsti and me. But if the itinerary was his, it was I who was expected to realise it, poring over timetables, haggling over charges, or, as now, arguing because we had been told that something that we had long since booked was not booked.

B The boys, having finished their task, were now awaiting their tips. Kirsti opened her bag and gave each a note. Then she gave me an apologetic glance, conscious of having usurped my role.

C 'Always get people to write things down,' my father muttered. 'If it's not down in writing, there's not an awful lot you can do, is there?' He smiled up at me, to draw the barb from the implied criticism.

D 'Sir, I regret. But, as I have already told you, the hotel is full. We have a party of Americans coming. They should be here at any minute now. Many people. Perhaps you should try the Lantern Hotel.'

E 'We'll find somewhere else. In a town as large as Indore, there are bound to be any number of hotels. Maybe Rajiv knows of a good one.' As always in these crises, Kirsti was reassuring.

F I went over to where my father was slumped in an armchair. Kirsti stood beside him, cigarette in hand. Behind them, I could see Rajiv peering in through the glass revolving door, a hand shielding his eyes. No doubt he had been put off entering by both the opulence of the lobby and the condescending self-importance of even the humblest members of the staff.

G On the veined red marble slab, the colour of a slice of raw beef, of the reception desk, a notice announced 'Mr Gerald Singh' and, under that in smaller letters, 'Assistant Manager'.

H Another moment passed as Mr Singh continued to stare down at the offending item lying between us. Then, picking it up with an air of faint disdain, he opened a drawer in the desk and dropped it in. He crossed over to the telephone.

You are going to read an extract from a book about the origins of mathematics. For questions **34–40**, choose the answer (**A**, **B**, **C** or **D**) which you think fits best according to the text. Mark your answers **on the separate answer sheet**.

Ancient Origins

Preceding the use of astronomy and of mathematics for navigation and calendar reckoning there must have been centuries during which men, filled with instinctive wonder and an awe of nature, with irrepressible philosophical drives, patiently observed the movement of the sun, moon and stars. These seers, obsessed by the mystery of nature, overcame the handicaps of lack of instruments and woefully inadequate mathematics to distil from their observations the patterns which are described by the heavenly bodies.

The early farmer learned to watch the face of the sky. He hunted, fished, sowed, reaped, danced and performed religious ceremonies at the times the heavens dictated. Soon particular constellations received the names of the activities their appearance sanctioned. Sagittarius, the hunter, and Pisces, the fish, are still in the sky.

The heavens decided the time of events. But such imperious masters would tolerate no delay in compliance with their orders. The farmer in many hotter countries, who made his living by tilling the soil which the river covered with rich silt during its annual overflow of the fields, had to be well prepared for the flood. His home, equipment, and cattle had to be temporarily removed from the area, and arrangements made for sowing immediately afterwards. Hence the coming of the flood had to be predicted. Not only in hotter countries, but in all lands, it was necessary to know beforehand the time for planting and the coming of holidays and days of sacrifice.

Prediction was not possible, however, by merely keeping count of the passing days and nights. For the calendar year of 365 days soon lost all relation to the seasons just because it was short by a quarter of a day. Prediction of a holiday or a river flood even a few days in advance required an accurate knowledge of the motions of the heavenly bodies and of mathematics that was possessed only by the priests. These holy people, knowing the importance of the calendar for the regulation of daily life and for provident preparation, exploited this knowledge to retain dominance over the uninformed masses. In fact, it is believed that many early priests knew the solar year, that is, the year of the seasons, to be 365.25 days in length, but deliberately withheld this knowledge from the people. Knowing also when the flood was due, the priests could pretend to bring it about with their rites, while making

the poor farmer pay for the performance.

Wonder about the heavens eventually led, via the respectable science of astronomy, to mathematics. Meanwhile, religious mysticism, itself an expression of wonder about life, death, wind, rain and the panorama of nature, became concerned with mathematics through astrology. Of course, the importance of astrology in ancient religions must not be judged by its current discredited position in most cultures. In almost all these religions, the heavenly bodies, the sun especially, had personalities and cosmic influences over events on Earth. The wills and plans of these bodies might be fathomed by studying their activities, their regular comings and goings, the sudden visitations of meteors, and the occasional eclipses of the sun and moon. It was as natural for the ancient priests to work out a formula for the divination of the future based on the motions of the planets and star constellations as it is for the modern scientist to study and master nature with his techniques.

Even if the heavenly bodies had not been thought to have their own personalities, a scientifically immature people would have had good reasons to associate the positions of the sun, moon and stars with human affairs. The dependence of crops upon the sun and upon the weather in general, the mating of animals at definite seasons of the year, and numerous other similar associations, all made such a doctrine credible. To ancient peoples, the coming of the annual flood on just the day that Sirius, the brightest star in the sky, appeared at sunrise meant only one thing: Sirius caused the flood.

Religious mysticism expressed itself directly in the construction and orientation of beautiful temples and pyramids. Although these monumental structures are to be found in many countries today, it is the pyramids of Egypt which have received the most attention in recent times. The pyramids of Egypt were built with special care because they were royal tombs, and the Egyptians believed that their construction according to exact mathematical prescriptions was essential for the future life of the dead. The orientation of these religious monuments in relation to the heavenly bodies is well illustrated by the temple of Amon-Ra at Karnak, which was devoted to worship of the sun. This building was so positioned that, on the longest day of the whole year, the sun shone directly into the temple and illuminated its rear wall.

34 What was the initial urge which prompted man to study the stars and planets?

   A the need to develop methods of navigation

   B the need for life to be regulated by an accurate calendar

   C a desire to improve the woefully inadequate mathematics of the time

   D the desire to unravel the wonder of nature

35 Primitive farmers made a careful watch of the sky

    A to see when certain activities should be performed.

    B to receive the blessing of particular constellations.

    C to receive comfort in times of hardship.

    D for guidance in their religious rituals and ceremonies.

36 Farmers in hotter countries needed to know when rivers would flood because

    A the results could potentially be disastrous.

    B various rituals had to be prepared.

    C their prosperity was dependent on it.

    D their cattle needed to be moved elsewhere.

37 What was the principal benefit to the priests of Egypt of possessing an accurate calendar?

    A It enabled them to maintain their power over the people.

    B They knew when they had to perform religious rites.

    C They could pretend to cause the annual flood of rivers.

    D They received payment from farmers.

38 The writer says that in ancient times astrology was

    A scorned by astronomers and mathematicians.

    B held in similar esteem to the standing of science today.

    C discredited, in comparison with astronomy.

    D primarily used to try to divine the future.

39 What is the 'doctrine' referred to by the writer in the penultimate paragraph?

    A That the growth of crops was entirely dependent on the sun and weather.

    B That animals were aware of the position of the sun and moon.

    C That events on Earth were connected to the movements of heavenly bodies.

    D That Sirius was the most important star in the sky.

40 The writer mentions the temple of Amon-Ra as an example of

    A the importance of the sun in early Egyptian religion.

    B a temple which was also used as a royal tomb.

    C the advanced building techniques of the ancient Egyptians.

    D the mathematical precision with which such monuments were built.

PAPER 2 – WRITING (2 hours)

Answer the Part 1 question and **one** question from Part 2.

PART 1

You **must** answer this question. Write your answer in **300–350** words in an appropriate style on the following pages.

1 You have read the following extract as part of a newspaper article on the disadvantages of living in a large modern city. Readers were asked to send in their opinions. You decide to write a **letter** responding to the points raised and expressing your own views.

Write your **letter**. Do not write any postal addresses.

> After more than thirty years of living in one of the biggest cities of the world, I am finally admitting defeat and going to live in a small village in the country. There is quite simply too much noise and traffic, too much ugliness, too much stress and too much pollution to make living in a large modern city worthwhile any more. Overcrowding has resulted in high levels of crime, and there has been a corresponding decline in social and community values. It is an unnatural way to live. In every respect, the countryside is a safer, cheaper and better place to live.

PART 2

Write an answer to **one** of the questions **2–5** in this part. Write your answer in **300–350** words in an appropriate style on the following pages. Put the question number in the box at the top of the page.

2 As a student representative for your school or college, you would like to set up an English Club, which would aim to promote a general interest in Britain and the English language. You decide to write a proposal to the Director, outlining the kind of activities you think should be organised, and saying how you think the English Club would benefit both the school or college and individual students.

   Write your **proposal**.

3 You recently saw an old black and white film, which you thoroughly enjoyed. Write a review of the film for a media arts magazine and say in what ways such older films are often superior to many films produced today.

   Write your **review**.

4 Your school or college magazine has invited readers to contribute an article entitled, 'It was an experience I will never forget …' Write an article in which you describe a visit to a restaurant which was memorable in some way, explaining what happened and how you felt.

   Write your **article**.

5 Based on your reading of **one** of these books, write on **one** of the following. Write **(a)**, **(b)** or **(c)** as well as the number **5** in the box.

   (a) Set book 1
   'They were so completely different, it was as if they inhabited different worlds.' Write an essay for your tutor discussing this statement, comparing the lifestyles of _____ and _____ , and explaining what role their relationship plays in the story as a whole.

   Write your **essay**.

   (b) Set book 2
   A student magazine has invited readers to send in articles entitled 'More than just a love story' on books they have read. Write an article about _____ (Set book 2), describing how the relationship between _____ and _____ develops, and showing how these developments are influenced by the political situation of the time.

   Write your **article**.

   (c) Set book 3
   Your school or college library has invited its members to suggest books they should have on the theme of 'European settings in English literature'. Write a letter to the library staff recommending _____ (Set book 3). Describe the characters of _____ and _____ , and say how the setting of the book influences their relationship and the development of events in the novel.

   Write your **letter**. Do not write any postal addresses.

PAPER 3 – USE OF ENGLISH (1 hour 30 minutes)

PART 1

For questions **1–15**, read the text below and think of the word which best fits each space. Use only one word in each space. There is an example at the beginning **(0)**. Write your answers **in CAPITAL LETTERS on the separate answer sheet**.

HERBS

Over the last hundred years, **(0)** ..*much*.. of the art of using herbs in cooking and medicine has been lost, especially in industrialised societies. Until recently, **(1)** .... people in the crowded cities had the space to grow plants or vegetables, and so **(2)** .... in the country did knowledge of herbs linger on. **(3)** .... the advent of refrigeration, however, **(4)** .... meant that the strong smell of old meat no **(5)** .... had to be disguised, and the appearance of packaged food and easily-available medicines, the growing of herbs declined rapidly.

Nowadays there is **(6)** .... anyone who does not have a small patch of garden, or a **(7)** .... sill or balcony large **(8)** .... for a pot or two of herbs. These facts, coupled with the beginnings of a revolt **(9)** .... standardised foods and perhaps also a mistrust of the side **(10)** .... of some of today's medicines, mean that herbs have taken **(11)** .... a new popularity.

The culinary uses of herbs are endless and they can be used **(12)** .... good effect all year round, **(13)** .... dried form or cut fresh. **(14)** .... aids to beauty and for medicinal **(15)** ...., there is now a vast range available. Herbs are for all occasions and all seasons.

PART 2

For questions **16–25**, read the text below. Use the word given in **capitals** at the end of some of the lines to form a word that fits in the space in the same line. There is an example at the beginning **(0)**. Write your answers **in CAPITAL LETTERS on the separate answer sheet**.

The Importance of Symbols

A symbol is a word or even a picture that may be familiar in **(0)** .*daily*.. life,	**DAY**
but possesses specific connotations over and above its standard and obvious	
meaning. It points to something vague or **(16)** ...., something which is	**MYSTERY**
normally hidden from us or may even be quite **(17)** .... On Cretan	**COMPREHEND**
monuments, for instance, **(18)** .... in the form of a double-headed axe are	**ENGRAVE**
often found. We know what this object is, but we do not know what it	
symbolises or what its **(19)** .... were for the people who used it.	**IMPLY**
Since there are **(20)** .... things beyond the range of human understanding, we	**NUMBER**
use symbolic terms all the time to represent concepts that are shrouded in	
(21) .... or that we cannot fully understand. This is one reason why religions	**OBSCURE**
(22) .... employ symbolic language or images.	**WORLD**
Man also produces symbols spontaneously in the **(23)** .... of the unconscious	**DEEP**
mind, in the form of dreams. Our **(24)** .... of reality is enormously complex,	**PERCEIVE**
and it is not **(25)** .... clear how events in our lives are recorded by our minds.	**WHOLE**
What is clear, however, is that the unconscious aspect of any event is revealed	
to us in dreams – not as a rational thought but as a symbol.	

PART 3

For questions **26–31**, think of one word only which can be used appropriately in all three sentences. Here is an example **(0)**.

Example:

0   If you ....*clear*............ all those books off your desk, you'll have a lot more room.
After the heavy snowfall last week, snow-ploughs had to be called in to ....*clear*............
the main roads.
When the jury hear the new evidence, they'll have no other option but to ....*clear*............
him of the charge of murder.

Write only the missing word **in CAPITAL LETTERS on the separate answer sheet**.

26   With the help of a team of psychologists, the police are trying to .... up a
profile of the killer.
After decades of totalitarian rule, it will not be an easy matter for that country to
.... a more democratic society.
We must .... on our recent successes in the area of research and
development if we are to develop into a leading international company.

27   The bank's regulations state clearly that you must show your cheque card whenever you
want to .... any money.
After two months of hard fighting, it seems very unlikely that the attacking army will admit
defeat and ....
Unless you are prepared to face a lengthy court case, you will have to ....
that negative remark you made about the organisation's activities.

28   I wish you would .... up all your clothes and put them away in the
cupboard.
Come on, children! Sit up straight and .... your arms!
In order to protect the delicate manuscript, we decided to .... it carefully in
a large piece of silk.

29   According to the forecast, there's going to be a .... of really hot weather
next month.
I had a dizzy .... this morning, but I think I've got over the worst of my
illness and can return to work tomorrow.
The villagers were so superstitious that they believed a .... to have been
responsible for the death of their animals.

30   The .... colours she uses in all her paintings make them difficult to miss at
an exhibition.
He gave us such a .... account of his journey across the desert that we
could almost feel the heat and the dust.
I have a very .... memory of the time I spent as a child with my mother in
France.

31   Don't be surprised if the managers .... your suggestion as being unrealistic
and follow another course of action.
The judge may decide to .... the case owing to the lack of evidence.
It's quite likely that Mr Hawkins will .... his secretary if he finds out about
her part in the theft.

PART 4

For questions **32–39**, complete the second sentence so that it has a similar meaning to the first sentence, using the word given. **Do not change the word given**. You must use between **three** and **eight** words, including the word given. Here is an example **(0)**.

Example:

0   Whatever happens, you are not to embark on the journey alone.
circumstances
Under ………… *no circumstances are you to set* ………… out on the journey alone.

Write **only** the missing words **on the separate answer sheet**.

32   If sales decreased dramatically, the company might go bust.
fall
Were …………………………………………….. sales, the company might go bust.

33   His efforts to find a solution didn't deserve such savage criticism.
criticised
He shouldn't …………………………………………….. his efforts to find a solution.

34   Nowadays I consider gossip to be far less important than I used to.
nearly
Nowadays I don't attach …………………………………………….. I used to.

35   This is the first time I've seen her in my life!
eyes
I …………………………………………….. her before!

36   Since my arrival, you have shouted at me constantly.
nothing
From the …………………………………………….. shout at me.

37   In all probability I can convince Dave that I'm right.
likelihood
There's …………………………………………….. to my way of thinking.

38   They'll soon discover what she's been doing.
before
It …………………………………………….. out what she's been doing.

39   Didn't you realise that he had invented that story about rescuing those people?
occur
Didn't …………………………………………….. up that story about rescuing those people?

PART 5

For questions **40–44**, read the following texts about following a career in scientific research. For questions **40–43**, answer with a word or short phrase. You do not need to write complete sentences. For question **44**, write a summary according to the instructions given. Write your answers to questions **40–44 on the separate answer sheet**.

What does the job of a research scientist have to offer the young, the bright and the ambitious? The pay is poor, the hours are long and the job security is virtually non-existent. But picture yourself in a quiet room, holding a piece of knowledge in your hand that no-one else in the world yet knows or has ever known. You feel a rush of excitement. For three minutes, three hours, three days, that piece of knowledge is yours and
5   yours alone, until you choose to share it with the world. You have stepped from the calm of the boat and into uncharted territory. This is the moment that every scientist dreams and hopes for.
What a scientist has to endure on the journey into the unknown will often be long days of despair: experiments that won't work, funding that disappears before you've even got off the ground, or a competitor who appears from nowhere and pips you at the post. In the shadow of defeat, you disconsolately shuffle back to the lab
10 and begin seriously rethinking your career options.
But the journey itself can be fun, even if the outcome or the final destination turns out to be not quite what you had expected. The challenge of pitting yourself against nature's myriad complexities can be endlessly rewarding. Why would anyone want to find out how the internal organs of a worm or snail develop, you might ask? Because – quite simply – we are not as distant from our fellow organisms as we would like to think. We
15 are one small component in a wonderfully complex, deeply mysterious machine.

40   What do the words 'you have stepped from the calm of the boat' (line 6) suggest about sharing a scientific discovery with the world?

....

....

41   In your own words, explain what image the writer creates of scientific research in paragraph 2.

....

....

Yeast. What's so special about it? It makes bread rise, of course, but so what? Unless you're a devotee of home-baked cottage loaves, there's not much in the humble yeast plant to get really excited about. But wait a minute. Understanding how yeasts grow and divide helps us understand how our own cells replicate. Since a number of serious illnesses are caused by cells that are unable to control their growth or replication, this knowledge might eventually lead us to new methods of treatment. And that, of course, is what makes scientific research so worthwhile and so rewarding.
If you already know this to be true and happen to be working in the field of pharmaceutical research, our company would be very interested in hearing from you. You may be just the person we are looking for. Of course, we'll need you to tell us about your particular areas of interest. We'll also need to know whether you posses the expertise we require. But, in a sense, we feel that we already know a lot about you. We know, for example, that what you really love about your work as a research scientist is that it is so personal – there is nothing in the least bit remote or abstract about it. It occupies all your waking moments, all your thoughts and energy; it never really leaves you alone. On a good day you are puzzled or even thrilled and amazed by what your work produces. On a bad day … well, every job has them, doesn't it?
If this really is true of yourself, then give us a call. You might be just the person we are looking for.

42 What point is the writer making about scientific research in the first paragraph by reference to the 'humble yeast plant'?

....

....

43 Which **two** words in paragraph 2 echo the 'rush of excitement' described in the first text?

....

....

44 In a paragraph of between **50 and 70** words, summarise **in your own words as far as possible**, the factors mentioned in the texts which make scientific research so rewarding.

PAPER 4 – LISTENING (Approx. 40 minutes)

PART 1

You will hear four different extracts. For questions **1–8**, choose the answer (**A, B** or **C**) which fits best according to what you hear. There are two questions for each extract.

Extract One

You hear a woman talking about her last holiday.

1 How does the woman feel about the island of Skopelos?

  A It has retained its character.

  B It has been spoilt by tourism.

  C It is friendlier than other islands.

[ ] **1**

2 The woman mentions The Golden Fleece as an example of a place where

  A there is a wide variety of local dishes available.

  B the food is very expensive.

  C the food is good and well-priced.

[ ] **2**

Extract Two

You hear an elderly woman speaking to someone in a supermarket.

3   Who is the elderly woman speaking to?

   A   the assistant manager

   B   another customer

   C   one of the cashiers

	3

4   What is the elderly woman's view of the signs?

   A   They are confusing.

   B   They are illegible.

   C   They are full of mistakes.

	4

Extract Three

You hear an extract from a programme on the radio.

5   What type of programme is being introduced?

   A   an interview

   B   a weekly book review

   C   a radio play

	5

6   The speaker mentions the effect of looking at old photographs in order to

   A   describe the nostalgia felt by older people at the circus.

   B   emphasise the family nature of a trip to the circus.

   C   emphasise how little circuses have changed over the years.

	6

Extract Four

You hear a conversation between two friends on a skiing trip.

7 Where are the speakers?

   A   on a bus

   B   on a train

   C   on a two-seater ski-lift

	7

8   What is the woman worried about?

   A   She will feel the cold.

   B   She may still be ill.

   C   She is out of practice.

	8

PART 2

You will hear part of a radio programme in which Dr Heather Clark talks about her job as a doctor and her passion for dancing. For questions **9–17**, complete the sentences with a word or short phrase.

Dr Heather Clark hit the headlines recently when she performed | **9**
in a London pub.

She travels | **10** | to get to people who need her help.

When she responds to an | **11** | she never knows what awaits her.

She likes her job because people can be saved | **12** | by the doctor.

Although she carries a heavy | **13** | she often has to run to get to patients.

At school, she loved dancing but she was not | **14** | to become a ballerina.

She now stays fit by dancing at least | **15** | a week.

The rehearsals she attends with a | **16** | may last until the small hours of the morning.

She often needs to discuss | **17** | with her colleagues after work.

PART 3

You will hear an interview with the presenter of a popular radio series about food and cooking. For questions **18–22**, choose the answer (**A**, **B**, **C** or **D**) which fits best according to what you hear.

18   What has made 'Just a taste' so popular?

    A   It gives advice about how to cook traditional dishes.

    B   It features interviews with professional chefs.

    C   It presents food and cooking in a more personal light.

    D   It takes a humorous approach.

        18

19   The presenter of the programme believes that smells

    A   will one day be made available to listeners.

    B   can never be part of a radio cookery programme.

    C   are more important than sounds in the kitchen.

    D   cannot be successfully imagined by listeners.

        19

20   What makes describing a dish particularly difficult?

    A   There are too many ingredients to describe.

    B   Listeners are mainly interested in what they should be aiming for.

    C   Each stage of the cooking process needs to be described.

    D   There is a lack of appropriate vocabulary.

        20

21   The presenter of the series mentions Iceland because

    A   it has a particularly unusual cuisine.

    B   fish-based dishes are particularly popular there.

    C   it has turned natural features to its advantage.

    D   it produces large quantities of fruit and vegetables.

        21

22   The spices asafoetida and turmeric are used in South Indian cooking

    A   mainly for their taste.

    B   mainly for their therapeutic properties.

    C   by filtering them into the food.

    D   for traditional reasons only.

        22

PART 4

You will hear two friends, Andy and Joe, talking about possible reasons for the increase in crime in recent years. For questions **23–28**, decide whether the opinions are expressed by only one of the speakers, or whether the speakers agree.

Write   **A** for Andy,
               J for Joe,
or   **B** for Both, where they agree.

23 Fewer crimes are reported to the police nowadays.   **23**

24 People used to be shocked by even minor offences.   **24**

25 Crimes increase as people become richer.   **25**

26 When people were poorer they had more reason to steal.   **26**

27 Sentences were much heavier in the past.   **27**

28 Many criminals are not convicted by courts these days.   **28**

PAPER 5 – SPEAKING (19 minutes)

Important notes

- In the actual exam, you will be interviewed together with another candidate, and the examiner will encourage you to take it in turns to talk or to interact naturally with each other. In order to do the activities in this part of the Practice exam you will need to **find a partner** to work with.
- Instead of reading printed instructions for each part of the interview, you will be told what to do by the examiner. These instructions will probably be a little different from the instructions printed here.
- It is important to listen to what the other candidate says during the interview, because you will be asked by the examiner to respond briefly in some way after he or she has finished talking.

Part 1 (3 minutes)

Take it in turns to answer the following questions on your own. Make sure you talk for no longer than **one and a half minutes each.**

You

Where are you from?
What are the things you like about your home town?
Could you tell us a little about your plans for the future?
Are there any countries you would particularly like to visit?

Your partner

Where are you from?
What kind of journey did you have to get here today?
Could you tell us a little about what you like doing in your free time?
Would you say that you are an ambitious person?

Part 2 (4 minutes)

In this part of the test you are going to do something with your partner. Look at the five photographs below, which show animals and people together, and then follow the instructions.

1 Look at pictures 1 and 2, and talk together for **1 minute** about how you think the animals and the people might be feeling in each photo.

2 Imagine that a photographic exhibition is being assembled on the theme of 'Man and animals'. All these photographs are to be included.

Talk together for **3 minutes** about the different aspects of man's relationship with animals illustrated by the photos. Then suggest two other aspects which you think should be represented in the exhibition.

Part 3 (12 minutes)

In this part of the test you and your partner are going to talk on your own for about **two minutes each**. (**Note:** In the actual exam, you also have to comment on what the other candidate says and talk a little about his/her topic.)

When you have both finished, you will have a discussion with your partner for **four minutes** to explore the topics you have spoken about further.

Follow the instructions below.

1 Look at the card with a question written on it and say what you think. There are some ideas on the card for you to use if you like. Speak for **two minutes each.**

You

> When a new product is launched, what things make it a success?
>
> • advertising
> • price and packaging
> • product quality

Your partner

> What should a shop or supermarket do to ensure customer satisfaction?
>
> • staff attitudes
> • prices
> • range of products

2 To finish the test, have a discussion with your partner about **changing attitudes to shopping**. Use as many of the questions below as you need in order to keep your discussion going. Talk together for **four minutes.**

• How is the way people shop today changing?
• What effect has technology had on the way people shop?
• Is shopping nowadays more pleasurable than it was 50 years ago?
• Do customers have greater expectations of products and services nowadays?
• What kind of things make customers angry these days?
• Are people becoming more materialistic?

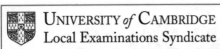

UNIVERSITY *of* CAMBRIDGE
Local Examinations Syndicate

SAMPLE

Candidate Name
If not already printed, write name in CAPITALS and complete the Candidate No. grid (in pencil).

Candidate Signature

Examination Title

Centre

Supervisor:
If the candidate is ABSENT or has WITHDRAWN shade here ☐

Centre No.

Candidate No.

Examination Details

0	0	0	0
1	1	1	1
2	2	2	2
3	3	3	3
4	4	4	4
5	5	5	5
6	6	6	6
7	7	7	7
8	8	8	8
9	9	9	9

Candidate Answer Sheet CPE Paper 1 Reading

Instructions

Use a PENCIL (B or HB). Mark ONE letter only for each question.
For example, if you think B is the right answer,
mark your answer sheet like this:

0 | A | B | C | D

Rub out any answer you wish to change using an eraser.

Part 1

1 A B C D
2 A B C D
3 A B C D
4 A B C D
5 A B C D
6 A B C D
7 A B C D
8 A B C D
9 A B C D
10 A B C D
11 A B C D
12 A B C D
13 A B C D
14 A B C D
15 A B C D
16 A B C D
17 A B C D
18 A B C D

Part 2

19 A B C D
20 A B C D
21 A B C D
22 A B C D
23 A B C D
24 A B C D
25 A B C D
26 A B C D

Part 3

27 A B C D E F G H
28 A B C D E F G H
29 A B C D E F G H
30 A B C D E F G H
31 A B C D E F G H
32 A B C D E F G H
33 A B C D E F G H

Part 4

34 A B C D
35 A B C D
36 A B C D
37 A B C D
38 A B C D
39 A B C D
40 A B C D

CPE 1

DP479/346

142

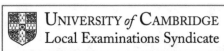
UNIVERSITY of CAMBRIDGE
Local Examinations Syndicate

SAMPLE

Candidate Name
If not already printed, write name
in CAPITALS and complete the
Candidate No. grid (in pencil).

Candidate Signature

Examination Title

Centre

Supervisor:
If the candidate is ABSENT or has WITHDRAWN shade here ▭

Centre No.

Candidate No.

Examination Details

0	0	0	0
1	1	1	1
2	2	2	2
3	3	3	3
4	4	4	4
5	5	5	5
6	6	6	6
7	7	7	7
8	8	8	8
9	9	9	9

Candidate Answer Sheet CPE Paper 4 Listening

Mark test version (in PENCIL) A B C **Special arrangements** S H

Instructions
Use a PENCIL (B or HB).
Rub out any answer you wish to change using an eraser.

For **Parts 1 and 3:**
Mark ONE letter only for each question.
For example, if you think B is the right answer,
mark your answer sheet like this:

0 | A | B | C

For **Part 2:**
Write your answer clearly in
the space like this:

0 | example

For **Part 4:**
Write ONE letter only, like this:

0 | A

Part 1
1	A	B	C
2	A	B	C
3	A	B	C
4	A	B	C
5	A	B	C
6	A	B	C
7	A	B	C
8	A	B	C

Part 2
		Do not write here
9		1 9 0
10		1 10 0
11		1 11 0
12		1 12 0
13		1 13 0
14		1 14 0
15		1 15 0
16		1 16 0
17		1 17 0

Part 3
18	A	B	C	D
19	A	B	C	D
20	A	B	C	D
21	A	B	C	D
22	A	B	C	D

Part 4
		Do not write here
23		1 23 0
24		1 24 0
25		1 25 0
26		1 26 0
27		1 27 0
28		1 28 0

CPE 4

DP440/349

Answer key

Abbreviations used in the key

adj = *adjective*   adv = *adverb*   colloc = *collocation*
conj = *conjunction*   dep prep = *dependent preposition*
fixed exp = *fixed expression*   for = *formal word or expression*
inf = *informal word or expression*   infin = *infinitive*   insep =
inseparable   no = *number*   p. = *page*   para. = *paragraph*
phr vb = *phrasal verb*   prep = *preposition*   prep phrase =
prepositional phrase   reflex = *reflexive*   rel pron = *relative
pronoun*   sb = *somebody*   sem prec = *semantic precision*
sep = *separable*   st = *something*   vb = *verb*   word comp
= *word complementation*

UNIT *1*

Language Focus: Vocabulary p.8

2

I   1   exam (*inf*); passed; take; examined on
    2   examined; for; detailed
    3   under (*being examined*)
    4   cross (*legal term*)

2   1b)   2c)   3a)   4d)

3

1 F (*scientific examination is normally uncountable*)
2 F (*not in fixed expressions and collocs like 'under
examination' or 'cross-examination'*)
3 T
4 F (*you examine sb* on *information they have learnt*)
5 F (*I've passed …*)
6 T

4

I **vast** majority   2 **do** well   3 information (*uncountable*)
4 meaning(s) **of**   5 pro**nun**ciation   6 insight **into**
7 confirm (*no prep is needed*)   8 **phonetic** transcriptions
9 make room for   10 **on** a regular basis

Language Focus: Grammar p.10

1

1 When the mistake **was discovered** yesterday, she
denied all knowledge of it.
2 By the time I finally **won** the lottery, I **had been playing**
it for thirty years.

3 Once she **had overcome** her initial reservations, she
actually **enjoyed** the concert.
4 By the time his latest novel **was published** last week,
tens of thousands of pounds **had been spent** on
promoting it.
5 She **didn't go** to bed until she **had checked** all the
safety catches on the windows.

2

When I **was** a little girl … **used to go/went** every New
Year (*repeated past action or routine*) … it **was** rumoured to
be haunted … it **had been** snowing heavily (*until that
point*) … all of us **were** sitting (*this was interrupted by the
crash*) … **had** galloped (*when it was finished*) … **had**
snapped (*before the moment we arrived*) … I **have never
been** so scared (*she was talking about all of her life, an
unfinished period of time*) …

Reading p.11

Always use a good **monolingual** *dictionary to help you check
your answers when practising Paper 1, Part 1. It will help you
identify precise meanings for words, as well as the collocations
and contexts they are typically used with.*

1

1C (*colloc*)   2A (*colloc*)   3D (*word comp*)   4B (*colloc*)
5B (*fixed exp*)   6D (*word comp*)   7A (*sem prec*)
8C (*sem prec*)   9B (*phr vb*)   10D (*word comp*)   11C (*idiom*)
12D (*fixed exp*)   13C (*idiom*)   14D (*colloc*)   15A (*phr vb*)
16D (*fixed exp*)   17A (*phr vb*)   18B (*idiom*)

2

keen interest, dense forests are examples of adj + noun
collocations; *clearly defined* is an adv + adj collocation;
exercises his right is a verb + noun collocation

Language Focus: Vocabulary p.12

1

2 b) *Sentence two is wrong because of word order. The position
of the object can vary with phrasal verbs, and a good dictionary
shows you this information. This verb appears as* keep sb on
(*not* keep on sb), *and this means the verb is separable:*
I'm afraid we can't afford to keep on you. ✗
I'm afraid we can't afford to keep you on. ✓

Always record whether a phrasal verb is separable or not when you make a note of it in your vocabulary notebook.

2

1 keep in with (*insep*) 2 Keep out of (*insep*) 3 keep to (*insep*) 4 kept them up (*sep*) 5 keep up (*sep*) 6 keeping back (*sep*)

Use of English p.12

*Make sure your **spelling** is correct, as you lose marks for such mistakes in this part of the exam.*

3

1 place 2 contrary 3 made 4 great 5 no 6 as 7 up
8 come 9 addition 10 would 11 which 12 of 13 all
14 part 15 did

Writing p.14

1

1 c) – a) *too general* b) *too specific* 2 c) – a) *too general*
b) *too specific* 3 a) – b) *too specific* c) *too general*

2   *Sample answers*

4 The government could do a lot more to improve the lives of the elderly. (*Note the critical tone of the paragraph.*)

5 The leisure centre has a wide range of facilities for the disabled. (*The paragraph goes on to examine these in detail, and has a very positive tone.*)

3

Change is a part of life … for the worse (*this is more appropriate to a discursive essay*)   I've always longed … approve of long hair (*this is not relevant to her sister*) … and there were plenty of those, I can tell you! (*this doesn't add anything to the description of the sister, and is a rather distracting detail*)

4

para. 1D   para. 2A   para. 3C   para. 4B   para. 5B

UNIT 2

Language Focus: Grammar p.16

1

1 If I **hadn't been so** nervous, I **would have written** much better in the exam.

2 If the weather **doesn't get** better/improve, we**'ll have to** cancel the school outing.

3 I wish they **would reconsider** their plans.

4 If I **hadn't had to** revise every night, I **wouldn't have been so** bad tempered throughout my exams.

5 I wish my car **would** start on cold mornings.

6 If we **hadn't received so much** money, we **wouldn't have been able to** build a new library.

7 If I **don't hear** from you, I**'ll continue** with my plans.

8 If I **hadn't had so much** work to do, I **might have been able to** go to the lecture.

3

1 1 was given 2 time he took 3 better answer the
4 if he'll/he will do 5 you didn't/did not shout 6 rather make 7 you kept 8 if we were

Use of English p.17

You may find it helpful to keep a separate 'word formation' section in your vocabulary notebook. Whatever you do, make sure you use a dictionary to make a note of related nouns, adjectives, verbs, etc. when you record new words.

2

1 upbringing 2 strikingly 3 formality 4 besieged
5 overcrowding 6 inability 7 disregarded 8 meaningless
9 boredom 10 requirement

Listening p.18

1

1 1B 2A 3D 4C

2 1 practically everything 2 contributions 3 easy
4 achievements

3 different register – sentence 1; different forms of words – sentences 1 and 4; different word order – sentences 1 and 4

2

1 translation 2 origins of the Nile 3 forty languages
4 extraordinary 5 systematic 6 long periods of time
7 abroad 8 play with local children 9 adolescence

Tapescript

My talk tonight will be the last in the current series of talks about famous artists, scientists and scholars in history. If a competition were to take place to decide on the person in recent history whose achievements at learning have been the most stunning, my vote would go to the nineteenth-century Englishman, Sir Richard Burton. It would be wrong to claim that his contributions to mankind are on a par with those of a Darwin or an Einstein, both of whom chose to concentrate their energies in particular directions, maximising the impact of their work. <u>But Burton's achievements were on a broader front.</u> <u>He excelled at practically everything.</u>

A list of Burton's feats gives at least a faint indication of the man's phenomenal powers. He is best known for his translation into English of sixteen volumes of the stories known as the Arabian Nights. He also translated large quantities of Portuguese literature, the folklore of many countries and Latin poetry. His own poems were published in two volumes. What is more, in an age of Victorian heroes, he was outstanding as an explorer and traveller. He journeyed in search of the origins of the Nile, and he made numerous dangerous expeditions of discovery in northern Africa and the Near East.

Perhaps the most impressive of all Burton's achievements, though, was his mastery, to a high level of proficiency, of no fewer than forty separate languages, plus a substantial number of related dialects.

<u>Is there any key that can help account for Burton's amazing achievements? I think motivation provides such a key, at least to his success at mastering foreign languages.</u>

<u>Burton did not hit upon any particular method or technique for language learning that might have made the task especially easy for him, or given him a special advantage.</u> He has left an interesting account of the methods and study habits he followed when he was learning a new language, and there certainly seems to have been nothing extraordinary about his techniques for studying. In fact, he reported that he did not find acquiring foreign languages at all easy, and he wrote with feeling about the difficult and time-consuming nature of the learning tasks he set for himself.

By all accounts, Burton was extremely systematic in his approach to learning unfamiliar languages and he went about the task with extraordinary persistence. Undoubtedly, it was this refusal to give up, together with his remarkable powers of energy and determination which really set Burton apart as a learner. He would spend long periods of time studying a new language, and he steadfastly refused to be put off. He worked and worked, and he kept at the task, persevering in the face of all the discouragement, boredom, frustration and fatigue that can wear down any normal student.

The young Richard Burton was a bright lad, although no infant prodigy. His early life reveals few hints of future intellectual excellence, but it's in his childhood that we find the key to the determination which made his efforts to learn so persistent, and eventually so successful. An unusual feature of his childhood is that it was mostly spent abroad. His father had a limited income and no paid profession, so it was financially necessary for the family to spend much of their time away from Britain, in various parts of continental Europe. So if the high-spirited Burton children wanted to play with local children of the same age, they had to learn the relevant language. Richard Burton, then, was repeatedly placed in a position in which the effort of learning a new language was amply justified and quickly rewarded.

By the time he reached adolescence he had gained

considerable language skills, in addition to a good deal of general experience in acquiring new languages.

Language-acquisition tasks that might have appeared dauntingly and excruciatingly tedious to others looked very different to Burton. He knew that he could succeed because he had reaped the rewards of his own efforts in the past.

In later life, Burton often said that …

Use of English p.19

1

3 The omitted information is either irrelevant to the summary question, or is repetitive, and does not add anything to the underlined parts of the text.

2

The student still needs to edit the summary to the correct length (30–40 words).

3

extremely important = vital; *spend their time only on things which are important* = prioritise; *things they need to do by certain times* = deadlines; *which are organised and cover all points* = thorough; *preparing for exams* = revising

Sample answer
It is vital for students to prioritise, making lists of deadlines. They should also develop effective reading habits and keep thorough notes. Finally, when revising, it is essential for students to leave themselves enough time.   (*35 words*)

4

2 1 relentless diet 2 they reward success 3 he is highly skilled/competent 4 they are successfully used to teach pre-school children reading and writing

5

The key words in the summary task are 'educational benefits' (*not problems, or other types of benefits*) and 'mentioned in the texts' (*this reminds you to look only in the text, and not to add your own opinions about the topic*).

6

The information mentioned here also appears in the first text, so it does not form a separate point.

7

1 concentration and memory 2 attitude to school work; them to 3 differently/in parallel; quickly and effectively 4 pre-school children; to read and write/reading and writing skills

8

Sample answer

Computer games may increase children's powers of concentration and memory. They may also have a positive effect on children's school work by encouraging them to look for greater challenges when they complete tasks successfully. It is believed by some that game players think differently and learn to deal with problems more quickly and effectively. Finally, computer games can even be used by pre-school children to learn to read and write.   (*70 words*)

Writing p.22

1

1 The writing task asks you to discuss the points raised in the letter <u>and</u> to express your own views. (You don't have to agree with the writer!) The essay should discuss the value of educating children at home (instead of at school).
  The three points you need to respond to are:
- children need the company of their peers …
- the personal attention and support … can only be positive (*2 points*)

2

Introduction – family relationships/effect of TV responsible for low standards
1st supporting para. – school buildings often in bad condition
2nd supporting para. – important for tutors to be reliable/trustworthy
3rd supporting para. – need to be given time to relax from studies
Closing para. – the education laws should be changed in many countries

3

1 **large numbers of** children … (*replaces* many);   2 **it would seem that** educating … (*replaces* we can say that); 3 **it is a sad fact that** many children … (*replaces* it is well known that);   4 **an increasing number of** parents … (*replaces* many more);   5 **it is important to point out that** children … (*replaces* we must say that)

4

1 This essay covers the points raised in the letter very effectively.   2 The essay is 'balanced'.   3 Method C has been used – generally speaking, the details are mentioned in order of emphasis.

Statement of topic – Perhaps another option … should be for parents to be able to educate their children at home if they wish to do so.

Topic sentence (1st supporting para.) – The first … the emotional support that they would receive at home from their parents and tutors.
Topic sentence (2nd supporting para.) – Educating children at home … particular needs and abilities.
Topic sentence (3rd supporting para.) – However … children might suffer in their personal and social development if they were educated only at home.
Summing up phrase – In conclusion …

UNIT *3*

Language Focus: Grammar p.24

1

1 At no time **did it seem** …   2 Only **when/after** our visas had been double-checked **were we allowed** … 3 Under no circumstances **are you to visit** …   4 Never before **has television played** …   5 Seldom **do you come** across …   6 **Had he not been** listening to the radio … (Hadn't he been *is incorrect*)   7 No sooner **had we sat** down **than** … (*but we say* hardly … when) 8 Never again **will I work** …   9 Little **did she realise** what was …   10 So well **does he act** that …   11 Not for another six months **did Sally meet** …   12 Rarely **does he <u>do</u>** his fair share of the work.

2

1 anyone had   2 did he congratulate   3 account are 4 having read   5 pleased/impressed were they   6 the worst   7 could he be   8 have we been/gone   9 few people   10 only did he leave

Language Focus: Vocabulary p.25

1 She didn't want to leave the room **for fear of** missing …
2 What I am telling you is **in confidence**.
3 We must avoid a scandal **at all costs**.
4 **To the best of my knowledge**, she is still …
5 I wanted to find a new job because **I was in (a bit of) a rut**.
6 They **are not on good terms with** their neighbours.
7 I had something particular **in mind**.
8 There's **no question of our selling** this painting./It would be **out of the question for us** to sell this painting.
9 Mr Smith said a few words at the board meeting **on behalf of** the older employees.
10 The book you want is **out of print**, so it may …

Reading p.26

1

d) romantic or e) detective

2 and 3

The parts of the text which give you the answers are included here to help you.

1B (… *in whether the employer would satisfy hers*)
2D (… *regarded a secretary as a status symbol*) 3C (… *was convenient both for the City and for the towering offices of Docklands. Neither had so far produced much in the way of business*) 4C (… *while other agencies foundered in the waves of recession, Mrs Creasley's small … ship was still … afloat*)
5D (*It was probably the cosy which kept Mandy faithful to the agency … [it] represented all Mandy had ever known of the comfort and security of home*) 6B (… *in acrimonious camaraderie … the main cause of dispute being*) 7C (this is not directly stated, but is implied by the embarrassment she felt about her feelings about the cosy, and the general picture we get of Mandy as an apparently tough character)

4

a) 4 b) 1 and 6 c) 3 and 5 d) 2 and 7

Language Focus: Grammar p.28

1

1b) 2a) 3c) 4c) 5d) 6a) 7b) 8c) 9e) 10c)

2

2

Sitting under a palm tree, **sipping** his cocktail, Tom Sloane kept his eye on the exceptionally fat man who was moving ponderously towards him. Something about him was not quite right. Maybe it was the slightly insane grin which made him feel uneasy. **Not having brought** his gun with him to the beach, Sloane naturally felt vulnerable. He wondered what he should do. **Putting** his glass down, he stood up and strolled towards the man, **whistling** nonchalantly as he went. **Even though exhausted** from his previous mission, he understood that a moment's carelessness could cost him his life. **Having been attacked** by a knife-wielding nun the previous week, Sloane was ready for anything. Especially a fat man wearing a black bowler hat – the steel hat! Why hadn't he noticed it before? **Seeing** the man reach for the weapon on his head, Sloane dived for cover. Zzzzzz! The steel hat just missed him, **burying** itself in the sand beside him. **Unperturbed**, the fat man continued to grin at Sloane. 'Good afternoon, Mr Sloane. How nice to see you,' he muttered, **clenching** his teeth.

Listening p.29

1

1c) 2e) 3a) 4b) 5f) 6d)

2

1A (… *TV journalism is very superficial … you don't get the detail or objectivity …*) 2C (… *I actually found it quite daunting … just the sheer quantity of information available*) 3A (… *cinemas also employed … pianists*) 4B (… *this never ceases to amaze me – it took film studios years before they were willing to embrace the new technology*) 5C (The speaker mentions the woman immediately after describing withdrawal symptoms) 6A (… *there are professional people who have found Captain Picard's dedication … a shining example*) 7C (*The odds* **seem** *to favour Vanessa O'Connor, although it* **may** *be that Jenny Jarvis … pulls it off*) 8B (… *the resounding success of … took even the most vocal advocates of his work by surprise*)

Tapescript

1

If we were to examine the causes of the decline of industry in the area, we would have to admit that they sprang from the unwillingness of the government to implement …

I'm not sure I go along with you on that … um … up to a point, maybe … but don't you think that there's been too much bickering about what should or should not be …

It always seemed to me, when I was a young man, that life in the city was far, far superior – much more sophisticated and glamorous somehow – than life in a small village in that backwater of Britain could ever …

If you look at these figures carefully, and compare them with the ones in front of you, I'm sure you'll agree that the new approach to marketing will …

The atmosphere here today is quite incredible … thousands … literally thousands of people have come to see what's going to happen tonight … I can see the organisers of the event making their way towards the …

I don't know that I'd put it quite that way … what you seem to be implying in your question is that we had little idea of how things would change when …

2

Extract One

A: *Well, let's get back to television. Do you* **honestly** *think there's such a difference between television and newspaper coverage of current events? Most people would say that television is the easiest* **and** *the best way of learning about what's going on in the world.*

B: The easiest, certainly. But most TV journalism is very superficial these days, isn't it? You know, the news has to **fit** between the commercials … so you don't get the detail or objectivity that you do, say, in a good newspaper.

A: I don't know. How can you be sure, anyway, that all that detail you talk about is unbiased?

B: You can't, I suppose. Which is why I always use the Internet as well when I want to find out what's **really** going on. I was using it yesterday to find out about that hurricane in Florida. I actually found it quite daunting … just the sheer quantity of information available … you don't know where to start.

A: Tell me about it! Perhaps you should just do what millions of other people do … and just watch the news in the evening on TV.

Extract Two

The real breakthrough came with the release of The Jazz Singer in 1927. Before this time, cinemas employed a variety of methods for adding sound to silent films, the earliest of which involved the placing of actors, musicians and noise-making machines directly behind the screen. I find it interesting that this practice was employed even as late as 1915 in special road-show presentations of The Birth of a Nation.

As I'm sure you all know, cinemas also employed improvising pianists … though you may not be aware that on occasion the more prestigious productions in the 1920s had the benefit of orchestral accompaniment. Film-makers like Charlie Chaplin even went so far as to compose their own orchestral scores for the films they made.

Live music, of course, often tended to be unreliable. This fact, coupled with developments in radio and electronic research, led to successful experiments at the beginning of the twentieth century in 'photographing' sound directly onto film. But – and this never ceases to amaze me – it took film studios years before they were willing to embrace the new technology.

Extract Three

I: Dr Wolfson, would you like to expand on what you've intriguingly termed 'Star Trek addiction'?

DR W: Yes, of course. My research has shown – quite simply – that an amazing five to ten per cent of Star Trek fans are so obsessed with the series that they show symptoms of addiction similar to users of hard drugs. For example, missing an episode will frequently result in what can only be described as withdrawal symptoms. You know – feelings of agitation … anger … frustration … depression … One woman I interviewed talked about how her holidays had been ruined because she couldn't stop worrying about whether she'd set her video recorder properly.

And many people … well, it's not uncommon for fans to spend hundreds – even thousands of pounds – on Star Trek merchandise.

I: So Star Trek fans beware?

DR W: Well, having said all that … Trek addiction does actually have its good points. It gets people talking to each other about a number of serious issues – issues such as racism and prejudice – and … um … there are professional people who have found Captain Picard's dedication and passion a shining example for their own careers. So it's not all bad, by any means.

Extract Four

Well, the atmosphere certainly is electric at tonight's ceremony. Rumours are rife as to who will finally walk away with that coveted Best Actress of the Year award. The odds **seem** to favour Vanessa O'Connor … although it may just be that Jenny Jarvis – still a relatively unknown quantity – pulls it off for her stunning performance in Beyond the Horizon, a movie which stirred up so much controversy at the beginning of the year. That the director of the film, Mike Winterley, will receive the award for Best Director would seem to most here tonight to be a foregone conclusion. Winterley, at 45, has already made a name for himself with a run of recent box office hits, but the resounding success of Beyond the Horizon took even the most vocal advocates of his work by surprise. The film, starring 17-year-old Jarvis as a bored but ambitious teenager, fatally attracted to the dazzle of the pop music world, has been cited by many critics as being as masterly and as penetrating in its insights into human nature as anything produced by the truly great directors of the century.

Writing p.30

1

Always read the instructions you are given carefully. In this task you have to describe the closure of the cinema **and** discuss the reasons **and** express your own views about changes in entertainment.
The reasons for the closure of the cinema:
rising prices; improved TV/video technology; smaller audiences. (Planners who want to turn the building into luxury flats is also relevant, though probably not a reason for closure.)

2

Para. 2: reactions/feelings of manager
Para. 4: views of manager about technological changes; manager powerless to bring down prices – why?

3

Direct speech makes more of an impact on the reader; it brings the news report alive. (In a similar way, news reports on TV usually include brief interviews with eye-witnesses or the people directly involved.)

4

'It really is awful …,' Mr Smythe **sighs**; 'It's progress of a sort, I suppose,' he **concedes**; 'People say I should cut prices,' Mr Smythe **smiles** (*notice the exclamation mark at the end of the sentence*)

UNIT *4*

Language Focus: Grammar p.32

1 the   2 it   3 these (*refers to the* factors *of the previous sentence*)   4 a   5 that (*meaning* the one)   6 might/could/may (*the gap is followed by a bare infinitive, suggesting a modal verb*)   7 there   8 a   9 It   10 this   11 it   12 It   13 play (*colloc with* role)   14 those (*meaning* the ones)   15 this

Use of English p.33

2

1   1 The **cost of petrol is very high** these days. (*You need to use the adjective* high *to collocate with* cost.)
   2 Over the past year there **has been a considerable increase in** the number of house buyers. (*The adverb* considerably *changes to an adjective, and the verb* rise *changes to the noun* increase, *plus its correct dep prep.*)
   3 The discovery of the theft **led to Mike's immediate** dismissal. (*As well as supplying the correct dep prep for the verb* lead, *you need to change the adverb* immediately *to its adjective form.*)
   4 We **were unaware of what had happened until** after the accident. (*The transformation of* only + when/only + after *to* not/negative form + until *is very common in the CPE.*)
   5 Alex **is suspected of having caused** the problem. (*Here the passive structure* is suspected *needs to be used, plus the correct dep prep.*)

2   1 I think you **should keep out of** this argument.
   2 Would it **put you out if I brought** a friend with me to dinner? (*Here you need to use a second conditional, as well as the correct phr vb.*)
   3 I **am baffled by his unwillingness** to tell us the truth.
   4 She **can be relied on to help** at the shop. (*Notice that a modal verb and a passive are necessary here, as the supplied form of* rely *is the past participle.*)
   5 The manager's **inefficiency contributed to the failure** of the enterprise. (*It is necessary to change both the form of the adjective* inefficient *and the verb* fail, *to fit the new sentence.*)

3   1 Mark's brother decided **on the spur of the moment to take** the bus home.
   2 I **have set my heart on** an exotic foreign holiday. (*This expression normally appears in the present/past perfect tense.*)
   3 Sandra **didn't get a wink of sleep/didn't sleep a wink** last night.
   4 The mistake only **came to light when we** counted the money.
   5 I don't mind lending you money but I **draw the line at paying for** a new car.

4   1 I don't **spend nearly as much on groceries as** she does.
   2 There **is hardly any difference between** these two brands of ketchup.
   3 Her **(desperate) craving for popularity is something** I really can't understand.
   4 Over the past ten years this **shop has doubled its** turnover.
   5 No **sooner had the match started than** a fight broke out.
   6 She only had your **safety at heart when** she asked you to leave.
   7 It was **virtually impossible (for him) to understand** what they were saying.
   8 When we returned to the shop **there was no sign of the** manager.
   9 Heather didn't **take up ballroom dancing until** she was eighteen.
   10 George has **been out of work/out of a job for** six months.
   11 Unless we **run out of fuel** we'll be fine.
   12 Can you **keep an/your eye on my children while** I'm away?

3

☑ *Watch out for this **checklist sign** after exercises. These questions about the exercise are designed to help you to notice **what each particular task is really testing**, to be aware of typical mistakes, and to **learn from your own errors** throughout your course. Keep a record of your mistakes in a separate place in your notebook, and refer to it regularly, to help you to improve your performance in the same type of task in the future.*

Listening p.35

2

1 cool   2 luxury   3 expensive fashions   4 carelessly
5 race track   6 designer label   7 changing room   8 flatter
9 smells

Tapescript

I: In America and in many parts of Europe big fashion stores are employing psychologists to help them boost their profits. Sandra Adams reports on how the modern clothes shop may have more tricks in store for us than we might have imagined.

SA: If you're lucky – or perhaps unlucky enough – to have such a shop near you, many of the things I'm going to say will already be familiar to you. You'll know – perhaps from experience – that every little thing in a shop like this is thought out in minute detail to coax the money out of your pocket.

On entering, for example, you – the unsuspecting customer, that is – are met by a blast of cool air. This relaxes you and refreshes you, of course, and puts you in the right frame of mind from the very start. You'll also notice that there's a large open space in front of you, with absolutely no clutter anywhere. This gives you a corresponding sense of luxury. The fewer the garments on display here the better, as far as the retailer is concerned.

From there, you turn right. 'The Invariant Right', researchers call it … because most of us do it instinctively. You usually find three things when you do this. You find the best and most expensive fashions here … also a casually-dressed assistant who smiles and greets you … asks how you are … and then you see the tables. On these tables are fashion's latest must-haves. Skirts and blouses are displayed carelessly – thrown about even – so that you the customer don't feel bad about opening them up and holding them up for closer examination. All at buy-now prices of course.

Angled tables coax you further into the shop and mirrors in the aisles keep you moving along a pre-determined route – rather like a race track in fact … although, of course, you're taking your time … and probably picking up accessories as you go. Towards the back of the shop are what retailers call Fashion Black Spots. The shop tries to draw you into these areas. One trick is to have clothes at bargain prices displayed here … 'everything in the basket less than £10' or something similar. The fact that there may be some items with a designer label buried at the bottom of the pile makes all that rummaging around seem worthwhile. If you can't find anything, never mind. You can go on up the escalator. These are also placed at the back of the shop … and people can't resist them!

When you want to buy something – I say 'when' and not 'if' – you need to try it on first, so you look for a changing room. These are traditionally a place of torture for many women as they see just how bad their bodies look in this season's clothes … but it's not like that here.

The mirrors are now tinted to make you look tanned … and slimmer. You'll also find that there's make-up available … and of course sales staff – or 'style consultants' as they are known in America – to flatter you and say how wonderful you look in that dress you've just tried on.

Everything … and I mean everything … works against you. As you would expect, clever use is made of colour throughout the store. Orange, yellow, red or purple are widely believed to make people feel more positive and self-confident. Like me, though, you might be taken aback to learn that many retailers make use of particular smells to ward off tiredness in their customers. Artificial coffee, citrus or lavender smells are circulated in the store – in the air-conditioning perhaps – to keep you awake … and spending.

So … when all is said and done … it is money – and making lots of it – that is the motivating factor behind everything in a shop like this. It is the future of fashion retailing. A sad reflection on society, perhaps, but people nowadays are set on being stylish … and prepared to pay through the nose for the right 'look'.

I: That report was by Sandra Adams.

Language Focus: Grammar p.36

1 It **isn't necessary for anyone to work** during the …
2 I found <u>it</u> rather **strange that she was reluctant to** … 3 It looked **as if the burglar <u>had</u> broken in** …
4 It doesn't **interest me whether you succeed or** fail.
5 I'll leave <u>it</u> **up to you to decide** what time you …
6 It's **surprising how/so many people** still believe whatever … 7 There **seems to be no point in <u>your</u> continuing** to write to him … 8 Didn't it **occur to you that he might not be telling** … 9 I have **no intention of commenting** on the recent decision.
10 The claims of the advertisement **can easily be shown not to be** true.

Language Focus: Vocabulary p.36

Phrasal verbs and expressions: set

1

1 set off 2 set off 3 set up 4 set off 5 set up 6 setting up 7 set up 8 set off

2

Expressions with set *tend to be quite emphatic in tone.*
1 I've never **set eyes on** him (before). 2 'Never (again) will I **set foot in** this house!' she screamed. 3 She's **set her heart on** winning … 4 He's too **set in his ways** to cope … 5 When I go to a restaurant I **set great store by** the attentiveness …

Connectors and adverbial phrases

1

1 While/Even though (despite *is a prep, and can only be followed by a noun or participle clause, not a full clause*) 2 thus/consequently 3 Furthermore (also *would appear between the subject* they *and the verb* shake; besides *is rather too informal for this context, and is usually used to add reasons for a particular course of action*) 4 Due to/Owing to (since *would need to be followed by a full clause*) 5 As a matter of fact/Actually 6 Or rather/At least

2

1 extent/degree 2 words 3 though (*notice the two commas*) 4 with 5 bounds 6 longer (*this comes before an inversion*) 7 By 8 more 9 example/instance 10 come (*phr vb*) 11 having 12 result/consequence 13 some 14 What 15 despite

Writing p.38

1

The letter is being written to the manager of a restaurant by a customer who was very dissatisfied with the standard of the food and service on a recent visit.

2

1f) 2b) 3a) 4g) 5d) 6e) 7c)

3

Answers provided in the letter on p.39.

5

1A (*at the same time*) 2B (*immediately after he had returned*) 3A (*adding a further complaint*) 4C 5C

UNIT 5

Language Focus: Grammar p.40

1

1 could you have (*you can't shorten this to* could you've) 2 should've had more 3 can't/couldn't have 4 didn't have/need to 5 must've 6 they might/may not (couldn't *is incorrect here*)

2

1 Although he **should have telephoned yesterday he didn't get** round to it.
2 Registration **with the police is obligatory for anyone/everyone** who stays …

3 You **could have had** him **arrested for such** bad behaviour.
4 You **might have told me to call** off the meeting.
5 Given the staff's lack of interest, she **needn't have bothered trying to find** a solution …
6 The robber **didn't need to use force because** the cashier …

Reading p.41

1

1 *incarceration* = imprisonment 2 *desolation* = a feeling of loneliness and sadness 3 *stem the flow* = stop the spread/development/continuation of st (*here, negative emotions*) 4 *take stock of* = think carefully about a situation/events, in order to decide what to do next 5 *pariah* = sb who is hated and avoided by others

2

1B 2B 3D 4C 5A 6C 7D 8B

Use of English p.44

1

2 develop

2

1 nature 2 gather 3 demonstrate 4 dense 5 stamped 6 point

Use of English p.45

1

1 disagreeable 2 improbability 3 dissatisfied 4 irreversible 5 unused 6 thoughtlessness 7 disloyalty 8 incurable

2

1 ensure 2 underlies 3 inheritance 4 disuse 5 survival 6 contradictory 7 concept 8 increasingly 9 influential 10 acknowledge

Writing p.46

1

You have to imagine that you are the leader of a team of social workers, and that you are writing a formal proposal for a project designed to encourage young offenders not to reoffend. You need to mention:
• the main features of the project
• <u>how</u> the young people would benefit
• how they would be monitored.

2

The answer is provided in Exercise 4.

3

the most effective way … (*replaces* a good) **be made fully aware of** the consequences … (*replaces* see) **humiliating and often violent** conditions … (*replaces* awful) **former inmates** … (*replaces* people who have been in prison) **monitored closely** by a social worker … (*replaces* checked)

4

1b) 2d) 3a) 4e)

UNIT 6

Language Focus: Grammar p.48

1

1 The best architect **will be presented with a prize by** the mayor.
2 This year an **increased number of drivers have been arrested** for speeding.
3 The cliff face in this area **is gradually being worn away by** the sea.
4 A **total ban on smoking takes effect** from next month.
5 You **could be arrested for refusing to obey** local laws …
6 My brother **was made to fill** in all …
7 The project was **(due/supposed) to be/have been completed** last month.
8 The housing problem **needs to be solved/needs a solution as quickly** as possible.

2

1 was blown 2 will have been made 3 (should) be made
4 is being looked 5 has been added 6 is included

Listening p.49

1

1 Agree (*I think … it's about time the council spent a bit of money doing them up* / **I wouldn't argue with you on that.** *It does seem …*)
2 Disagree (*it's … a real eye-sore, amateurish in every sense of the word* / **I wouldn't go along with you** *on consigning it to the scrap heap …*)
3 Agree (*The woman begins by saying that she thinks it is good, then agrees with the man that there may be problems*

– *he says he has 'mixed feelings'. The woman* **signals agreement by continuing the man's sentence**.)
4 Disagree (*I'd give it a five-star rating anytime* / *I guess it depends on whether … The second speaker uses the turn of phrase* fork out quite a lot of money – *this is negative – and then* for the privilege of having your own room – *she is obviously being sarcastic*.)

2

1 A (*You may have been confused when Sally says* it's not that people don't want to use them, it's just that … *Sentences like this are quite common in spoken English*)
2 B (*Sally agrees by saying* That goes without saying …)
3 A (*Alan uses the word* dearth, *which means* a lack of st)
4 S 5 B (*Sally uses the idiom* it'll be the last straw …, *which means* the last problem in a series of problems that finally makes you give up or lose your temper) 6 B

Tapescript

1

Extract One

A: *I think it's a real shame that so many buildings in the town have just been allowed to fall down … they're in a terrible state. You know, it's about time the council spent a bit of money on doing them up, instead of just knocking them down, one after another and building office blocks or whatever in their place …*

B: *Mm, I wouldn't argue with you on that. It does seem rather short-sighted, doesn't it? I mean … when you look at the history of some of those buildings …*

Extract Two

A: *Well, I just couldn't believe my eyes when I saw what they'd built … you know … it's … a real eye-sore … amateurish in every sense of the word … and to think they put it slap bang in front of the National Museum. It's some kind of enormous, I don't know, an enormous pyramid, I suppose …*

B: *Yeah, I've seen it. It represents one of the pyramids in Egypt … or that's what I read anyway … and I wouldn't go along with you on consigning it to the scrap heap so easily, you know. The sculptor is quite a celebrity it seems. She is believed to have …*

Extract Three

A: *I think the new road system within the town should please a lot of the locals. It's so much better than how it used to be … don't you agree?*

B: *Well … I've mixed feelings about it, to be quite honest. Yes, on the one hand, um, it will benefit motorists … in that it's a lot easier to be more efficient, as it were, than the previous system … but I think that the new markings on the road …*

A: ... are likely to confuse motorists. Mmm, I must admit I wondered about that myself. It will be easier for them to take a wrong turning, won't it?

Extract Four

A: I was really sold on that hotel we stayed in – the Green Dragon ... or Golden Dragon ... I can't remember now. I think you stayed there as well, didn't you? I'd give it a five-star rating anytime ... brilliant service ... friendly staff ... good food ... what else do you want?

B: I guess it depends on whether you're a couple ... or a family. If you're a single person, you have to fork out quite a lot of money – over and above what other people pay – for the privilege of having your own room. One of these hidden charges that you learn about later and then ...

2

A: Yeah, well, pedestrianising the centre of town is one way of solving the traffic problem, I suppose ... it seems to be getting worse all the time, doesn't it? It's not really the lorries ... the passing traffic that's to blame – although it can get pretty awful at times – it's all the local traffic as well. People have just got lazy ... they'll take the car rather than, you know, even for the shortest journey they'll hop in the car and off they go. They could easily take the bus or something.

S: Yeah, though the fact of the matter is that people have almost forgotten what buses look like, haven't they? There've been so many cutbacks recently. It's not that people don't **want** to use the bus service, it's just that it's become so unreliable, I think.

A: Well, at least now the council's doing **something** to improve the life of this town. You must give them their due.

S: Mmm, I suppose so. But I'm sure they won't feel the need to do much more than they're already planning to do. They certainly don't see the buses – or rather the lack of them – as a problem ...

A: I don't know. I think we should give them the benefit of the doubt. They'll probably come up with some bright idea for a tram or something. Anyway, they'll have to do something about all the traffic which is going to be diverted ... build a bypass or something.

S: That goes without saying. The roads which already go round the town are too narrow and unsuitable for heavy traffic ... there'd be absolute chaos. That wouldn't go down very well with that green, we-really-care-for-the-environment image they're always trying to project, would it?

A: You're such a cynic! This place'll be much more attractive, I think. There's such a **dearth** of anything green in the centre at the moment ... a few trees will be nice.

They're also going to put up a few statues here and there, I hear ...

S: Mmm, commissioning local artists to make them. Yes, I heard that too. I must admit, it all sounds pretty impressive. What with all their proposals to do up those run-down houses in the centre as well ... You certainly can't accuse them of lacking in ideas, I'll say that for them. I only hope they haven't bitten off more than they can chew, that's all ... they're planning to do so **many** things.

A: No ... they must know what they're doing. Although, my dad doesn't agree with any of it. Says that pedestrianising the centre will put loads of little shops out of business. The more I think about it, the more I think he's got a point.

S: It'll be the last straw for lots of those people, I think. They've already been hit by those new taxes which were introduced a couple of years ago. Plus the recession. Now they'll lose out on all the passing trade that's probably kept them going for so long ...

A: Right. Makes you wonder, doesn't it? And then there'll be all the hassle ... what with all those bulldozers ... and digging up the streets ...

S: And the noise – the road drills, lorries, buildings being knocked down, everything covered in concrete ... It doesn't bear thinking about really. I don't know, I really am in two minds about the whole thing. Like you, I can see the benefits to the town, but ... well, I suppose I've just grown a bit cynical of late.

A: You're not the only one, I can tell you. Still, I can't believe that this present council won't ...

Use of English p.50

2

1 That rich and poor people often live very close to each other. 2 Pioneers are people who go to settle in an unknown region or county; the expression 'urban pioneers' conveys the idea that people with vision and courage are needed to go and live in these areas. 3 Planners had not taken into account the wishes of local people. 4 Making / Creating an attractive, integrated urban environment / a lively, flourishing city.

3 *Sample answer*

It is important to encourage people to take advantage of low property prices in the poor and run-down neighbourhoods surrounding many city centres. Both rich and poor should be encouraged to live in the inner city, and planners should take into account the desires and needs of the residents. Finally, it is essential for individuals and groups to agree to work together.   (*62 words*)

Language Focus: Vocabulary p.52

1

1 He might have **made up** that story so that we would …
2 The lecturer told us that atoms were **made up of** even smaller particles.   3 … and **made off with** my wallet.
4 They **made out** that the money was being collected for charity.   5 What do you **make of** the new mayor?
6 Due to the fog, we couldn't **make out** any of the signposts.

2

1 How can I **make amends** for forgetting …   2 You are **making heavy weather of** …   3 I can't **make sense of** these …   4 I can't **make up my mind** where …

Language Focus: Grammar p.53

1

1 whom   2 living (*fixed exp*) 3 answer/solution (*fixed exp*)
4 among (*several facilities are mentioned*)   5 majority (*colloc*)
6 themselves (*reflex vb*)   7 number (*fixed exp*)   8 both (*two problems are mentioned*)   9 to/for (*notice that the rel pron. is* whom)   10 but (*this often appears with* nonetheless, *between two dashes or commas*)   11 times   12 upon (*fixed exp*)   13 little/scant   14 but (*fixed exp*)   15 longer

2

1 People **working** in large cities often long to escape from the 'rat race'. (*Although it is impossible to omit just the rel pron, because it is the subject of the rel clause, you can replace the rel clause with a participle clause.*)
2 Most houses **built** more than a hundred years ago have problems with damp. (*As 1. Here, the participle is a past one, which has a passive meaning.*)
3 The tram starts from the castle, the oldest surviving building in the town. (*The rel clause can be omitted altogether with no loss of meaning.*)
4 The house I lived in as a child has just been knocked down. (*This is a defining rel clause, and the rel pronoun is* **not** *the subject of the rel clause. The pronoun can therefore be omitted.*)
5 The City Council, **well known** for its radical ideas, recently developed this dock area. (*As 3.*)
6 Visitors **caught** taking photographs inside the church are usually asked to leave. (*As 2.*)
7 The mosaic was discovered by workmen digging in the street. (*As 1.*)
8 The square is surrounded by old buildings, now on the verge of collapse. (*As 3.*)
9 The river **flowing** through the town centre is liable to flood in winter. (*As 1.*)
10 The man I have been talking to used to live in this neighbourhood. (*As 4.*)

Writing p.54

1

1a)   2c)   3c)   4a)   5b)   6a)   7a)   8b)   9c)   10c)

2

1 His behaviour can at **best be described as unhelpful**.
2 I would **like to express my disagreement with** …
3 We should be making **every effort to prevent** …
4 That restaurant is a **favourite/popular destination for** …
5 I strongly **believe that their proposal is not as beneficial as** they pretend.
6 I regret that **I am / shall be unable to see** …

3

2   1 I would like to express my disagreement
2 are unable to   3 can at best be described as impersonal   4 a favourite/popular weekend destination for local people   5 making every effort   6 as beneficial

UNIT 7

Language Focus: Grammar p.56

1

1 If you **had gone** on the expedition, you **might have been killed**.   2 The disaster **could have been avoided** if the government **had taken more** action.   3 Had **more people listened** to the warnings of the ecologists, some species of animals **could have been saved**.   4 Should I **be prevented from** entering the USA, I'll have to reconsider my options.   5 Were I **(to be) made to take** the exams again, I **would** probably stop doing the course.
6 Had the Minister of Agriculture **ignored** the advice of so-called 'experts', large tracts of farmland **might still be** productive.

2

1 as long   2 unless the   3 must/have to take
4 can't you tell   5 think about/consider   6 we are to find

Reading p.57

1

para. 2C   para. 3E   para. 4A   para. 5D   para. 6B
para. 7F

3

1C 2F 3A 4B 5G 6E 7D

Language Focus: Vocabulary p.60

Dependent prepositions and prepositional phrases

1 with 2 to 3 for 4 in 5 at 6 under 7 on/upon
8 to 9 inside 10 in 11 as 12 to 13 with 14 with
15 on 16 at 17 on 18 in 19 in 20 in

Phrasal verbs and expressions: *run*

1

1 I **ran into** someone I …   2 She said we would soon **run out of** … / were **running out of** …   3 While he was at college he **ran into** debt.   4 The government's proposal **ran into** a lot of …   5 An old woman **was run over by** a car today.   6 I object to **being run down** by my colleagues.   7 Don't let your imagination **run away with** you.   8 Would you mind if I **ran through** what you have to do again?

2

1 … eat those mushrooms, you **run the risk** of being …
2 … as we are careful we **won't run short** of …
3 My **blood ran cold** when I heard …   4 … **run of the mill** …

Listening p.61

1

1 B
2 1D (*there is no mention of* climate *in the extract*) 2C (*the word* asteroids *is used in the extract, but the meaning is different from what the statement says*) 3A (*this information is correct, but it is not the answer to the question*)

2

1D (*calculations of the timings of nearby neutron star collapses … just like mass extinctions …*) 2C (*the muons have enough energy to irradiate and kill almost every living thing …*) 3B (*Muon radiation can be fatal even hundreds of metres underwater / a lethal burst of atmospheric muons would explain the massive extinctions deep underwater*) 4D (*insects can … tolerate up to 20 times the radiation dose that kills …*) 5D (*It's rather unsettling, but until we see them, we can't know when they will merge*)

Tapescript

1

AD: *Geological records, as you may know, show there have been five major mass extinctions in the past 500 million years. Scientists believe the most recent one – which wiped out the dinosaurs 64 million years ago – was caused by the impact of a meteorite. Some 300,000 tons of the element iridium was laid down in the Earth's crust at this time, and high levels of iridium have also been found in asteroids. What caused all the other extinctions, however, is still an open question.*

2

I: *As if you didn't have enough to worry about already, it turns out we're 100 million years overdue for a mass extinction. The apocalypse could happen at any time. At least – that is – if you accept the theories of Arnon Dar, a space physicist at the Israel Institute of Technology. Arnon, can you tell us a little more about the findings of your research?*

AD: *Yes, of course. Geological records, as you may know, show there have been **five** major mass extinctions in the past 500 million years. Scientists believe the most recent one – which wiped out the dinosaurs 64 million years ago – was caused by the impact of a meteorite. Some 300,000 tons of the element iridium was laid down in the Earth's crust at this time, and high levels of iridium have also been found in asteroids. What caused all the **other** extinctions, however, is still an open question. Um …*

I: *Yes, but haven't scientists suggested that volcanic eruptions were to blame?*

AD: *Yes, they have, and they've also suggested that supernova explosions were the cause. However, it turns out that there is **no** geological evidence for coincident volcanic activity … and supernova explosions don't occur close enough at a sufficiently high rate. My theory is that collapsing neutron stars were the cause. Um … calculations of the timings of nearby neutron star collapses show that – just like mass extinctions on Earth – they seem to occur about once every 100 million years. Um … unfortunately … unfortunately for us, that is … the evidence suggests that the **last** one probably happened 200 million years ago.*

I: *I see. Why are collapsing neutron stars so dangerous though?*

AD: *Well, when a pair of neutron stars collapse, cosmic rays are produced and become a very serious threat. I and my colleagues have been studying the likely effects of jets of cosmic rays flung out by neutron star collapses for several years now, um, and … on entering the Earth's atmosphere … the cosmic rays create showers* *of lethal high-energy subatomic particles known as muons. As …*

I: *I'm sorry. The cosmic rays create particles – smaller than atoms – called **muons**, did you say?*

AD: *Yes, yes … that's right. Muons. As cosmic ray jets rain down on the Earth, the muons have enough energy to irradiate and kill almost every living thing in their way. Um, they would also destroy the ozone layer, irradiate the environment, and damage vegetation.*

I: *So muons are extremely dangerous?*

AD: *Yes, extremely dangerous. Muon radiation can be fatal even hundreds of metres underwater … or underground. So a lethal burst of atmospheric muons would explain the massive extinctions deep underwater. The fossil record's reported extinction of marine life – as well as continental life – begins to make sense.*

I: *Mmm. And I also believe, Arnon, that you can explain other features of previous mass extinctions that current theories leave to one side.*

AD: *Indeed I can. Insects, for example …*

I: *Insects?*

AD: *Yes, insects. They have been the great survivors of mass extinctions. This is not surprising as insects can, in general, tolerate up to 20 times the radiation dose that kills most other animals. The only time they were severely affected was in the largest mass extinction, 251 million years ago. Even then, only 30 per cent of insect species were destroyed, compared with up to 95 per cent of other orders of species. I find that very interesting.*

I: *Mmm, interesting, but also rather worrying … since we are apparently 100 million years overdue for another bout of mass extinction.*

AD: *Well, astronomers have examined the orbits of the five pairs of neutron stars observed in our galaxy and it seems that we probably have a breathing space before the first ones collapse. However … the data they have gathered seems to indicate that our galaxy also contains neutron star pairs that no-one has yet seen. It's rather unsettling, but until we see them, we can't know when they will merge.*

I: *So nobody can actually be sure that the apocalypse is not just around the corner?*

AD: *I'm afraid that's right.*

I: *Well, thank you very much, Arnon Dar.*

AD: *Thank you.*

I: *Now to turn to another subject …*

Writing p.62

3 *Sample answers*

para. 1 – Background information   para. 2 – Environmental benefits   para. 3 – Safety   para. 4 – Benefits to the community   para. 5 – Comments and recommendations Paragraph 3, about safety, would be better placed after the current para. 4. (*This would group the positive and negative points in the report together, and would also link with the concerns about safety in the final para.*)

4

1 to recommend the plan to build a car factory
2 1 The plan to build a car factory in the suburb of Westham **has much to recommend it**. 2 **Offering** over 2,000 jobs to the local population, it would **solve the problem of unemployment** and **increase the wealth of** the whole area. 3 **In addition, not only would it provide** opportunities for work, **but it would also** offer **a number** of other services, **including** baby-sitting facilities, a free health-care scheme, and a company pension. 4 **The major drawback, however**, seems to be that the factory is **to be located** 30 miles from the town centre. 5 This would **undoubtedly** be a problem for **those who do not possess their own means of transport**, as bus and train services to Westham **are infrequent**. 6 **Should the factory management be reluctant to** provide company transport, the town council would have to **consider** improving existing services.

UNIT 8

Language Focus: Grammar p.64

1

1 The **mere thought of climbing that mountain makes me** afraid.
2 I'm not **in the least (bit) surprised that you/about your** having won the race.
3 Jack Calton **is without exception the best** player in the team.
4 Never **(before) have I** met so quick a learner.
5 I've told you **time and time again/time after time** not to do that.
6 The **one thing he is good at is** long distance running.
7 I'm afraid that **there is no chance/possibility whatsoever of** a rematch.
8 Although they are a good team, they **are by no means the** best.

2

1 was very little 2 earth didn't you tell 3 poor/bad was the 4 whatever you 5 make a bit 6 so strong

3

1 On (*when they find*) 2 their (*their + own*) 3 whatsoever (*no + whatsoever*) 4 merest/barest/briefest (*notice the before the gap, suggesting a superlative*) 5 Whatever (*notice* may *later in this sentence*) 6 least 7 purely 8 a 9 such 10 Above 11 though/although 12 very (*very + indeed*) 13 so (*notice the inversion which follows*) 14 in 15 unless

Language Focus: Vocabulary p.65

1

1 This matter should have **been brought up** at the meeting … 2 His chances of **bringing off** such a difficult dive in the competition tomorrow are … 3 Sponsorship **brings in** more than half of what … 4 An old lady **brought her round** by … 5 This campaign **has brought about** a huge change in the habits of … 6 I'm sure he can **be brought round to** our way of thinking.

2

1 … if/that she'll **be brought to her senses** by … 2 … failure in the championships **brought home** (to him) the importance of … 3 … will **be brought into disrepute** by the … 4 … what he did **I couldn't bring myself to** talk to him … 5 … **brought the house down** …

Reading p.66

1 Sample answer

The voyage will probably be rather tough, with poor weather conditions, and it doesn't seem that the two people aboard the boat will get on at all well.

2

1A (*instead of the champagne parting … there had only been …*) 2C (*if the forecast held good then I could not hope for a better departure wind*) 3B (*I had lost count of how many times I had …*) 4D (*I was not at all sure I wanted her on board*) 5D (*the notion of Jackie coping on the boat had energised David and Betty with a vast amusement*) 6D (*… sharing a boat with a complete novice*) 7C (*I had felt an inexplicable allure towards … I did not want that irrational feeling to be nurtured by the forced intimacy of a small boat*)

3

1 Sample answers
slipped = moved smoothly, easily and quietly

splash = the noise made by water hitting a solid surface
hiss = a sound like 'sss', such as that made by a snake
shift = move something heavy or awkward, probably rather slowly
winked = turned on and off
faded = slowly became dimmer
pattered = made a soft light sound as it landed
dripped = fell in small drops of liquid
flickering = weak, unsteady (usually used to describe light)
tear = move quickly, possibly both noisily and violently

2

Movements: slipped, shift, dripped, tear
Sounds: splash, hiss, pattered
Lights: winked, faded, flickering

4

1 pattered 2 to slip 3 to flicker/flickering 4 hiss 5 tore 6 winked 7 splash 8 to shift 9 to drip/dripping 10 faded

Listening p.68

1B (listen to her intonation) 2A (*Nobody drives a car just like that … They have to spend a lot of time and money learning how to drive …*) 3C (*he was so full of himself … you had a real problem if he felt you were taking the mickey …*) 4B (*it all seemed so out of place … I found it utterly impossible to keep a straight face*) 5B (*who have braved the elements …*) 6A (*Given all the problems I'd been having with my ankle*) 7C (*No more was sport to be the preserve of a leisured elite*) 8A (*It is no coincidence, for example, that two years earlier the Football Association …*)

Tapescript

Extract One

A: *I just can't believe it! You really are determined to go hang-gliding again this weekend, aren't you? I think you're out of your mind! Do you know how many fatal accidents involving hang-gliders there have been this past year? It must be at least five or six …*

B: *Come on, Sue. It's not that bad, it really isn't like that at all.*

A: *Isn't it? That's not what the magazine I was reading yesterday said!*

B: *Look, provided you take it step by step … that you have someone who's qualified to take you through all the things you need to do – you know, how to fix the harness correctly, how to position your body, how to work the controls – I honestly can't see what all the fuss is about. It's like driving a car. Nobody drives a car just like that, do they? They have to spend a lot of time and money learning how to drive before they're allowed on the roads. There's no difference in my mind.*

A: *Well there is in my mind – and I think you're absolutely mad to want to do it!*

Extract Two

Japanese sword fighting – or kendo, as it's known – was something I did when I was still at school. I didn't do it for very long because, well, the teacher we had – or 'master' as he liked us to call him – insisted on our kneeling in front of him before each lesson and, well, he was so full of himself that you had a real problem if he felt you were taking the mickey or something. He used to get so worked up … it was quite unbelievable really. Another thing was, all the Japanese words you had to scream each time you made a thrust with the sword … one word for a thrust to the body, another for a thrust to the head, all that shouting at the top of your voice, plus the paraphernalia you had to dress up in … You know, it all seemed so out of place among a group of scruffy schoolboys – all that rushing around in a suburb of London screaming words in Japanese. I found it utterly impossible to keep a straight face, which, of course, annoyed the teacher no end.

Extract Three

A: *The athletes have just this moment got off the plane and are making their way through the crowd which has gathered here to greet them … making their way through what must be hundreds of enthusiastic on-lookers, who have braved the elements today to welcome back the men and women who so brilliantly represented this country at the recent Olympic Games. There they are. There're moving towards the line of taxis now which … one moment – here's Steve Oaks. Let me see if … Mr Oaks? Mr Oaks? Just a few words … have you a moment?*

B: *Yes?*

A: *How do you feel on your return after what can only be described as a tremendous personal victory in the Olympic stadium last week?*

B: *Absolutely great! I still can't take it all in! Given all the problems I'd been having with my ankle – that was the major stumbling block – and then all those totally unfounded allegations about drug abuse, you know, I find it amazing that I managed to walk away with a medal at all – let alone a gold medal. It's … well …*

A: *You're glad to be back, I imagine?*

B: *Oh, yeah, and I'm just thanking my lucky stars I had such wonderful support … in the stadium itself and among people here back at home …*

Extract Four

On July 14th 1865 a young English illustrator and mountaineer, Edward Whymper, climbed the Matterhorn, or Monte Cervino, at the seventh attempt. On the way down from the 4,440 m pyramid of rock, which towers over Zermatt, four of Whymper's party fell to their deaths.

This was by no means the first major alpine ascent, but Whymper's tragic feat was noteworthy because it publicised the new sport of alpinism, and underlined changing attitudes to recreation. No more was sport to be the preserve of a leisured elite. Nor was it to be confined to the traditional pursuits of hunting, shooting, fishing, riding, 'taking the waters', and the Grand Tour. Europeans of all sorts were looking for new sports, new challenges, and new sources of physical fitness.

It's no coincidence, for example, that two years earlier the Football Association had been founded at a meeting in the Freemason's Tavern in London, the aim of which was to standardise the rules of football, and to provide the framework for organised competition in the future.

Language Focus: Vocabulary p.68

1 from 2 on 3 to 4 for 5 in 6 in 7 of 8 of 9 with 10 upon/on 11 on 12 with

Use of English p.69

1 delicate 2 firm 3 struck 4 impose 5 crack 6 motion

Writing p.69

1

The main points to be covered are:
- the value of <u>team</u> sports in developing a sense of discipline in children
- their value in developing a competitive spirit
- their value in developing an ability to co-operate with others.

2

3 Method A has been used. The writer compares and contrasts the benefits of team sports with other activities. (Many examples, of course, are also provided to support the arguments outlined in the essay.)

3

1a) 2b) 3a) 4a) 5b) 6a) 7a) 8b) 9b) 10b) 11a) 12a) 13b) 14a) 15b) 16b) 17a) 18a)

4

1a) 2b) 3a) 4b) 5c) 6b) 7b) 8c) 9a) 10c)

UNIT 9

Language Focus: Grammar p.72

1

Notice the adverb + verb collocations in several of the sentences in this exercise.

1 He appears **to be having** difficulty **(in) finding someone to** replace her.
2 I'm **looking forward to the completion of** the new theatre.
3 I bitterly **regret paying so little attention** to his warnings.
4 I've arranged **for the tickets to be sent to us** next week.
5 Robert confessed to **forgetting/having forgotten to put off** the appointment.
6 He categorically **denied having been lent** the money.
7 I'm not used **to having to make such an early** start.
8 The workmen hope to **have finished knocking the wall** down by the end …
9 I strongly **object to being** made to work overtime.
10 Did you honestly **forget to get in touch with us** when …

Language Focus: Vocabulary p.73

Verb + noun collocation

1 slap 2 gestures 3 decision 4 try 5 glance
6 recollection 7 recovery 8 gulp 9 offer 10 effect
11 smile 12 think 13 cry 14 intention

Dependent prepositions and prepositional phrases

1 of 2 on 3 In 4 at 5 with 6 on 7 at/on 8 at
9 in 10 in 11 of 12 out 13 to/from 14 on 15 in
16 after 17 about/around 18 under 19 to 20 In

Reading p.74

1C (*colloc*) 2B (*phr vb*) 3A (*sem prec*) 4B (*colloc*) 5C (*sem prec*) 6B (*fixed exp*) 7B (*colloc*) 8C (*fixed exp*) 9A (*colloc*) 10A (*phr vb*) 11D (*colloc*) 12B (*fixed exp*) 13B (*phr vb*) 14C (*colloc*) 15D (*idiom*) 16A (*sem prec*) 17C (*fixed exp*) 18A (*fixed exp*)

Use of English p.75

2

1 Games are highly organised/meaningful + they are not invented by teachers/parents, but invented by children themselves.

2 They are proud or lack self-confidence and so are afraid of making mistakes/don't want to look stupid in front of other children.
3 that it is hidden/not usually seen/undesirable
4 trivial

3 *Points required*

Games:
1 reveal children's attitudes/prepare them for the future
2 help children to be co-operative/sociable/develop social skills
3 provide opportunities for children to lead/organise/be in charge of others
4 allow children to be creative
5 may indicate future careers

4 *Sample answer*

Games are important because they reveal children's attitudes and prepare them for their future lives as adults. In addition, they help children to learn to be co-operative and sociable, as well as providing opportunities for organising and being in charge of others. Games are particularly important because they allow children to express themselves and be creative, and may even indicate careers children will follow in the future. (*67 words*)

Language Focus: Grammar p.76

1

1 1A, 2B 2 1A, 2B 3 1B, 2A 4 1A, 2B 5 1B, 2A
6 1B, 2A

2

1B 2A 3B 4A 5B 6A

Tapescript

1

I

1 A *What I'd like to know is …*
  B *What I'd like to know is …*
2 A *Actually, he didn't help me …*
  B *Actually, he didn't help me …*
3 A *What I can't understand …*
  B *What I can't understand …*
4 A *It was a comedy we saw last night …*
  B *It was a comedy we saw last night …*
5 A *What's happening now …*
  B *What's happening now …*
6 A *The first time I knew something was wrong …*
  B *The first time I knew something was wrong …*

160

2

1 A *What I'd like to know is not important, so it seems.*
  B *What I'd like to know is how on earth did they do it?*

2 A *Actually, he didn't help me, she did.*
  B *Actually, he didn't help me to fix the car.*

3 A *What I can't understand is this problem on page 66.*
  B *What I can't understand is why he didn't ask her to marry him.*

4 A *It was a comedy we saw last night at the cinema.*
  B *It was a comedy we saw last night, not a thriller.*

5 A *What's happening now is that more and more people are breaking the law.*
  B *What's happening now doesn't concern you at all.*

6 A *The first time I knew something was wrong was when he didn't come to work on time.*
  B *The first time I knew something was wrong I suddenly broke out in a cold sweat.*

2

1

1 *No, I'm sure **he** couldn't have turned up late.*
2 *Really? I couldn't believe how **rude** he was.*
3 *Yes, I can't believe how **hard** he studies.*
4 *Well, why didn't he **do** it then?*
5 *Are you sure? I thought **Saturday** night was a problem for her.*
6 *So it's only been tried out on **animals** in the past?*

2

1 *I think it was Peter who waltzed in over an hour late for the meeting. No, I'm sure he couldn't have turned up late.*
2 *It was his dishonesty which amazed me more than anything else. Really? I couldn't believe how rude he was.*
3 *He always seems to have his head buried in a book. Yes, I can't believe how hard he studies.*
4 *What he really wanted to do was go abroad to study. Well, why didn't he do it then?*
5 *I think it's tomorrow night that Anna can't come to the party. Are you sure? I thought Saturday night was a problem for her.*
6 *What's new is that this test is being done on a human subject. So it's only been tried out on animals in the past?*

3

1 What is really interesting/really interests me is that …
2 What I really like/enjoy is going …   3 All he ever does is (to) complain about the weather!   4 What I remember most is my father playing …   5 The only thing I can remember is the doctor giving …

4

1 … **must have been her twin sister (that)** you saw …   2 What **I can't understand is why** you didn't telephone me …   3 It's **his arrogant attitude that**

I find …   4 All **you think about is** going out to parties.
5 What **baffles me is** his lack …   6 It's not **so much** your finishing the job **that concerns me as** the state of your health.   7 What **they have decided to do is** of no interest to me.   8 What **they will ask you to do is** (to) attend an interview.   9 The person **you should complain to** is the manager.   10 The first **time** I realised something was wrong **was when** …

Listening p.77

1 biological reason   2 money or penalties   3 working properly   4 random events   5 won't happen   6 remember events   7 a reputation for   8 an underlying attraction   9 intuition

Tapescript

I: *For thousands of years philosophers and ordinary people have pondered the question of luck and good fortune. Just why is it that some people seem to have 'all the luck', as the saying goes? What is it about these people that makes them different from others? In the studio with us tonight is a psychologist who has made luck and intuition the subject of serious scientific research. I'd like to welcome to our programme Dr Sandra Beckett, from the University of Manchester.*

SB: *Good evening.*

I: *Dr Beckett, perhaps you would like to tell us a bit about what exactly it means to be lucky or unlucky, and what you have discovered in the course of your research at Manchester …*

SB: *Yes, of course. Before I talk about my own research, however, I'd like briefly to mention a study which was carried out in America recently, at the Iowa College of Medicine, which seems to suggest that good or bad luck might be something biological. Whether or not this is actually true, of course, is open to question, but the study itself was very interesting. Um, scientists at the University of Iowa had isolated a type of mildly brain-damaged person who, um, despite good intelligence and memory … had a tendency to 'foul up'. In the study, um, they set up an experiment whereby two groups of patients were given cards, some of which awarded money and others penalties. Now, what they found was that the group with brain defects took longer to access the difference between the cards – and, in fact, even after finding out the difference, still chose the penalty card.*

I: *In other words …?*

SB: *In other words, unlike the control group, they acquired no 'hunch', as it were, that the cards were duff.*

I: *I see. And what conclusions did they draw from that?*

SB: *Well, they concluded that the mildly brain-damaged*

probably made bad decisions because, um, whatever part of the brain which allows other people access to 'intuition' or 'gut feeling' was not working properly.

I: *Mmm. That's interesting. Now, you mentioned your own research, Dr Beckett. What kinds of conclusions have you reached about what makes lucky people different from others?*

SB: *Well, first of all, let me say that it is true that some people do seem to be exceptionally lucky … and their luck is not just manifest in health and wealth, but, um, even more … random events seem to go in their favour. Just **why** this is so is still a bit of a mystery, but there do seem to be a number of factors involved. Um, one important factor is that lucky people are optimistic … whereas unlucky people tend to be more pessimistic. They believe that good things won't happen to them … and sure enough, bad things happen instead …*

I: *And this outlook on life is also reflected in other areas, I imagine?*

SB: *Yes, there's a great difference in the way lucky and unlucky people remember events, for example. People who are lucky remember good times, while unlucky people tend to focus on personal failures.*

I: *Mmm. And what about the impression people give to others? That's important as well, isn't it – I think?*

SB: *Yes, that's true. Some people do seem to acquire a reputation for bad or good luck. Because behaviour is mediated by those around you, I suppose. If people expect you to knock a wine glass over, you will. Um, body language is also important. We've been studying the body language of children recently in Manchester … even in small children this reciprocal process seems to start as early as six months old. Whether we like it or not, some people **do** create an underlying attraction that brings good things to them.*

I: *Yes, that's very true. What then **is** luck, would you say?*

SB: *Well, that's the big question, isn't it? The lucky often put their good fortune down to intuition – which is not something mysterious or magical, but based on learning and expertise. In the business world, for example …*

I: *Yes, I was going to mention that. Business people …*

Writing p.78

1

2 In your proposal, you need to:
- outline the measures you think will reduce stress
- say *why* you think these measures would be effective.

4 Answer provided in the proposal on p.79.

3

1 The extract would be more appropriate in an informal letter to a colleague.

2

Sample answer

I suggest that employees **should be allowed to work at home if they** wish to do so. This **may not be** feasible for some jobs, where collaboration **is important**, but it should be possible for many activities which have traditionally been carried out at the office. Were **this step to be taken**, efficiency and quality of work would probably improve, and levels of **stress would almost certainly decrease**.

U N I T *10*

Language Focus: Vocabulary p.80

Adjectives

1

1C 2C 3D 4B 5A 6C

2

1 **Almost nobody** turned up …   2 I know you are **capable of producing** good work …   3 I am **proud to be meeting/will be proud to meet** …   4 His **sole intention in joining** the project is to …   5 It will be **virtually impossible to** find someone to …   6 I am **baffled by your unwillingness to** give …   7 … the sale of tobacco is **restricted to people over** the …
8 Harry's homework **wasn't quite perfect**.

Determiners and pronouns

1 … no business of 2 … matter what …   3 … reason/right to be/feel …   4 … both of …   5 …contacted by anyone …   6 … need to make/point in making …
7 … neither (of them) …   8 … none of which …

Use of English p.81

1 It **comes as no surprise to hear** that Charles has …
2 Everybody appears **to go along with** the new plans.
3 His recent remarks **have <u>given</u> rise to bitter resentment** among the staff.   4 It is **a foregone conclusion that the company will totally** collapse.
5 The manager **is alleged to <u>have been accepting</u>** bribes.   6 It is **by no means easy to predict** the result …   7 Under **no circumstances <u>must you</u> try** to contact me.   8 But **for his help we would not have met** the deadline.

Reading p.82

1

a newspaper or magazine (*it's a current news item*)

2

1B (*the revival in green woodworking*) 2C (*the chairman … emphasised that nobody should see the cutting-down of ancient trees as an act of destruction or vandalism*) 3D (*His words were to the point, but he rather gave away his own lack of practical skills …*) 4A (*… trees which, by their natural bend, lend themselves to forming the curved beams …*)
5B (*Thereafter, hand-tools will be the order of the day*)
6A (*They will also need to be fairly impervious to scrutiny … visitors … will doubtless flock around*) 7A (*… a striking blend of ancient and modern … the most striking innovation … since the arboretum was founded in 1829*)

Use of English p.83

1 order 2 which 3 on 4 make 5 up 6 had (*notice the past participle* implanted *which follows*) 7 able 8 his (+ *every*) 9 where 10 be (*fixed exp*) 11 it (*refers to* the system) 12 as/when 13 likely (*collocates with* highly) 14 have (*colloc*) 15 for (+ *which, referring to* companies)

Language Focus: Vocabulary p.84

Adverb + adjective collocation

1

1 deadly dull 2 wildly exaggerated 3 widely available 4 highly skilled 5 deeply moved 6 closely guarded 7 entirely convinced 8 strictly forbidden

2

1 deadly dull 2 closely guarded 3 deeply moved 4 widely available 5 strictly forbidden 6 highly skilled 7 wildly exaggerated 8 entirely convinced

Phrasal verbs and expressions: *work*

1

1 work out **why** 2 work out **how** 3 working out **between** 4 work up **any** 5 worked up **over** 6 works out **at** 7 working up **to** 8 work out (**much/ far**) 9 work up **an** 10 **all** worked out

2

1 short 2 cut 3 rule (= *protest by doing work slowly, stating that you have to obey all the rules exactly*) 4 bone
5 frenzy (= *get extremely upset/hysterical*) 6 courage
7 wonders 8 line (= *kind or type*) 9 dirty (= *unpleasant or illegal*) 10 donkey (= *hard, unrewarding, boring*)

Language Focus: Grammar p.85

Future forms

1

I
1b) (= *it's already arranged*) 2b) (= *do you intend to …? you've kept me waiting for so long. The speaker is being sarcastic.*) 3a (= *what the timetable says, as opposed to when trains actually run*) 4b (= *it's already decided*)
5a (= *we can see what is about to happen*) 6b (= *I've already planned this*) 7a (= *I'm planning to do this anyway, so it's easy for me to do you a favour*) 8b (= *a threat about the future*)

2 *Sample answers*
1 I'll/I might play tennis with Roger tomorrow …
2 Will you marry me … 3 The train will be delayed by over an hour … 4 He will have resigned … 5 That tree will/may have fallen down … 6 I'll wear/I could wear a red pullover … 7 I'll go to the supermarket later …
8 You may have to work overtime every day next week …

2

1 It won't **be long before he gets** promoted. 2 … he **is unlikely/not likely to come** first. 3 His **refusal to work overtime is bound to** create problems.
4 Scientists **are on the verge of discovering** a cure …
5 My licence **is due to expire/be renewed** next month.
6 The house **is expected to have been sold/sale is expected to have been completed** by the end …

Writing p.86

1

1 Extract 1 comes from a report.
2 a), c), d) and e)

2

2 The most appropriate conclusion is C (*it is more appropriate than A, because it comments on what their views* reveal about the hopes and aspirations …); conclusion B would be appropriate for an essay.

UNIT *11*

Language Focus: Grammar p.88

Reflexive pronouns

1

1 Anne **prides herself on being able/her ability** to speak … 2 She wants **to distance herself from** the

scandal … 3 Danielle Steel's latest novel **lends itself to being made** into a film. 4 You do **not need to commit yourself to supporting** the proposal now. 5 She knew she **couldn't trust herself not to eat** the bar … 6 He **resigned himself to hav<u>ing</u> to travel on his** own.

2

1 should/must pull yourself (*this expression sounds rather critical; it might cause offence*) 2 wear yourself 3 couldn't concentrate 4 assert yourself 5 couldn't help

Use of English p.88

1

They believe that very limited communication may be possible, but certainly not *natural* conversation.

2

1 The false belief among computer researchers that talking to computers will be natural/commonplace in the future.
2 That these would be understood by a human being, but not by a computer.
3 'inhabit different worlds'
4 Users must not be polite/must overcome politeness.

3   *Sample answer*

Most people today are unable to give short, unambiguous orders. Many would feel strange talking to a machine, and workplaces would also become very noisy. Additionally, computers do not share the kind of life experiences that make communication natural and enjoyable between people. Consequently, computers are not very effective interpreters of human speech, and there would probably be numerous confusions and mistakes in their attempts to carry out commands. (***69 words***)

Reading p.90

1B (*The irony … so-called information revolution … consumers neither like nor expect …*) 2A (*the writer's attitude is apparent throughout the extract; the phrase* brevity and blandness *is particularly indicative of his attitude*) 3D (*Since then, nothing much has changed. The same mental toolbox …*) 4B (*like monkeys and apes, we are visual animals … So we invented graphs …*) 5A (*Getting out and about with your digital camera is now a practical proposition*) 6B (*it is very much a photographer's camera. You will need to have a good knowledge of …*) 7C (*the journal … to track and cheer on current advances … breathless editorials*) 8B

Reading p.92

1B 2A 3D 4G 5H 6C 7E

Writing p.93

1

1 2 = too blunt and direct
2
1 **In all probability/There is every likelihood/It is likely that** this trend will continue 2 have **to a large extent/largely** been ignored; **seem/appear to** have been ignored 3 People **are apt to/tend to** dismiss; **There is a tendency for** people to dismiss 4 It is **rather** sad 5 do not **seem/appear to** worry

2

2 2, 3 (*only in the briefest terms at this stage*), and 5 (*try to 'echo' the essay title in both your introduction and conclusion*)
3 2 (*the first two sentences outline the situation today*), 3 (*mobile telephones and the Internet*) and 5 ('*people have perhaps become more isolated from their immediate surroundings*')

3

1a) 2c) 3b) 4a) 5b) 6b)

4

Conclusion A is more balanced, echoes the question, and ends in a constructive point for action. Conclusion B, on the other hand, is rather extreme in its views, and contains the distracting new detail about the health risks of mobile phones.

5

Outline B has been used to plan this essay.

UNIT *12*

Language Focus: Grammar p.96

1

1 … **blamed her for their missing/having missed** the train (their *is necessary, to include Sandra's mother in missing the train*) 2 She **advised me not to** say anything about it to the manager. (*notice that we cannot say* to not say) 3 Our mother **threatened not to give us** our pocket money if we **didn't behave** ourselves. 4 She **promised never to tell** anyone about the money **I had given** her. (*not + ever = never*) 5 He **denied stealing/having**

stolen/that he had stolen the money. 6 She **urged me not to** pay any attention … 7 He **complimented us on** the (excellent) job/work we **had done/on doing** an excellent job.

2

1 me of stealing/having stolen 2 her against 3 the blame on 4 would/might have taken 5 (that) they should keep/have kept 6 to put us

Use of English p.97

1

1 occurrence 2 explosive 3 unaffordable 4 references 5 mileage 6 modernisation 7 insistence 8 wastage 9 incomprehensible 10 triumphant

2

1 unquestionably 2 invasion 3 destructive 4 pretence/pretension(s) 5 nobility 6 overcharged 7 realisation 8 beneficial 9 Mercifully 10 boundless

Reading p.98

1A (*phr vb*) 2B (*colloc*) 3C (*idiom*) 4B (*sem prec*) 5D (*sem prec*) 6A (*idiom*) 7B (*phr vb*) 8C (*idiom*) 9D (*sem prec*) 10B (*word comp*) 11D (*sem prec*) 12A (*fixed exp*) 13B (*fixed exp*) 14D (*colloc*) 15A (*fixed exp*) 16C (*fixed exp*) 17D (*phr vb*) 18A (*fixed exp*)

Use of English p.99

1 matures 2 restore 3 pale 4 burst 5 pour 6 settle

Language Focus: Grammar p.100

1 He **is alleged to have had** no knowledge/**not to have known** … 2 He **is thought to be arriving** … 3 The police **are reported to have already arrested** … (*notice* the police are, *not* is) 4 It **is believed that she had been using** … 5 It **is thought that she was not** involved/It **is not thought that she was** involved … 6 He **was said not to have been** aware of … (*notice that* he was not said to have been aware *has a slightly different meaning*) 7 He **is claimed to have known** exactly what … 8 She **was rumoured to have married** …

Listening p.100

1D (*the air was growing thinner … breathing was pretty difficult*) 2A (*Our first night in tents was cold, though nothing like the night we had spent at Chivay, earlier in the holiday*) 3B (*… refused to join the first arrivals sitting waiting until I*

was absolutely positive I had no further to climb*) 4B (*The sense of awe I experienced just took my breath away*) 5C (*the group was large enough to dilute … but small enough to maintain …*)

Tapescript

I: *At one time or another, many of our listeners will have dreamed of visiting that mysterious city of the Incas, Machu Picchu. Tucked away, high up in the Andes mountains of Peru, its very remoteness is a source of wonder. Someone who recently climbed the Inca Trail to Machu Picchu is Sarah Chapman, who is here in the studio tonight to tell us about her experiences. The going was tough, I understand, Sarah?*

SC: *Yes, very. There was a moment, in fact, as I scrambled along the Inca Trail, when I really thought I would die. I was facing the so-called Dead Woman's Pass, and at 14,000 feet, nothing seemed to have been more aptly named!*

I: *But you obviously managed it!*

SC: *Well, I hadn't gone all that way just to give up at the last moment, but it was incredibly tough. All I could see was this wall of mountains in front … the air was growing thinner as well, and breathing was pretty difficult. Even the porters looked over-stretched. Conrad, who was another member of our party, had come up alongside me and we calculated every movement forward. Ten or fifteen steps and then a pause. Ten, fifteen steps … then another pause. It was painfully difficult.*

I: *Although – as you were telling me earlier – there had been some relatively easy bits before.*

SC: *Oh yes. Actually the first day of the climb had not been too bad. Our first night in tents, was cold – though nothing like the night we had spent at Chivay, earlier in the holiday, where the water froze in our water bottles and the tents were stiff with ice by morning. At Chivay, even a sleeping bag designed for temperatures down to minus ten seemed to offer no more protection than a sheet. Anyway, here on the Inca Trail life seemed a lot less demanding.*

I: *But that obviously changed during the second day.*

SC: *Yes, definitely. We all set off together, but soon became separated by the steepness of the path. Mark and Liz, our tour leaders, leapt on ahead, with Monica and Abigail close behind them. The rest of us, I'm afraid to admit, straggled onwards at whatever pace we found bearable. When I reached the top, I staggered to the edge and refused to join the first arrivals sitting waiting until I was absolutely positive I had no further to climb. Conrad and I posed for photographs, and, eventually, after all of the members of the group were reunited, we went down to where the porters had prepared lunch.*

INT: *After that, I believe you used pathways built by the Inca. Is that right?*

SC *Yes, it is. From that moment our journey continued up and down on stone steps – some of them knee-high – where the Inca messengers had once run from the city of Cuzco. On the morning of the fourth day, we set off when it was still dark and got to the Sun Gate by dawn. That was when we saw Machu Picchu. It was enormous! The sense of awe I experienced just took my breath away … nothing could have prepared me for what I saw or felt at that moment! Everywhere there were the ruins of palaces and temples … some of them dating from the fifteenth and sixteenth centuries. It was simply too much to take in!*

INT: *Yes, I was going to say that. You must have felt rather like an explorer discovering a lost world!*

SC: *Yes, it's funny you should say that. It's one of the things we all said when we talked about it later. You know … the walk to Machu Picchu had made all of us feel like real explorers. It had also welded us together into a team. Fortunately, everyone in the group got on well together … and the group was large enough to dilute those irritations that inevitably emerge on an organised tour, but small enough to maintain the sense of adventure. Walking the Inca Trail is something none of us will ever forget. To anyone thinking about doing it, my advice would be … just get up and do it. You'll never regret it.*

INT: *Good advice to all our listeners, I'm sure. That was Sarah Chapman talking about her visit to Machu Picchu.*

Language Focus: Vocabulary p.101

1 What is **your attitude to/towards people who take** advantage … 2 At least she will **be in good hands** at the clinic. 3 The building **is in urgent need of complete** renovation. 4 Dr Jenkins is **out of touch with recent developments in** technology. 5 I **am not averse to occasional** hard work. 6 Her homework **hasn't been up to scratch** recently. 7 There will be problems in **the long run unless** we … 8 The escaped prisoner is **still at large in the south** of England. 9 At first we **were doubtful about employing** Alan. 10 … **as she is allergic to** them.

Language Focus: Grammar p.101

1 The bodies of cars **might/may/could be made of plastic** in the future. 2 The meeting **might/may not have finished by the** time you arrive. (could *is not possible here*) 3 You **should have completed that report** by tomorrow. 4 You **should not get involved** in this matter. 5 … people **might/may/could be living in colonies** on the Moon.

Writing p.102

2

1 Introduction 1 is more appropriate. Introduction 2 is more complex, and certainly well written, but would be more appropriate for a discursive essay.

2 No, the article fails to answer the second part of the task, in which you should explain *why it affected you so much.* It is also too short for Proficiency.

3 *very cold* = bitterly cold *had no lights on* = was shrouded in darkness *the streets* = the narrow cobbled streets *looking at* = gazing up in awe at *to be in* = to grace *the old buildings lining the streets were mysterious* = there was an air of mystery about the old buildings lining the streets *a layer* = a thick blanket *softening* = muffling *I will never forget New Year's Eve* = New Year's Eve was particularly memorable

3

1b) 2a) 3e) 4f) 5c)

4 *Complete improved article*

Cracow, the ancient capital of Poland. Just the name of the place is enough to bring back a flood of happy memories. It was around Christmas time, a few years back, when I first visited the city with a group of friends.

We arrived in Cracow at around midnight. I remember that it was bitterly cold and there was a lot of snow about. Our hotel was shrouded in darkness when we arrived, but fortunately the receptionist was on duty. What amazed us was how friendly and hospitable she was, even though it was late and she was obviously tired.

Our first few days in Cracow were spent looking around the old Polish capital, exploring the narrow cobbled streets and castle, and gazing up in awe at the statues and monuments which seemed to grace every public square we came across. There was an air of mystery about the old buildings lining the streets, and throughout our stay in the city, we were frequently overwhelmed by the sense that we had somehow walked back into a magical kingdom belonging to another age.

The snow continued to fall constantly, reminding me of scenes from novels I had read by Tolstoy and other Russian and Polish writers. Everywhere was covered in a thick blanket of snow, which had the effect of muffling the sounds of cars and passing trams. It also made us feel like travellers in some mysterious, silent land, far away from the noise and bustle of modern city life.

New Year's Eve was particularly memorable. An enormous crowd had gathered in the main square of the city, and most people were dancing. The fact that everyone seemed so happy and well-behaved – and intent on enjoying themselves – made an enormous impression on us.

Our week in Cracow was something I shall never forget. I have been back several times since, and each time I am struck by the beauty of the city and the friendliness and openness of the inhabitants. Cracow is one of those places which reminds us of the splendour that has unfortunately been lost or destroyed in many of our cities today. (*350 words*)

UNIT *13*

Language Focus: Grammar p.104

1

1 1a), 2b) 2 1b), 2a) and c) 3 1b), 2a) 4 1a), 2b) 5 1b), 2a) and c) 6 2a) and b)

2

1 They **have been negotiating** a settlement for over … 2 The minister's policies **have been attacked** by journalists several times. 3 The fact that **he was being sarcastic** was … 4 Politicians **have already begun** talks to … 5 By the time he was eighteen **he had left** home to go … 6 They **have been trying to sell** that house for …

3

1 help/stop thinking (that) 2 hasn't been keeping your 3 he's making a/some kind of 4 thought it 5 must've been having 6 morning doing/washing the 7 has run 8 has been telling

Language Focus: Vocabulary p.105

1

1 **stand by** him, whatever 2 REM **stand for** in this 3 **stand for** such 4 make the sign **stand out** 5 had **stood up for** him when they started making 6 you unfairly until you **stand up to** 7 **stands out** among/as the best of 8 **standing in for** Robin while

2

1 Abrams will **stand trial** … 2 Their marriage has **stood the test of time**. 3 How do our sales **stand in relation to** those of other firms? 4 He **stands little chance of** winning … 5 If you really want to leave, **I'm not going to stand in your way**. 6 It **stands to reason that** hard work and …

Use of English p.106

2

1 To show that educationalists do not question the point of exams, as generals did not question the killing.

2 They are unwilling to study.
3 As top managers, they are in the best position to say whether exam grades are important for later success.
4 To the fact that it is not essential to have high exam grades to be able to carry out leading research.

3 *Sample answer*

Although school and university exams do not necessarily indicate intelligence or talent, they often cause people to feel like failures. In addition, many retail companies do not find them helpful, and use their own tests for applicants instead. In business and industry, exam results do not determine later success, and even in scientific research a good degree does not mean that someone can think originally or be self-motivated. (*69 words*)

Use of English p.107

1

1 between 2 recent 3 made 4 way/means 5 such 6 same 7 paid (*you* pay attention to st, *but in this sentence we have* attention (which is) paid to …) 8 anything (*fixed exp*) 9 With (*meaning* since managers are …) 10 never 11 in 12 their/the 13 about (*phr verb*) 14 variety/ number 15 able

Language Focus: Vocabulary p.107

Verb + noun collocation

1 take 2 made 3 handled 4 jump 5 set 6 seized 7 get/achieve 8 achieve 9 set 10 made 11 take 12 made

Dependent prepositions and prepositional phrases

1 on 2 under 3 To 4 into 5 in 6 for

Use of English p.108

1 We can **take it as read that** Maria will … 2 Why **not go halves on (the cost of)** a taxi … 3 I only knew that **I wasn't cut out to be/for being** a lawyer … 4 There **is no point whatsoever in trying** to get … 5 Little **does he realise how damaging** the changes … 6 Failing this test will result **in your not being allowed to** take … 7 Pensions have failed **to keep pace with** inflation. 8 James **hasn't got over the cold he caught** at Christmas.

Listening p.108

▶ Paper 4, Part 4

1B (*the most common mistake is lack of preparation/Mmm, yes. Another thing …*) 2R (*Most candidates need to display* more confidence in themselves and their skills/there's too much <u>over</u>confidence about these days …) 3B (Candidates should go into the interview with their minds fixed on the four or five key strengths that they want to get across/making sure, of course, that they can back up any claims they make … – finishing someone else's sentence is a common way of signalling agreement) 4A (I think it's best to be honest with the employer/which could cost you the job, I think. It's probably best to steer clear of such areas if you can) 5B (Instead, say, of listing all the duties you had in your previous job, I'd mention …/there's certainly a lot to be said for being as specific as possible) 6B (most employers will have a few tricky questions up their sleeve/… or 'Where do you see yourself in five years' time?' That's a common one)

Tapescript

I: Thank you, Dave, for that report, which I'm sure our listeners found very interesting. We're going to move on now to a related topic … job interviews. How can you make sure that that all important job interview you go for doesn't turn into your worst nightmare? Giving us their views on the matter tonight are Angela Simpson, of the Alpha Recruitment Agency, and Rita Gilbert, who works for Drake Ream Tollin, an agency which specialises in finding jobs for people who've been made redundant.

AS/RG: Hello.

I: Without further ado then … Angela, what's your advice to our listeners about what they should do in an interview … and – perhaps more importantly – what they should not do?

AS: Well, the most common mistake is lack of preparation. Recruitment companies are always reporting that most candidates still don't make enough effort to find out about their prospective employer and the business they're in. And they don't think enough about what they're going to say when the interview takes place. It is a pitfall that even those going for senior jobs fall into. You see, I think that candidates really need to sit down and study the organisation's annual report and accounts, and maybe look at any relevant websites as well.

RG: Mmm, yes. Another thing they could do is look at the company's market … you know, determine whether it is expanding, consolidating or declining, and the company's likely direction and aims for the future.

AS: Yes, that would be good as well.

RG: I'm not sure, though, that lack of preparation is the most common mistake. I would say it's probably lack of confidence. Most candidates need to display more confidence in themselves and their skills in the interview situation … um … they need to be a lot more sure of themselves … impress the employer that they're up to the job …

AS: Yes, well, there's too much <u>over</u>-confidence about these days, I'd say … especially if people are being headhunted. There's a sense of … well, you know, 'I've been headhunted so they must want me. I'll walk in and give them a short spiel about myself and that will convince them'. Well, that really isn't enough – invariably they will be up against five or six candidates as well-qualified as themselves … some of whom will have done their preparation.

RG: Well, confidence or lack of confidence aside … you mention the importance of preparation, Angela … and … well, the other side of the coin is knowing what the employer is looking for and matching it to your own skills and experience. Candidates should go into the interview with their minds fixed on the four or five key strengths that they want to get across …

AS: … making sure, of course, that they can back up any claims they make.

RG: Oh, of course. If you say you are good at managing people, for instance, you should be able to cite an example of a job or a team project in which you have managed people well. Um …

AS: But, what about areas you might not know very much about … or know that you are weak in? You see, I think it's best to be honest with the employer. Say that you're willing to learn … or that your knowledge of something is fairly limited.

RG: … which could cost you the job, I think. It's probably best to steer clear of such areas if you can … you know … focus more on your strengths … your achievements. I'd also not focus too much on things which are run of the mill. Instead, say, of listing all the duties you had in your previous job, I'd mention things like … um … 'I increased turnover by x per cent' or 'I completed this project ahead of schedule' …

AS: Mmm … well, there's certainly a lot to be said for being as specific as possible. I'm sure you've found as well, Rita, that most employers will have a few tricky questions up their sleeve which the interviewee should have prepared for. You know, the obvious ones, of course … like … um, well, let's think, …. 'Tell me about yourself' or 'Why are you leaving your present job?'

RG: … or 'Where do you see yourself in five years' time?' That's a common one. It catches a lot of people out … you know … they start to babble, or even worse, try to say something clever in reply. I once knew someone who, when asked what he would do to improve the company's turnover, said that he would …

Language Focus: Vocabulary p.109

1 to 2 of 3 for 4 between 5 as 6 between 7 from
8 to 9 for 10 on 11 about 12 of 13 to 14 on
15 with 16 at 17 beyond 18 to 19 in 20 in

Writing p.109

1

1 Statements 3, 4 and 6 could be interpreted as slightly
  sceptical. All of the statements are neutral or slightly
  formal, with statements 3 and 6 being the most formal in
  tone.
2 1c) 2f) 3d) 4b) 5a) 6e)

2

1 be seen to be believed 2 thing that strikes you is …
3 more like a warehouse than a place for wining and dining
4 as the eye can see 5 is now making/turning a handsome
profit

4

1a) 2b) 3c) 4a) 5b) 6a)

5

A is the more appropriate conclusion, as the tone is more
personal and light-hearted, and so fits the rest of the article
better.

UNIT 14

Reading p.112

1B (*sem prec* staring *at*) 2C (*colloc*) 3A (*idiom*)
4D (*word comp*) 5D (*fixed exp*) 6D (*fixed exp*)
7C (*word comp*) 8A (*sem prec*) 9C (*fixed exp*)
10B (*colloc*) 11D (*phr vb*) 12A (*fixed exp*)
13B (*colloc*) 14C (*sem prec*) 15A (*colloc*)
16A (*phr vb*) 17C (*fixed exp*) 18C (*fixed exp*)

Language Focus: Vocabulary p.113

1 keep to 2 made off with 3 be getting up to 4 brought
about 5 put up with 6 taken aback 7 came across
8 have run up 9 are getting at 10 has got away with

Reading p.114

1C 2H 3A 4F 5B 6G 7E

Language Focus: Vocabulary p.115

1 to; at 2 on 3 of 4 in; in 5 out of 6 in; In 7 on; on
8 of; out of 9 in; at

Use of English p.116

1 to (*used to + st or -ing*) 2 reason 3 whom (some of
*before the blank indicates that a pronoun is required, the
commas indicate that this is a relative clause*) 4 with 5 up
6 What 7 however (*notice the commas around the blank*)
8 in 9 unable (*the meaning here is negative*) 10 around
11 until 12 all 13 anyone/anybody (hardly *cannot be
followed by* nobody, nowhere, *etc.*) 14 so (*notice an* after
the adjective comfortable) 15 another

Use of English p.116

1 pianist 2 extraordinary 3 unnoticed 4 sobering
5 outstanding 6 doubtless 7 clarity 8 compulsion
9 regardless 10 unwilling

Use of English p.117

1 claim 2 maintain 3 handle 4 sharp 5 measure 6 bind

Use of English p.118

1 She **is alleged to have been receiving** large bribes.
2 The government **has come in for heavy criticism**
over its immigration policy. 3 There is **little likelihood
that he will be given** the sack. 4 Charles **was bound
to have been taken** in by all … 5 Sarah has **set her
heart on winning** first prize … 6 She made **(very)
little attempt/effort to get** along with … 7 Since we
have **come up against serious problems, we should
call/put** a halt to … 8 It was difficult to **keep a straight
face when he told/ticked us** off about such …
9 There **is no question of our agreeing** to their terms.
10 She seems **intent on making them stay/keeping
them** in the building. 11 Had **it not been for your
contribution** I would not … 12 She was **under no
obligation to take** part in the discussion.

Use of English p.119

The first draft of the summary is too long.

Sample answer
Buying books from an Internet bookshop is often cheaper
than buying them from a conventional bookshop. It is also
possible to find almost any book in print and to order it
quickly and easily. As well as providing information about
books by the same author or on a related subject, many
Internet bookshops also encourage readers to send in
reviews of books they would recommend to others.
(*67 words*)

Practice exam

Paper 1 – Reading p.122

Part 1 p.122

One mark per question (total = 18)

1D (*phr vb*)   2C (*sem prec*)   3B (*sem prec*)   4A (*fixed exp*)
5B (*sem prec*)   6D (*fixed exp*)   7B (*fixed exp*)   8C (*colloc*)
9A (*colloc*)   10D (*phr vb*)   11B (*colloc*)   12A (*fixed exp*)
13B (*word comp*)   14C (*fixed exp*)   15C (*colloc* – virtually
can only be used with an adjective that has a fixed meaning,
like perfect or complete, *which has the wrong meaning for
this context*)   16C (*colloc*)   17A (*fixed exp*)   18C (*sem prec*)

Part 2 p.123

Two marks per question (total = 16)

19C (*conservation was initially thought of as only being
relevant to endangered species … Now is it recognised that
conservation must also be applied to the environment in which
…*)   20A (*If those people's welfare, let alone their survival, is
at stake, then these must take priority.*)   21C (the writer's
surprise at the ignorance of the local people as regards the
sharks' feeding habits is evident when he remarks that *Even
now, after all the publicity … daily papers in the Scottish
Hebrides still report plagues of Basking Sharks 'in pursuit of
herring shoals', and there are many fishermen who believe this
to be true*)   22B (*They destroyed their nets, passing through
them as an elephant would pass through …*)   23D (*To find
out what part you can play …* It is not obvious from the
advertisement that the organisation is asking people to
send in donations – although, of course, this may be true.)
24A (There is no evidence of resignation or bitterness in
the opening remarks, and the writer is certainly not being
humorous.)   25B (*The ill-conceived notion that oil and gas will
imminently run out, together with worries about the greenhouse
effect, is responsible for the despoliation of wild landscapes in
Wales and Denmark by ugly wind farms.* The writer's view of
wind farms here is obviously a negative one.)   26C (*They
(environmentalists) are quick to accuse their opponents of
vested interests, but their own incomes, advancement and
fame …*)

Part 3 p.126

Two marks per question (total = 14)

27G   28A   29F   30C   31E   32D   33H

Part 4 p.128

Two marks per question (total = 14)

34D (*These seers, obsessed by the mystery of nature,
overcame …*)   35A (*He hunted, fished, sowed, reaped, danced
and performed religious ceremonies at the times the heavens
dictated*)   36C (*The farmer … who made his living tilling the
soil which the river covered with rich silt during its annual
overflow … had to be well prepared … His home, equipment,
and cattle had to be temporarily removed … and
arrangements made for sowing immediately afterwards.* A and
D are true, but only **partially** answer the question.)   37A
(*These holy people … exploited this knowledge to retain
dominance over the uninformed masses.* The question asks
what the **principal** benefit was.)   38B (*It was as natural for
the ancient priests to work out a formula … based on the
motions of the planets and star constellations as it is for the
modern scientist to study and master nature with his
techniques.* D was **one** use of astrology, but the text does
not suggest that it was the **primary** one.)   39C (*a
scientifically immature people would have had good reasons to
associate the positions of the sun, moon and stars with human
affairs. The dependence of crops … all made* **such** *a doctrine
credible.*)   40D (*The orientation of these religious monuments
in relation to the heavenly bodies is well illustrated by … This
building was so positioned that …* The writer focuses here
on the **precision** with which the temple was built.)

Paper 3 – Use of English p.131

Part 1 p.131

One mark per question (total = 15)

1 few (*the quantifier* many *makes no sense here – the
sentence has the opposite meaning*)   2 only (*notice the
inversion which follows*)   3 With (*fixed exp*)   4 which
5 longer (*note that* more *is incorrect here*)   6 hardly (*hardly
+ anyone – you have to read the whole sentence to find the
meaning*)   7 window (*colloc – notice the comparision with*
balcony)   8 enough   9 against   10 effects (*colloc*)   11 on
(*phr vb*)   12 to   13 in   14 As (*you need to read the whole
sentence here; you use something* as *or* for)   15 purposes

Part 2 p.131

One mark per question (total = 10)

16 mysterious   17 incomprehensible   18 engravings
19 implications   20 numerous/innumerable   21 obscurity
22 worldwide   23 depths   24 perception   25 wholly

Part 3 p.132

Two marks per question (total = 12)

26 build   27 withdraw   28 fold   29 spell   30 vivid
31 dismiss

Part 4 p.133

***Two marks per question; one mark for each item
marked (*) (total = 16)***

32 Were **there to be** (*) a dramatic fall in (*) sales, the
company might go bust.   33 He shouldn't **have been so**
(*) **savagely criticised for** (*) his efforts to find a
solution.   34 Nowadays I don't attach **nearly as/so
much importance** (*) **to gossip as** (*) I used to.
35 I **have never** (*) **set eyes on** (*) her before!

36 From the **moment/time I arrived** (*) **you have done nothing but** (*) shout at me.   37 There's **every likelihood that** (*) **I can bring Dave round/around** (*) to my way of thinking.   38 It **won't be long before** (*) **they find** (*) out what she's been doing.   39 Didn't **it occur to you** (*) **that he had made** (*) up that story about rescuing those people?

Part 5 p.134

Two marks per comprehension question (total = 8)

40 It is likely to generate/be greeted with noise/fuss/controversy.

41 It is often difficult and frustrating / requires great patience and persistence.

42 That something common/mundane may lead to important scientific/medical breakthroughs.

43 thrilled, amazed

Summary. Total = 14 marks.
One mark per point marked (*) (total = 4)

44   *Sample answer*
Scientific research is challenging because it involves wrestling with a large number of complex natural phenomena every day. (*) It is also a very personal activity, occupying all your thoughts, time and energy. (*) Knowing that you have discovered something nobody else knows about (*) is extremely exciting, as is the knowledge that the study of something mundane and apparently unimportant could eventually bring tremendous benefits to mankind. (*)
(*65 words*)

Up to 10 marks for:

- **organising** the points to make a logical and coherent argument
- **linking** the sentences together appropriately
- evidence of **using your own words**, rather than 'lifting' vocabulary from the text
- writing with a **concise style**, within the **required length**

Paper 4 – Listening p.135

Part 1 p.135

One mark per question (total = 8)

1A (*Skopelos … doesn't seem to have succumbed to the tourist-bar-on-every-street mentality that has spoilt some of the other islands*)   2C (*… tavernas where you don't have to pay through the nose for the kind of food … My friend and I discovered such a place … The Golden Fleece*)   3C (*you've totted all these things up, have you? … I hope you don't mind if I give you this refers to the banknote she hands over*)   4B (*some of us oldies have problems with our eyes … all I can see is line upon line of squiggles …*)   5A (*it is apparent that the presenter is building up to introducing Harold*

Summers)   6A (*That feeling of sadness, tinged with regret perhaps, as you look at those smiling faces and remember your childhood*)   7B (*All the carriages are packed …*)   8C (*I'm a bit rusty I suppose … it's been donkey's years since I was last on skis*)

Tapescript

Part 1

Extract One

Last summer I went with a friend of mine to Skopelos, which is one of the Greek islands in the middle part of the Aegean. Um … we didn't go as a group, but rather travelled on our own, taking the ferry boat from Volos on the mainland, and then looking around for a room ourselves when we arrived. It actually wasn't very difficult to find something, though I think it would have been much harder on the neighbouring islands, which have a lot more tourism. Skopelos is popular as well, of course, but doesn't seem to have succumbed to the tourist-bar-on-every-street mentality that has spoilt some of the other islands. Um … it's probably not so different from what it was like twenty or thirty years ago, in fact. The local people are very friendly and there are quite a few tavernas where you don't have to pay through the nose for the kind of food and wine most people dream about before coming to Greece. My friend and I discovered such a place on our second day in Skopelos … The Golden Fleece, I think it was called. It was really magical. We ended up going there every evening!

Extract Two

A: *Right. Have you got that? Um … what about the fruit juice? It's a wonder I found it actually. You'd think they'd do something about the signs in this shop, wouldn't you? I don't mean you, personally, of course … but … well …*

B: *Mmm, I know. I can see your point. I'm sure something will be done, though … I'll talk to Mr Higgins again if you like.*

A: *Well, that would be marvellous if you could. Um … you've totted all these things up, have you? Lovely. I hope you don't mind if I give you this, by the way … I've got nothing smaller …*

B: *No, that's all right. Thank you.*

A: *Anyway. They'll have to do something. They don't seem to realise that some of us oldies have problems with our eyes. Whoever wrote those signs should try putting himself in my shoes … they may well be intelligible to you younger people, but all I can see is line upon line of squiggles, dots and dashes. It's not as if they're misleading or anything like that … it's just that … You know what I mean, don't you?*

B: *Yeah. I find them pretty awful myself, to be quite honest.*

Extract Three

A trip to the circus is something that the whole family can enjoy. Young children cannot fail to be enthralled by the feats of the acrobats or the daring of the trapeze artists, while many of us who have more than a few grey hairs will feel much the same under the canvas as we do looking through an album of family photographs. That feeling of sadness, tinged with regret perhaps, as you look at those smiling faces and remember your childhood, is much the same feeling you experience as you sit in that enormous tent and laugh at the antics of the clowns as they squirt each other with water, or watch the lions and the tigers. It is a world of magic and glamour ... it draws you in and makes you forget those niggling little worries that beset so much of adult life. Someone who has been visiting the circus all his life is Harold Summers. He has written numerous articles about circus life and lore, and has even been known to follow circus troupes around the world. He is not an easy man to track down. Tonight, we are lucky ...

Extract Four

A: *Isn't it exciting that we're eventually on our way? After all those set-backs we had in Vienna!*

B: *You can say that again. I never thought we'd get away, to tell you the truth. Still, here we are. A bit squashed perhaps ... but never mind ... at least we're moving in the right direction.*

A: *Mmm. All the carriages are packed, I think ... not just this one. Look at that view! How far do you think those people are down there? A thousand feet?*

B: *Who knows? A long way, that's for sure.*

A: *Mmm. I bet they're all in better shape than I am. I know I've got over that cold I had last month, but I'm still not convinced I should be doing this. It's not that it's the first time I've been on those slopes ... it's just that ... well, I don't know ... I'm a bit rusty I suppose ... it's been donkey's years since I was last on skis.*

B: *Don't worry. You'll be fine. I'll help you if you need it.*

A: *Mmm. Well, I wish I shared your sense of optimism.*

B: *No really – you'll be great! Teaching me a thing or two, I shouldn't wonder!*

Part 2 p.137

One mark per question (total = 9)

Relevant parts of the tapescript have been marked in **bold** to help you locate the answers in the text.

9 open-heart surgery   10 by helicopter   11 emergency call
12 on the spot   13 pack   14 tall enough   15 two nights
16 professional company   17 cases

Tapescript

I: *In the first part of 'It's all in a day's work' we are fortunate in having someone who has been much in the headlines recently. Familiar to most of our listeners as the doctor who turned a busy London pub into a makeshift operating theatre last week, Heather Clark talks to us today about the two loves of her life: medicine and dancing. Dr Clark?*

HC: *Yes ... thank you. Well ... as you say ... I unwittingly found myself in the headlines last week when I **performed open-heart surgery** on a man on the floor of an East End pub. I was lucky it turned out so well. But as a member of the Royal London Hospital's helicopter emergency service – or Hems for short – I can't honestly say that ... for me at least ... it was such an unusual experience. I'm whisked off **by helicopter** to situations like that all the time ... and it's not always easy, I can assure you. Actually my heart's in my mouth and my whole body floods with adrenaline when I get that **emergency call** and head for the helicopter, you know. It's certainly a buzz. When you get in, you never know what you are going to – it could be a major incident with lots of casualties, or a road accident or anything. But I do fortunately have an incredibly low boredom threshold. With this job, the day's always varied, you never know what you could be doing. Also, it's the only area of medicine where **you really save people on the spot**, as it were. Where you really know right away whether you've been able to make a difference.*

*Um ... people sometimes ask me where I find all the strength and energy to cope with such a demanding job. The answer, I suppose, is that I keep myself in pretty good shape. You have to be for this job, because we often have to run quite a way from the helicopter to the patient, **carrying a pack** weighing 15 kilos or so. Then there's all the kit in my suit, which is another 8 kilos at least.*

*I stay fit because I dance any spare minute I can. Dancing, as you mentioned earlier, is the other love of my life – apart from medicine, that is. It's probably more of an obsession, actually. As a teenager growing up in Bristol I desperately wanted to be a dancer. I had a place to train with the Royal Ballet as a teenager, but **I just never grew tall enough** to be a ballerina, and my parents drew the line at my idea of giving up my scholarship at school. I knew my own mind, but they won through in the end, so I stayed on at the sixth form and did my A-levels. But **I still manage to dance two nights during the week ... usually more**. It keeps me in good shape and it's also a fantastic way to relax. Believe me, in this job, you really need to be able to switch off! **I dance for a professional company and we rehearse** at all hours, often till one or two in the morning. When I finish work, I go straight off to rehearsals. In fact, I'm going to be in a BBC programme ... a programme about jive dancing ... some time soon. I get very tired, of course, but I just love dancing and* *cramming lots into my life. I have loads of energy. I'm not too bothered about relaxation.*

*Um ... having any kind of social life at all while you do this job is nigh on impossible. I just never know where I'm going to be and I often end up staying late at the hospital ... to talk to my colleagues, you know ... **about what cases we've had to deal with** during the day ... we sort of debrief each other. Um ... I suppose I've got used to working long unsociable hours. As a junior doctor I regularly did a 100-hour week. If you can do that, you can do anything!*

Part 3 p.138

One mark per question (total = 5)

18C (*it's more a programme about food and the relationship that people have with it ... describing what the food means to them*) 19A (*we'll see developments in so-called 'scratch and sniff' radio*) 20D (*you're not helped at all by the fact that there are so few words to describe smells and tastes*) 21C (*some cultures have adapted climates to meet their needs. Take Iceland ...*) 22A (*whilst he included them for the flavour and not necessarily for their properties ...* Traditional reasons are important (D) but not the **only** reasons these spices are used.)

Tapescript

I: *Television programmes about food – and ways of preparing and cooking it – have been riding a wave of popularity in recent years. Not surprisingly, the same is also true for programmes designed for radio. Many of our listeners will have already sampled the delights – at least in their imaginations – served up by the recent series 'Just a taste' and will agree that listening to people from different countries talking about cooking and eating ... and sharing their recipes ... can be a fascinating, as well as a mouthwatering, experience! Anne Winslop asked Katherine Hodgson – the presenter of 'Just a taste' – to explain what she felt lay at the heart of the series' success.*

KH: *Oh, food is a very meaningful part of our lives, I'd say. Um ... although 'Just a taste' does feature people cooking, eating and telling us about their favourite recipes, of course, I don't really like to call it a cookery programme as such ... it's more a programme about food and the relationship that people have with it. The people featured are not necessarily professional chefs ... they're simply lovers of food who prepare traditional, everyday dishes whilst describing what the food means to them ... or what special memories it might have for them.*

AW: *Mmm. How difficult was the series to make, Katherine? On the face of it, television would seem to be a much easier medium for a programme about food, wouldn't it? How does such a programme translate to radio?*

KH: *Well, in a blind situation listeners rely almost entirely on their sense of hearing. There are so many sounds in the kitchen which are very evocative ... there are the wonderful sounds of chopping and boiling, for example, which do conjure up a picture of somebody's kitchen surprisingly well. Smells, of course, are another matter ... um ... I think that in the not too far future we'll see developments in so-called 'scratch and sniff' radio ... but until that day arrives, listeners, I'm afraid, will just have to do it with their imagination, when it comes to the smell of the food being described.*

Describing food, of course, is not as easy as it might seem and there can be problems. When you first taste a dish all you can say is 'Mmm' and then you have to try to put that into words ... what it looks like, what it tastes like, the texture and feel of it, so that people have some idea of the process the dish goes through and what sort of taste you should be aiming for ... and you're not helped at all by the fact that there are so few words to describe smells and tastes.

AW: *What things, Katherine, did you find particularly surprising or interesting while you were making the series?*

KH: *Oh, the influence of geography and culture on food, I think. Oh, yes ... and the way they interact. For example, if you live in a very barren climate, you'd think that you'd be less likely to have recipes based around fresh salad vegetables. However, rather than be dictated to by the weather, some cultures have adapted climates to meet their needs. Take Iceland ... it's called the land of ice and fire and it really is. There are huge volcanic, black plains. Now, how can people have anything else to eat but fish? But then you see that they have great greenhouses where they grow all sorts of vegetables and fruits which are heated by the natural thermal hot springs. Food can also be literally infused by the culture that it is made in ... for example ... when we did South Indian foods in the first series, the man cooking the food explained how the different spices that he used have different health benefits. He explained the benefits of asafoetida and turmeric, and whilst he included them for the flavour and not necessarily for their properties, traditional medicine and beliefs are so part of the Indian culture, so part of his life, that it has filtered through into his everyday food.*

AW: *And for many cultures food is also heavily entwined with notions about hospitality, isn't it?*

KH: *Yes. One of the nicest things about making this series is that we have experienced some amazing hospitality. We haven't been able to leave a house without having a feast. But the best thing about the series is that we get to eat all of the food and nobody has ever asked us to do the washing up!*

Part 4 p.139

One mark per question (total = 6)

23J (*It could just be that more crimes are reported to the police/it's probably the other way round*) 24B (*we've come to accept a lot of things nowadays that people didn't accept in the past/people have become hardened to crime, haven't they ... ?*) 25J (*crime tends to increase along with wealth/I've always found that argument a bit ... glib*) 26A (*Are we to believe that when people were much poorer ... that the incentives to steal were smaller than they are today/Yeah ... anyway* – this signals disagreement) 27J (*They're more lenient these days/they are slightly tougher on the most serious crimes today*) 28B (*the criminals the police charge very often get off lightly .../... or scot free ...* Andy finishes Joe's sentence, which signals agreement.)

Tapescript

A: I wonder really if crime has not actually risen at all in recent years. It could just be that more crimes are reported to the police than in the past. Don't you think, Joe?

J Yes, I've heard that one too. But I think ... it's probably the other way round. And, for minor offences especially, I think it's true that nowadays a large number of crimes actually go **unreported** because we don't really consider them to be crimes anymore. You know – a short scuffle in a pub ... um ... a garden trampled by kids. No, I think that we **have** to accept the fact that crime really has increased over the past thirty or forty years.

A: Mmm ... it's true, of course, that we've come to accept a lot of things nowadays that people didn't accept in the past, isn't it? There are many people, I think, who can remember a time when – in some neighbourhoods – when houses could be left safely unlocked ... and bicycles could be left just propped up on a wall. They talk about the shock they felt when someone they knew experienced a crime ... or even vandalism ... um ...

J: Uh huh ... people have become hardened to crime, haven't they, Andy? The rot began to set in in the 1960s and 70s, I think. Who knows what went wrong? Maybe crime tends to increase along with wealth. People now have videos and colour televisions and what have you, all worth stealing, whereas they didn't before ...

A: Yeah. Frankly, I'd say I've always found that argument a bit ... too, er ... glib, if you know what I mean. What ... for example ... is the link between rising living standards and rising **violent** crime, would you say, Joe? Even when it comes to theft, er, the logic ... I don't know ... the logic seems a bit dubious to me. Are we to believe that when people were much poorer, or more in need of the bare necessities, that the incentives to steal were smaller than they are today? And people today can receive all sorts of benefits from the state if they really need them, can't they? Are colour televisions, for example, easier to steal now than pound notes were fifty years ago?

J: Yeah ... anyway. The courts have a lot to answer for, I think. They're more lenient these days. I read in the paper the other day that if you were found guilty before a judge in 1954, you ran more than a two-out-of-three chance of a prison sentence for an offence that was serious. For murder, you'd ... you'd hope you were insane. Of the 25 people found guilty of murder in 1954, apparently, 21 were sentenced to hang.

A: Well, they may be slightly more forgiving for the less serious crimes ... I don't know ... but I would say that ... that – in fact – they are slightly tougher on the most serious crimes today.

J: I don't know, Andy. Anyway, offenders today serve a much smaller portion of their sentence than they used to, don't they?

A: Well ...

J: And the police often say that there's no point in making arrests because nothing is going to happen to the culprits anyway. It's true, isn't it, that the criminals the police charge very often get off lightly or ...

A: ... or scot free, even. Yes, that's true ... for every category of crime, I think, the odds that you will be found guilty if you commit a crime have fallen by two-thirds or more in most cases. And you mentioned the criminals that the police **do** manage to catch, didn't you? Isn't that one of the problems today? That the police ...

Paper 5: Speaking p.140

The marking categories for the interview are:

- **grammatical resource** – demonstrating that you are able to use a wide range of grammatical structures to express your ideas accurately and fully
- **lexical resource** – you should be able to use a wide range of appropriate vocabulary to express your ideas; it should not be necessary to resort to simplification
- **discourse management** – this refers to your ability to link your utterances together in a logical and coherent way, and to develop themes and arguments where appropriate
- **pronunciation** – you are not expected to sound exactly like a native speaker, but you should be very easy to understand; your sentence stress, rhythm and intonation should be natural and effective
- **interactive communication** – maintaining a natural conversation, turn-taking, little or no hesitation in responding; listening to and understanding what is said to you.

When you are speaking, **don't worry about**:
- **making grammatical errors** – your grammatical accuracy is only a part of your overall performance; if you worry about making mistakes, you will probably speak less fluently and naturally than you would otherwise
- **your opinion being assessed** – the examiner is not interested in what you say so much as how you say it
- **speaking with an American accent** – this is not penalised in any way in the Proficiency exam.

Pearson Education Limited
Edinburgh Gate
Harlow
Essex CM20 2JE
England
and Associated Companies throughout the world.

www.longman.com

© Pearson Education Limited 2002

First published 2002

ISBN 0 582 507332

Set in Admark 10/13pt

Printed in Spain by Graficas Estella

Third impression 2002

The author would like to thank the following: Mike Gutteridge for
his comments on the first draft of the book; Jenny Colley
(Publisher), Helena Gomm (Project Manager), Frances Cook and
Susannah Reed for their editorial work and support.

We are grateful to the following for permission to reproduce
copyright material:

Dennis Publishing Limited for an extract from "Choosing a Digital
Camera Made Easy" published in *The Sunday Times Internet Guide*
19th November 2000; Guardian Newspapers Limited for extracts
adapted from "Star Trek good for humans says doctor" by Alex
Belos published in *The Guardian* 13th June 1997, and "City limits" by
Anne Power published in *The Guardian* 25th October 2000;
Independent Newspapers (UK) Ltd for extracts adapted from "Art
forger convicted of brilliant fraud" by Andrew Buncombe published
in *The Independent* 13th February 1999, "Raise high the roof beams"
by Duff Hart Davis published in *The Independent* 15th March 1999,
"What a stitch-up!" by Martin Raymond published in *The
Independent on Sunday* 22nd August 1999, and "How sport can help
you win" by Roger Trapp published in *The Independent on Sunday*
29th September 1998; the author's agent for an extract from *Original
Sin* by P D James published by Faber and Faber Limited; News
International Limited for extracts from "Companies seek chip
implants to control staff" by Stephen Bevan published in *The Sunday
Times* 9th March 1999, and "Amazon survival guide" by Mark Mann
published in *The Times Weekend Section* 22nd March 1997; Pearson
Education Limited for an extract from *Longman Dictionary of
Contemporary English*; Penguin Books Limited for extracts from
Stormchild by Bernard Cornwell published by Penguin Books 1992.
© Bernard Cornwell 1999, and *How the Mind Works* by Steven Pinker
published in *The Independent Weekend Review* 13th March 1999; and
The Random House Group Limited for extracts from *Europe – A
History* by Norman Davies published by Pimlico, *Venture to the
Interior* by Laurens Van der Post published by Hogarth Press, and
The Crocodile Bird by Ruth Rendell published by Arrow.

In some instances we have been unable to trace the owners of
copyright material, and we would appreciate any information that
would enable us to do so.

The Publishers are grateful to the following for their permission to
reproduce photographs:
Bryan & Cherry Alexander for 140 middle right; Friends of
Westonbirt Arboretum, Gloucestershire for 82; Getty One Stone for
60; Robert Harding Picture Library for 140 middle left, 140 middle
and 140 right; Impact Photos for 65, 97 and 100; Pictures Colour
Library for 35, 99 and 108; Rex Features for 140 left and Telegraph
Colour Library for 49.

Illustrated by Alan Rowe and Oxford Designers and Illustrators
Designed by Oxford Designers and Illustrators
Project Managed by Helena Gomm